THE AGE OF THE SAGES

THE AGE OF THE SAGES

THE AXIAL AGE IN ASIA AND THE NEAR EAST

MARK W. MUESSE

Fortress Press
Minneapolis

THE AGE OF THE SAGES

The Axial Age in Asia and the Near East

Copyright © 2013 Fortress Press. All rights reserved. Except for brief quotations in critical articles or reviews, no part of this book may be reproduced in any manner without prior written permission from the publisher. Visit http://www.augsburgfortress.org/copyrights/ or write to Permissions, Augsburg Fortress, Box 1209, Minneapolis, MN 55440.

Cover image: Zoroaster image © Torea Frey; Prince Siddharta, the Buddha, Gandhara, from Peshawar, Pakistan, Gandhara style, second century CE, Marble, Erich Lessing / Art Resource, NY; Statue of Confucius, Chinatown, New York, NY, © Vanni Archive / Art Resource, NY

Cover design: Tory Herman

Library of Congress Cataloging-in-Publication Data

Print ISBN: 978-0-8006-9921-5

eBook ISBN: 978-1-4514-3861-1

The paper used in this publication meets the minimum requirements of American National Standard for Information Sciences — Permanence of Paper for Printed Library Materials, ANSI Z329.48-1984.

Manufactured in the U.S.A.

This book was produced using PressBooks.com, and PDF rendering was done by PrinceXML.

For Dhammika Swarnamali Muesse
My wife, teacher, and friend

CONTENTS

Preface	ix
Acknowledgements	xv
Timeline	xvii
Introduction: What Was the Axial Age?	1

Part I. West Asia

1.	The Noble Ones	9
2.	The Life of Zoroaster	21
3.	Zoroaster's Legacy	27

Part II. South Asia

4.	South Asia before the Axial Age	39
5.	The Start of the Indian Axial Age	49
6.	Death and Rebirth	59
7.	The Quest for Liberation	67
8.	The Vedantic Solution	75
9.	The One and the Many	85
10.	The Life of Siddhattha Gotama	97
11.	"I Am Awake"	107
12.	Why We Suffer	115
13.	The Noble Path	123
14.	From Buddha to Buddhism	133
15.	Jainism	143

Part III. East Asia

16.	East Asia before the Axial Age	155
17.	The World of Confucius	165
18.	The Foundations of Confucianism	175
19.	The Cultivation of Virtue	185
20.	Early Confucianism and the Rise of Daoism	193

| 21. The *Daodejing* | 203 |
| 22. Daoist Politics and Mysticism | 213 |

Conclusion: Reflections on the Axial Age	223
Glossary	233
Bibliography	253
Index	261

PREFACE

The Age of the Sages is unlike most other introductory books in the study of religion. Most foundational religious studies texts approach their subject in one of a few basic ways. Some works focus on a single tradition, such Islam, Buddhism, or Christianity. Books of this sort usually unfold chronologically, starting from the tradition's inauguration (or shortly before) and proceeding historically to the present. The advantage of this general method is that it permits the study of a single religious tradition in some depth. If the book's approach is chronological, it adds the very important dimension of showing how a religion evolves over time. Without a historical perspective, one might be led to think that religious traditions are relatively static and that devotees of a particular religion believe and practice the same things. As someone whose job is to interpret religions, I am frequently asked questions such as "What do Hindus believe?" The truest answer one can give to a question like that is that Hindus believe-and have believed-many different things throughout their history. The same answer, of course, could be offered for all the world's major religions. Thus, one of the dangers in not taking historical development into account is that the great diversity manifested in all religions gets neglected. Focusing on the evolution of a single tradition can avoid that pitfall. The disadvantage to the single-tradition approach, however, is that it rarely allows for comparisons with other religions. Without the comparative dimension, one might be misled into believing that a particular religious tradition is completely unique or that it develops independently of other domains of culture or other religions. The comparative method ensures that a religious tradition is interpreted against the larger background of human experience beyond the specific religion under study.

Another kind of religious studies text takes the comparative approach seriously but in so doing sacrifices much of the depth one gains from studying the historical development of a single tradition. Many textbooks for introductory courses in world religions are structured in this manner. Such books are designed for courses in which one might spend the first two weeks on Hinduism, then two weeks on Buddhism, two days on Jainism, a week for the Sikhs, three weeks on Chinese religions, and so forth. The benefit of this method is the opportunity it affords to study traditions side by side to see how they differ and compare. It is difficult truly to understand any religion—including, and perhaps especially, one's own—without such comparisons and contrasts. In the same way that studying another language enables one to recognize the taken-for-granted features of one's native tongue, so too does the comparative study of religions bring to consciousness the dimensions of religious belief and practice that usually escape our notice. One might be tempted to think that all religions posit the existence of a creator god until one encounters a tradition like Buddhism, in which belief in god plays no role in accounting for the existence of the universe. Similarly, one could assume that Jesus originated the Golden Rule until one finds that Confucius uttered essentially the same principle five centuries earlier. In the words of Max Müller, one of the first comparativists of religion, "He who knows one, knows none."[1]

But the problem with the comparative approach of most textbooks is that each religion receives such short shrift that its treatment is often shallow and its historical development is glossed over or insufficiently addressed. Furthermore, a religion's evolution in the larger context of its culture can be easily neglected. Thus, one fails to see how traditions are related to other aspects of their social setting, such as art, economics, politics, and education. Because it lacks adequate attention to historical development, this two-weeks-per-religion approach can also disregard the ways in which religious traditions frequently influence and shape one another. This is also a hazard of the single-tradition method. In fact, one of the least appreciated aspects of the world's religions is the extensive ways in which they interact. To cite some small examples: Prayer beads seem to have originated among the Hindus and later adopted by Christians, Buddhists, Sikhs, and Muslims. Karma and rebirth are ideas shared by Jains, Hindus, Sikhs, and Buddhists, who appropriated these concepts in very different ways relative to one another. The Roman Catholic Church canonized a Saint Josaphat, who was a fictionalized character based on the life of the Buddha.[2] Such instances of cross-fertilization between religions can easily be ignored when one's approach tends to focus on religious traditions in isolation from one another.

---

1. F. Max Müller, *Introduction to the Science of Religion: Four Lectures Delivered at the Royal Institution in February and May, 1870* (London: Longmans, Green, and Co., 1882), 13.

2. John C. Hirsh, ed., *Barlam and Iosaphat: A Middle English Life of Buddha* (Oxford: Oxford University Press, 1986).

The present volume adopts a different approach. By examining the evolution of Asian religions over a six-hundred-year span known as the Axial Age (800–200 BCE) and against the background of their preaxial settings, we will have the opportunity to study religions both comparatively and developmentally. This method aims to combine the benefits of considering the historical evolution of religions, as championed in the single-tradition approach, with the benefits of regarding religious traditions in comparative fashion. The comparative dimension allows us to view how different religions respond to similar historical and social circumstances and to see the mutual interaction of religions in proximity to one another. But by limiting the time frame and the number of religions we cover, we gain a measure of depth in our investigation and connect them more fully with their social and political contexts. Thus, we will neither attempt to study all the major religions of the world, as most comparative introductions do, nor provide a comprehensive account of their historical developments, as many single-tradition introductions do. Rather, we shall examine several of the principal religions of Asia during a particular—and particularly important—period.

The great value of this book, however, derives not simply from the approach it adopts but from the era on which it is focused. The Axial Age, as we shall see, is simply one of the most intriguing periods in religious history. No other six-hundred-year epoch compares with its spiritual and philosophical richness. It is called "axial" because it marks a decisive turn in the evolution of the human spirit; it profoundly shaped who we are today, and it continues to offer us great insight for the living of our lives well over two thousand years later. It has lessons to teach us about the nature and function of religion in human experience as well as valuable guidance for the twenty-first century, whether we consider ourselves religious or not.

Overview of the Chapters

The book begins with a discussion of the Axial Age and its characteristics and contours. We note how brilliant and sensitive thinkers in this period began to reflect on life in new and sometimes unprecedented ways across several geographical regions we call "axial centers." Although these centers were located in numerous parts of Eurasia, we will attend principally to the traditions that emerged in three Asian sites to delimit the scope of our study: Zoroastrianism in Iran (with mention of its influence on Judaism, Christianity, and Islam); Hinduism, Buddhism, and Jainism in India; and Confucianism and Daoism in China.

Although not an axial center, we begin our analysis in Central Asia in order to study the early Indo-European peoples who later migrated to West and South Asia and decisively shaped the religious outlook and practices of those regions. Today, we refer to these migrants as the "Indo-Iranians" in recognition of their eventual destinations. We trace their movements first into Iran, where we examine the context out of which came the most mysterious of all axial sages: Zoroaster. Perhaps the world's first prophet, Zoroaster was responsible for reforming the ancient Iranian religious tradition and for popularizing ideas such as the Day of Judgment, the devil, and the apocalyptic redeemer. We will look at these conceptions both in their native Iranian context and as possible influences on Judaism, Christianity, and Islam.

In South Asia, we start with the indigenous Indus Valley Civilization and witness the impact of the migration of a branch of the Indo-Iranians (retrospectively called the Indo-Aryans) that eventually made its way to northwestern India. We will explore the elements of both Indus and Indo-Aryan religions to prepare for the examination of the axial transformation of Indian religion. Preaxial religion in India focused on this-worldly concerns, such as the acquisition of material needs and comforts, a long life, and successful reproduction, and was decidedly oriented toward ritual.

With the advent of the Axial Age, Indian sages began to question the values associated with the material world and ritual practices. Indian religion became increasingly preoccupied with understanding the destiny of the individual and the nature of the deepest reality underlying all appearances. After a great deal of speculation, the ideas of reincarnation and karma were widely accepted, creating a new problem for Indian religion: attaining release from the endless rounds of death and rebirth known as *samsara*. Individuals by the hundreds began to renounce worldly life and to experiment with solutions to this predicament. Among the scores of new spiritualities developed during this time, we examine three of the most important and most enduring: the mysticism of the Upanishads, which provided the foundational structure for the massive conglomerate of religious beliefs and practices later known as Hinduism; the teachings of the Buddha, based on an approach he called the Middle Way; and the beliefs and practices of Mahavira, whose movement became known as Jainism. Setting these traditions side by side will afford the chance to see how they responded to many of the same problems but offered distinctive and innovative solutions.

Our final destination is East Asia. We begin with a study of the preaxial culture of what was later called China. Understanding this early period, which is barely within reach of current historiography, is important for appreciating the axial transformations brought about by Confucius and the thinkers associated with the tradition of Daoism. We look at the earliest attestations of religious practices that have been important throughout Chinese history, including divination and ancestor reverence. Later, when we turn to Confucius and his followers and then to the Daoists, we observe how these practices were retained and reinterpreted to fit the new concern with moral behavior brought by the Axial Age. Claiming only to transmit ancient traditions, Confucius taught a comprehensive ethic of personal development that remained influential throughout Chinese history and provided the basis for the Chinese educational system. Daoism, often associated with the mythic figure of Laozi, was concerned with many of the same issues as Confucius but advocated alternative solutions. Throughout Chinese history, Confucianism and Daoism functioned as complements to one another in such a way that individuals could claim allegiance to both traditions.

Finally, the book concludes with a set of reflections on the axial transformations, emphasizing the common themes across the centers of development as well as their distinctive qualities. Only then can we consider the overall significance of this age for human history and its major contributions to human spirituality.

A Note about Terminology

The Age of the Sages uses transliterations of many technical terms from several languages, especially Sanskrit, Pali, and Chinese. I have tried to keep these terms to a minimum, but it is often helpful to use transliterations from the original languages because precise English equivalents are not always available. Keeping a word or phrase in its original tongue reminds us that sometimes much is lost in translation. Furthermore, learning the basic vocabulary is a fundamental feature of understanding any religious tradition.

Some technical terms will appear in *italics* and other will not. The basis of this distinction is simple: familiarity. Certain words from non-Western religions have been adopted into English and are recognizable to most English-speakers. Accordingly, words like karma, nirvana, and mantra will appear in plain type in recognition of their status as English words. Other terms, however, are not so familiar and hence appear italicized. These include words such as *tianming*, *anatta*, and *li*. In addition, the titles of some texts will be italicized while others will appear plain. References to collections such as the Vedas and the Upanishads are not italicized, much like similar conventions for the Bible and the Qur'an. But most texts, such as the *Bhagavad Gita* and the *Analects*, will be italicized in the standard way for such documents.

The scholarly transliteration of the languages of the traditions we will cover often involves certain standard diacritical marks to indicate sounds for which there is no precise English equivalent. To avoid creating unnecessary distractions, however, I have chosen to avoid diacritical markings and use transliterations that approximate the original as much as possible. The glossary provides the full transliteration of terms including diacritics in parenthetical marks. For direct quotations from other texts, I have reproduced the transliteration and capitalization scheme of the original, even though it might be at slight odds with my own. Chinese words have been transliterated according to the pinyin system rather the older Wade-Giles method. Hence, a word that might be familiar to Western readers such as *Tao* has been rendered as the more phonetically correct *Dao*.

Acknowledgements

Although I did not recognize it at the time, this book was conceived over thirty years ago when I was a graduate student. During that time, I was fortunate to study with many brilliant theologians and religious theorists, but two teachers stand out as inspiration for this particular volume: the director of my graduate program, Wilfred Cantwell Smith, and the director of my doctoral thesis, Gordon D. Kaufman.

From Professor Smith, I learned the value of thinking of religious traditions as dynamic, diverse, and mutually interactive realities. He taught his students to imagine the world's religions developing century by century, not simply tradition by tradition. I unwittingly began the research that culminated in this volume while preparing for a question Professor Smith posed for my general examinations for the Ph.D. His question involved selecting a specific century of human history and identifying all the major religious developments—regardless of tradition—that occurred within that time frame. My particular period revolved around 500 BCE, near the center of the Axial Age. Thus began my career-long fascination with what is clearly one of the most philosophically creative times in human history.

From Professor Kaufman, I gained a critical appreciation for the way religious concepts are humanly constructed by means of what he called the "theological imagination." Rather than being realities that are sent down from the heavens, Kaufman contended that religious ideas and symbols are created by human beings for human purposes. Because religions can function to our great benefit and to our great detriment, it is essential, he argued, to exercise a critical and conscious approach to the ways we create and appropriate our concepts. Kaufman's approach to theology, like Smith's, has left a deep impression on my own approach to the study of religion, and both have helped shaped the way this book has developed.

In addition to these two theological mentors who have helped fashion the way I think, I am indebted to several individuals whose labors have aided in the nuts-and-bolts process of crafting this text. I gratefully acknowledge the assistance of the following persons in preparing this book: Manoj Jain, Michael Turco, Nathan Redman, Philip Culbertson, Kaleb Yaniger, and Scarlett D'Anna. Each of these friends read the manuscript or a portion of it and offered their suggestions for its improvement. Almost invariably, I accepted their recommendations, and the book is a better volume as a consequence.

Finally, I am especially grateful for the love of my daughter, Ariyana Prabashwari Muesse, and my wife, Dhammika Swarnamali Muesse, who has deepened my understanding of Buddhism and supported me in every phase of this project. I am indebted to Dhammi for the title of this book, and to her it is dedicated.

Timeline

c. 3300–1500 BCE Indus Valley Civilization (South Asia)
c. 2300–1200 BCE Composition of the Rig Veda (Central and South Asia)
c. 1600–1000 BCE Migration of Indo-Aryans into the Indus Valley (South Asia)
c. 1500–1045 BCE Shang Dynasty (East Asia)
c. 1045–221 BCE Zhou Dynasty (East Asia)
c. 1045–771 BCE Western Zhou Dynasty (East Asia)
c. 1000 BCE Migration of Indo-Aryans into Gangetic Plains (South Asia)
c. 1000 BCE Zoroaster (West Asia)
c. 1000 BCE Composition of the Gathas of the Avesta (West Asia)
c. 800–200 BCE Composition of the Upanishads (South Asia)
771–221 BCE Eastern Zhou (East Asia)
722–481 BCE Spring and Autumn Period (East Asia)
595–573 BCE Ministry of Ezekiel (Judah)
586–536 BCE Babylonian Captivity (Judah)
582–507 BCE Pythagoras of Samos (Greece)
c. 551–479 BCE Confucius (East Asia)
c. 540–468 BCE Vardhamana Mahavira (South Asia)
535–475 BCE Heraclitus of Ephesus (Greece)
c. 490–410 BCE Siddhattha Gotama, the Buddha (South Asia)
475 or 403–221 BCE Period of the Warring States (East Asia)
c. 470–390 BCE Mozi (East Asia)
470–399 BCE Socrates of Athens (Greece)
c. 427–347 BCE Plato (Greece)
c. 385–312 BCE Mencius (East Asia)
c. 384–322 BCE Aristotle (Greece)
369–286 BCE Zhuangzi (East Asia)
327–325 BCE Campaign of Alexander the Great in India
c. 310–219 BCE Xunzi (East Asia)
273–232 BCE Reign of Ashoka (South Asia)
c. 250 BCE Composition of the book of Ecclesiastes (Judah)

221–206 BCE Qin Dynasty (East Asia)
206 BCE–220 CE Han Dynasty (East Asia)
c. 200 BCE–100 CE Composition of the *Bhagavad Gita* (South Asia)
c. 200–100 BCE First Buddha images in Gandhara (South Asia)
c. 167–164 BCE Final redaction of the Book of Daniel (Judah)
c. 150 BCE Pali Canon put in writing (South Asia)
c. 100 BCE–100 CE Rise of Mahayana Buddhism (South Asia)
c. 4 BCE–29 CE Jesus of Nazareth (West Asia)
c. 50 CE Introduction of Buddhism to China (East Asia)
570–632 CE Muhammad (Arabia)
c. 788–820 CE Shankara (South Asia)
960–1279 CE Song Dynasty (East Asia)
c. 1077–1157 CE Ramanuja (South Asia)
1844–1900 CE Friedrich Nietzsche (Germany)
1869–1948 CE Mohandas K. Gandhi (India)
1883–1969 CE Karl Jaspers (Germany)

Introduction: What Was the Axial Age?

The years between 800 and 200 BCE constitute one of the most astonishing periods in the history of humanity. During this epoch, a cohort of brilliant individuals appeared whose teachings radically changed the way human beings thought about themselves and the world around them. So pivotal and revolutionary were their ways of thought that we refer to this era as the Axial Age, a term coined by German philosopher Karl Jaspers.[1] Today, we are still living out and living through the ideas and ideals that were introduced in this period. In the Axial Age, observed Jaspers, "the spiritual foundations of humanity were laid. . . . And these are the foundations upon which humanity still subsists today."[2]

Remarkably, this burst of creativity occurred almost simultaneously in separate areas on the Eurasian continent. In East Asia, Confucius and his followers laid the religious, philosophical, and political foundations for the next 2,500 years of Chinese culture. At the same time, Daoist philosophers produced a compelling alternative to Confucianism, affecting Chinese society in an equally powerful but very different way. In South Asia, a countercultural movement of ascetics and mystics composed a diverse collection of profound teachings that gave ancient Hinduism its characteristic features. At the same time and place, the Buddha and Mahavira attained new insights that inaugurated Buddhism, the first major international religion, and Jainism, a small but highly influential Indian religion. In West Asia, Zoroaster inspired the religion that took his name and served as the state religion of three powerful empires. In the Middle East, the nations of Israel and Judah witnessed the rise of the prophets and the emergence of the religion later known as Judaism. Finally, in the region north of the Mediterranean Sea, thinkers such as Pythagoras, Heraclitus, Socrates, Plato, and Aristotle invented the Western philosophical

---

1. "Axial Age" is the usual English translation of *die Achsenzeit*, Jasper's actual term.
2. Karl Jaspers, *The Origin and Goal of History*, trans. Michael Bullock (New Haven, CT: Yale University Press, 1953).

tradition. Rarely in human history do we find such a dense concentration of creative individuals in such a short period of time, especially persons whose lives and teachings have had such an extensive and long-lasting impact. And just as fascinating as the density of genius in this era is the similarity of their ideas and modes of thinking, despite their geographical distance from one another. Although they did not come to identical conclusions or advocate common practices and beliefs, they grappled with many of the same fundamental issues: the nature and destiny of the self, the character of ultimate reality, the basis and practices of morality, and the highest goods of human life.

What was happening at this particular time and in these particular places that might account for this prodigious output of decisive ideas and the appearance of some of the greatest individuals ever known to the world? To begin to answer this weighty question, let us consider some of the significant developments occurring in the axial centers during this period.

Urbanization and Mobility

The Axial Age happened at a time and in places of increasing urbanization. More and more, persons were living nearer to one another, establishing new towns and cities and enlarging older ones. People had lived in urban settings prior to the Axial Age, of course, but now that practice accelerated and expanded. Nomadic peoples began to settle, take up agriculture, and enjoy the benefits of a more sedentary existence. Those who had lived in villages moved to larger towns and cities to take advantage of new economic opportunities.

The rise of urbanization was significant because of its effects on social structures and the human psyche. Urban life often disrupts one's sense of identity and places traditional values and beliefs in doubt. In towns and cities, one often meets others quite unlike oneself, and that fact frequently challenges a person to look at him- or herself in different ways. Conventional beliefs and ways of being are thrown into flux. Some people are challenged by such conditions to entertain new ideas, while others cling more resolutely to their old beliefs. In either case, customs and traditions often lose their taken-for-granted character.

Higher densities of people also intensify exposure to the realities of life. In urban areas, one sees more sickness and suffering, more death, more instances of our inhumanity to one another. Reinhold Niebuhr's classic work *Moral Man and Immoral Society* argued quite persuasively that persons who ordinarily behave very morally as individuals are often moved to act immorally as members of a collective.³ It is almost as if we humans tend lose our moral bearings when we congregate and engage in "groupthink."⁴

Political Disorder and Instability

The axial centers were also characterized by political and social upheaval. The Axial Age overlapped an epoch in Chinese history known as the Period of Warring States. The traditional and relatively stable feudal system was disintegrating, and small principalities began to vie for hegemony. Hundreds of thousands of Chinese lost their lives in the ensuing conflicts. Profound and rapid political and economic transformation in the area surrounding the Ganges River set the stage for the Indian ascetic movement and the emergence of Hinduism, Buddhism, and Jainism. The Axial Age in the land of Judah proceeded under the constant threat (and eventual actuality) of the tiny kingdom's engulfment by the larger empires that surrounded it. And Zoroaster's reform of Iranian religion was undertaken at a time of great lawlessness in West Asia, as his society was plagued by independent warlords and bands of warriors with little respect for human life.

Rapid political and social change generates great uncertainty and insecurity for many. But interestingly—and this is observed less frequently—such times are often the most creative and innovative for religious and philosophical thought. The context of political and social instability seems to foster just the right conditions to evoke the best (as well as the worst) in human beings. With their worlds in flux and their received traditions under question, the bold thinkers of the Axial Age experienced freedom to ponder and live their lives in new ways.

Selfhood and the Transience of Life

As they reflected on their lives, sages in all the axial centers became increasingly anxious about death and preoccupied with what, if anything, lay beyond it. Preaxial humans, to be sure, were not unconcerned with death, but they seemed more generally to accept death as a natural part of life and rarely gave attention to the idea of an afterlife. For the most part, they valued a long life with many descendants but hardly expected anything more than that. One's sense of identity prior to the Axial Age was more firmly rooted in participation in the family, the clan, or the tribe. Ideas about whom and what one was and what life was about were derived from being a part of a larger human reality.

---

3. Reinhold Niebuhr, *Moral Man and Immoral Society: A Study in Ethics*, 2nd ed. (Louisville: Westminster John Knox, 2013).

4. This term was coined in 1952 by William H. Whyte in *Fortune* magazine.

Accordingly, death could be accepted, knowing that the family would survive one's personal demise.

By the Axial Age, however, attitudes toward death began to reflect a greater concern with the experience of dying and what occurs after it. Increasingly, death was regarded with dread and fear, and speculation about what might lie beyond was filled with both hope and terror. Every conceivable possibility for the afterlife seems to have been entertained, from continued existence in a delightful place, to life in the most unpleasant realms of the underworld, to rebirth in this life, to the decomposition of body and soul back to the elements of the earth, to resurrection of the dead at the end of the age. These issues and proposals were passionately debated—an indication that something of great importance was at stake, something that marked an important change from the preaxial age.

Reflected in this shift in attitudes about death is the rise of a sense of individuality and selfhood. The Axial Age was the time when people began to experience themselves as separate, autonomous individuals—as selves. With this developing sense of selfhood came a greater consciousness of the human being as a moral agent, one who is accountable and responsible for his or her own actions. Although we today take individuality, moral agency, and personal responsibility as givens in life, the concept of a "self," in the sense just described, emerges at a particular point in time: the Axial Age. Humans have not always been "selves."

As people began to think of themselves as separate, autonomous individuals, death became a more dreaded reality. Selfhood promotes a feeling of isolation, or at least differentiation, from the rest of the human community and the rest of reality, making it more difficult to accept dying as a part of the natural process of living, as merely a passing event in a greater reality. With a sense of self, death means the end of the thing we hold most dear: ourselves. Knowing that the world, our descendants, or even our accomplishments live on after us is hardly any consolation. Woody Allen spoke in the spirit of this attitude when he said, "I don't want to achieve immortality through my work. . . . I want to achieve it through not dying."[5] The self does not wish to die, and it looks for ways to avoid death or to survive it.

Transcendental Consciousness

The growing sense of selfhood and anxiety about life's transience stimulated conjectures about the nature of the person and spurred the search to discover

---

5. Eric Lax, *Woody Allen: A Biography* (Boston: Da Capo, 2000), 183.

something within the human individual that might endure the dissolution of the body, something eternal or immortal. As part of this quest, axial sages developed a new way of thinking about the world and the place of humanity within it. S. N. Eisenstadt, one of the first scholars to study the sociological dimensions of the Axial Age, calls this way of looking at life "transcendental consciousness,"[6] the ability to stand back and see the world more comprehensively, as a totality, and to look at it more critically and reflectively, not merely accepting the world as it appears or as tradition says it is. Transcendental consciousness produced novel conceptions of the world's ultimate reality. In some cases, the axial sages were not content to accept the old anthropomorphic gods and goddesses as the highest realities or powers governing the universe. They often conceived ultimate reality in terms that transcended the ancient gods of the older, preaxial religions. They imagined sublime conceptions of ultimate reality, such the Hindu Brahman and the Chinese Dao, so great that they exceeded the human capacity to think or speak of them.

Thinking about the highest or deepest realities led these individuals to reflect more consciously on the process of thinking itself. Axial sages became progressively more interested in what we call epistemology: analyzing how we know what we know and the possibilities and limitations of our knowledge. Attention to epistemology, in turn, promoted a greater sense of self-consciousness and awareness of humanity's place in the universe.

From Cosmic Maintenance to Personal Transformation

Finally, the Axial Age marked a dramatic change in the very function of religion in human life. During this era, the purpose of religion shifted from what John Hick calls "cosmic maintenance" to "personal transformation."[7] When its purpose was cosmic maintenance, a religion functioned chiefly as a ritual means for human beings to collaborate with the divine powers to assist in keeping the world in good working order. The gods and goddesses relied on humans to help them provide the means to ensure reproduction and the productivity of the land, and to keep the sun and the seasons on course. Humans believed they had to provide sacrificial food and other pleasantries to the divinities to enable and encourage the gods to promote the processes of life. Divine and human beings worked together to maintain the well-being of the

---

6. S. N. Eisenstadt, *The Origins and Diversity of Axial Age Civilizations* (Albany: State University of New York Press, 1986).

7. John Hick, *An Interpretation of Religion*, 2nd ed. (New Haven, CT: Yale University Press, 2004).

world upon which they both depended. To understand this view of religion, one has to set aside the belief that gods are omnipotent and completely self-sufficient; the gods and goddesses certainly surpassed humans in power and dignity but were usually not considered supreme entities.

During the Axial Age, however, religion took on an unprecedented new role in human life: providing the means for the individual to undergo whatever change was necessary to achieve immortality, happiness, or whatever was considered the highest good in life. Selfhood and the heightened awareness of suffering and death prompted some religions to imagine wonderful afterlife experiences as ways to overcome the painful realities of this life. The achievement of these goals was connected to transforming the self from its ordinary state to another. It might mean accepting a new vision of the way the universe works, accepting the demands of a particular god with the power to bestow immortality or paradise, or subjecting the self to a discipline that reshaped it in more wholesome ways. However it was imagined, the rise of the self in the Axial Age meant that religions were faced with new problems. In response to this novel predicament, religion began to facilitate personal transformation by helping people understand the nature and cause of their problems and providing innovative ways to solve them.

Jaspers was certainly correct in his contention that the Axial Age laid contemporary humanity's spiritual foundations. In this book, we will probe this idea in much greater detail by carefully examining the specific and distinctive developments within the axial centers of Asia. To that study we now turn.

PART I

West Asia

1

The Noble Ones

Our study of the Asian Axial Age begins neither in the axial centers nor even in the Axial Age. We start, rather, with a collection of peoples who lived in Central Asia several millennia before the Axial Age got under way. Known today as the Indo-Europeans, these individuals were the ancestors of the axial communities of West and South Asia. Understanding the Indo-Europeans enables us to better grasp the developments that unfolded among their descendants.

The Indo-Europeans

Six thousand years ago, the Indo-Europeans occupied the area of the south Russian steppes just north of the Black and Caspian Seas. Today, this region roughly corresponds to the land stretching from Ukraine, across a portion of southern Russia, to west Kazakhstan. When the Indo-Europeans occupied this area, it was mostly a barren desert that suffered bitterly cold winters and harsh summers. It was not an easy place in which to live.

Scholars do not know a great deal about the inhabitants of this region during this period, but on one matter, most historians agree: many of the original occupants and their descendants gradually migrated to other parts of the world, including the northern Mediterranean area, northern Europe as far west as Ireland, and southward into Iran and the Indian subcontinent. This hypothesis suggests that many of the past and current residents of these sundry regions derive from a common ancestral stock. The basis of this theory is principally linguistic. The careful analysis of languages as diverse as Icelandic, German, Gaelic, Latin, Greek, Russian, Persian, Sanskrit, Sinhalese, and English has determined that they all evolved from what was once a single language known today as Proto-Indo-European (PIE). Because it fell into disuse before writing was invented, there is no direct evidence attesting to the existence of this original language. But by analyzing the dozens of extant languages that are believed to have developed from it, linguists have been able to reconstruct much of Proto-Indo-European. This reconstruction, along with some archaeological and archaeogenetic (the study of ancient DNA) evidence, has provided the means to hypothesize the migratory patterns of these Central Asians. While some of the specific details of these patterns continue to be the subject of debate, there is general (but not universal) agreement among scholars about the main features of the migrations.

The Indo-Iranians

Of the many groups that migrated out of Central Asia to other locations, the most important for our study are those who journeyed southward into the areas now occupied by the countries of Iran, Pakistan, and India. To differentiate these migrants from other Indo-European peoples, scholars often refer to them as the Indo-Iranians, but they called themselves the Aryans, a name that derives from *ariya*, which translates into English as "noble." They thus knew themselves as the "Noble Ones."

This group remained unified until about four thousand years ago, when it slowly split and moved in separate directions. Some of the Aryans settled in present-day Iran, and others traveled farther into Afghanistan and then the Indus Valley, gradually spreading across the northern Indian subcontinent. As they divided, their languages evolved away from one another, but they were still similar enough that communication was possible for some time. The Iranian tribes spoke a dialect we call Avestan, because it now exists only in a collection of sacred writings known as the Avesta. The group who migrated to India spoke a form of the language now known as Sanskrit.

When each group arrived at its final destination, it called its new territory the "Land of the Noble." The Indo-Aryans knew their new home not as "India" but as *Āryāvarta*, and the Irano-Aryans called theirs *airyana waējah*, an expression that later evolved into "Iran."

Society and Economy

Almost all we know of the Aryans comes from two sources: the Rig Veda, the oldest extant Indo-European text, taken to India in oral tradition, and the Avesta, a slightly later text from Iran, also preserved orally for much of its history. Because they were composed before the final division of the Aryans, the Rig Veda and the Avesta tell us a good bit about Indo-Iranian life prior to their migrations. These texts make clear that the Noble Ones were originally nomadic and seminomadic shepherds and cattle herders who wandered in relatively small areas, seeking pastureland for their animals. Since the Central Asian steppes were arid and barren, the Indo-Iranians were not great agriculturalists. The principal source of their food was the domesticated animals they kept and the wild game they hunted.

Their society was divided into two classes: the priests and the laity. Members of the lay class were called the "producers," because their occupations involved meeting the community's material needs. The Aryans arranged themselves loosely into tribes, with little to no formal governing structures. Early Indo-Iranian society appears to have been relatively peaceful and probably quite static, as it seems to have existed for centuries with few significant cultural changes.

The Religion of the Indo-Iranians

The religious life of the early Indo-Iranians, inasmuch as it can be reconstructed from our limited resources, suggests a rather commonsensical worldview for people living in the harsh environment of Central Asia. Like all ancient groups, the Indo-Iranians had their gods, their beliefs about the nature of the world, and rituals that helped them influence those gods and that world.

> "The religious life of the early Indo-Iranians ... suggests a rather commonsensical worldview for people living in the harsh environment of Central Asia. Like all ancient groups, the Indo-Iranians had their gods, their beliefs about the nature of the world, and rituals that helped them influence those gods and that world"

The Gods

The gods were of various sorts, each related to a different aspect of everyday life. Especially important to the ordinary people were the deities who controlled the natural world. These gods included the Sky and the Earth (Asman and Zam), the Sun and the Moon (Hvar and Mah), and the Winds (Vata and Vayu). Although not considered gods as such, trees were venerated, especially those growing beside rivers or streams, probably because the bark or fruit was thought to have healing properties. In India still today, certain trees growing by rivers are seen as highly auspicious and often mark the sacred site of a temple or shrine.

At one time, the Indo-Iranians worshiped an overarching sky god. This king of the gods was known in the Iranian dialect as Dyaoš and in the Indian dialect he was called Dyaus-Pitr. These names are cognates of the Greek and Roman terms for their chief god: Zeus (Dyaoš/ Dyaus) and Jupiter (Pitr). Over time, this Aryan sky god became so remote and distant from everyday life that he simply became irrelevant, and the Aryans effectively forgot about him.

In addition to the gods of nature, there were gods associated with ritual practices. Particularly important were the Fire, the Water, and Geush Urvan, or the "Soul of the Bull." Geush Urvan was the spiritual energy of a primordial bovine that had once lived on earth but had died and ascended to the heavens, where its powers continued to replenish the animal realm. The Aryans also deified a vision-inducing plant called Haoma in the Avestan dialect and Soma in the Sanskrit. Because of their importance in religious ceremonies, these divinities were especially significant to the priests.

Another category of divine beings were the *ahuras*, in Avestan, or *asuras*, in Sanskrit (names that simply mean "lords"). In this class, three gods were of greatest significance. The first two—Varuna and his assistant, Mitra—were associated with oaths and promise keeping. These gods were invoked to ensure that covenants among individuals and communities were fulfilled. The third and greatest was Mazda, the lord of wisdom.[1] As the Iranian tradition evolved, Ahura Mazda became the most important god of all, and perhaps for some, the *only* god; unlike the other ahuras, Mazda played no role at all in the development of the Indian traditions.

Finally, there were numerous lesser divinities known as *daevas* in Avestan and *devas* in Sanskrit. These words are ordinarily translated as "gods," but a more literal rendering would be "shiny ones." These Avestan and Sanskrit words have obvious cognates in other Indo-European languages. *Deus* in Latin, *divine* in English, and *diva* in Italian are just three examples. The shiny ones initially represented such qualities as courage, friendship, justice, obedience, and "glory," a charismatic characteristic that dwelled in gods and heroes. In the later Indo-Aryan tradition, *deva* and its feminine form *devi* became terms for the most important class of divinities, although, as we shall see, that was not the case in Irano-Aryan religion.

Morality and Order

In addition to this complex world of spirits and gods, the Indo-Iranians believed in an abstract, impersonal principle of order. The Sanskrit speakers called it *rita*, and those who spoke Avestan referred to it as *asha*. Both words designate a

---

1. The name of the Iranian god is spelled just like the automobile Mazda. According to the manufacturer, the car was so named for three reasons: first, to honor the god Mazda; second, because Mazda means "wisdom" in Persian; and third, because the family name of the Japanese manufacturer is Matsuda, which sounds much like Mazda.

natural reality that maintains cosmic order, keeping the astral bodies on their paths and the seasons turning in proper sequence. *Rita/asha* had moral as well cosmological dimensions, and in this sense, it was a principle for appropriate human and divine behavior; the deities, like humans, were also subject to it. Adherence to this moral law promoted harmony and well-being for the individual and for society.

The principle of order was opposed, however, by another power that prompted disharmony and chaos. The Iranians, for whom this element of disorder became very prominent in later theology, called it *druj*; the Sanskrit speakers called it *druh*. Because these two principles were diametrically opposed to one another in a constant struggle for dominance, the Indo-Iranians considered it necessary to help maintain and strengthen the orderly element. Proper observance of the religious rites, they believed, enhanced the power of order and promoted harmony in the world.

COSMOGONY: HOW THE WORLD CAME TO BE

To understand ritual in any preaxial culture, one must have a grasp of its beliefs about the origins of the world. Creation stories, or cosmogonies, provided prototypes or templates for ritual practices. The performers of religious rites often understood themselves as reenacting the original divine work of creation and thereby renewing creation and giving it a fresh beginning.[2]

This point can be well illustrated by considering an account of the world's creation from the Avesta and then studying its relationship to ritual practices. The Avestan cosmogony says the earth was created in seven stages, not unlike the seven-day scheme of the book of Genesis, which was written centuries later. The driving force behind creation in the Avestan story is not always clear, although sometimes it appears to be the Ahura Mazda, the Iranian lord of wisdom.

In the first stage, the sky came into being. The sky was conceived as something like a gigantic inverted bowl made of beautiful stone. Rather than believing that the sky was our perception of infinite space, as we moderns might think, it seemed obvious to the ancients that the firmament was a finite, solid structure.[3] During the second stage, water was created, covering the bottom of the sky shell. Imagine an upside down bowl floating on the surface of the

---

2. For an analysis of the connection between cosmogony and ritual, see Mircea Eliade, *The Sacred and the Profane: the Nature of Religion* (Orlando, FL: Harcourt, 1987).

3. I remember thinking as a child the same thing as I pondered the nature of the sky. When the first rockets were sent into outer space, I recall being deeply worried about the possibility of spacecraft literally shattering the sky and breaking it into pieces.

water in a sink. Next, in the third stage, solid earth came into being, floating on the surface of the water like a flat plate beneath the inverted bowl. Life was added to the physical world during the fourth, fifth, and sixth stages, with the successive emergence of one plant, then one animal (a bull), and finally, a man, named Yima. The seventh stage brought fire, an element that came to pervade the entire world, residing in seen and unseen places.

In the final act of creation, the gods assembled to perform the first ritual, a sacrifice. By crushing and dismembering the primordial plant, the bull, and the man, the gods created new lives, and the vegetable, animal, and human realms were populated. The world was set in motion following the course of *asha*. Death soon appeared, as did reproduction and new life, and the world was on its way.

RITUAL

In their own ceremonies, the Indo-Iranians reenacted the primordial sacrifices of the gods to maintain the cosmic and moral order and to ensure that new life properly replaced the old.

Among the simplest of their rituals were offerings of libations to the gods of Water and Fire, performed in the home by ordinary folk. In the arid and cold steppes, the importance of—indeed, the very sacredness of—these two elements is readily evident. To the Water was given an offering of milk and two plant leaves to represent the animal and vegetable realms. These libations returned to the divine powers the vital elements they required to continue productivity and harmony. Fire was of great importance not only for winter warmth but also for cooking meat, the staple of the Indo-Iranian diet. Because starting a new fire was difficult, fires were kept continually burning in fireplaces and terra-cotta pots. Like the libations to Water, the offerings to Fire were from the two kingdoms: incense and wood from plants and animal fat from cooked meat. The melting fat caused the flames to blaze, visibly fortifying the fire.

> "In their own ceremonies, the Indo-Iranians reenacted the primordial sacrifices of the gods to maintain the cosmic and moral order and to ensure that new life properly replaced the old."

For more complex rituals, a sacred space had to be created, and professional priests were required to conduct them. Because of their nomadic life, the ritual precinct was temporary, and portable implements were used. Sacred space was marked by lines drawn on the ground as prayers were uttered to keep out evil spirits. Fires burned in sacred vessels and pits dug in the earth.

The most sacred of all ceremonies were the fire rituals, and they often involved blood sacrifice, usually goats, sheep, or cattle. The Avestan word for sacrifice was *yasna*, almost identical to the Sanskrit *yajna*. The Indo-Iranians were awed by the act of taking life and did so reverentially. Animal sacrifices had to be performed with special prayers to enable the animal's spirit or life force to continue on. This ritual practice suggests a strong affinity between humans and animals. One of the Avestan texts says, "We reverence our [own] souls, and those of the domestic animals which nourish us . . . and the souls of useful wild animals."[4] The spirits of sacrificed animals were believed to become part of Geush Urvan, the "Soul of the Bull," the life energy of the animal world. Since blood sustained this deity, the Indo-Iranians understood themselves as helping the god to care for the animals on earth and thus guarantee their abundance. Consecrated meat was also offered to the other gods and then eaten by the participants of the sacrifice. Because of their respect for animal life, the Indo-Iranians believed that domesticated animals had to be sanctified before their flesh could be consumed. Even before killing a wild animal for food, hunters said prayers to ensure the animal spirit's safe return to the Soul of the Bull.

These sacred rites also utilized Soma. Like fire and water, Soma was regarded as a god. It resided in a special species of plant whose identity is unknown to us today. According to the ancient texts, the liquid essence of this plant was pressed out and mixed as a golden drink resembling honey. Soma had properties that allowed those who imbibed it to feel ecstatic, literally out of their ordinary world, and transported to the realm of the gods. This passage from the Rig Veda captures a sense of the experience of consuming this sacred libation:

I have tasted the sweet drink of life, knowing that it inspires good thoughts and joyous expansiveness to the extreme, that all the gods and mortals seek it together, calling it . . . [ambrosia].

When you penetrate inside, you will know no limits, and you will avert the wrath of the gods.

. . . .

We have drunk the Soma; we have become immortal; we have gone to the light; we have found the gods. What can hatred and the malice of a mortal do to us now, O immortal one?

. . . .

---

4. Yasna 39.1-2 quoted in Mary Boyce, *Zoroastrians: Their Religious Beliefs and Practices* (New York: Routledge, 2001), 5.

The glorious drops that I have drunk set me free in wide space . . . . Let the drops protect me from the foot that stumbles and keep lameness away from me.

Inflame me like a fire kindled by friction; make us see far; make us richer, better. I am intoxicated with you, Soma, I think myself rich. Draw near and make us thrive.

. . . .

Weakness and diseases have gone; the forces of darkness have fled in terror. Soma has climbed in us, expanding. We have come to the place where they stretch out life-spans.[5]

By ingesting Soma, the Indo-Iranians achieved what they considered the apex of existence: long life, freedom from suffering and fear, communion with gods and the spirit world, and intense pleasure. Little wonder that Soma was so highly prized and zealously protected. Its chief downside, however, was that it provided only temporary ecstasy. Eventually, the effects would wear off, and ordinary life would reassert itself. But the experience of divine communion was important in confirming the existence of the gods and expanding the mind to consider the deepest possibilities of human life. Soma allowed the Indo-Iranians to imagine a life devoid of pain and anxiety. In the centuries to come, the heirs of this tradition would seek similar experiences through the techniques of introspection and ascetic practice, rather than botanical substances.

These ritual practices reveal the fundamental elements of the worldview of preaxial Aryans. The central purpose of religion was to collaborate in the processes and functions of life. These forces were often personified as gods and goddesses or as abstract, impersonal principles. Human beings had to do their part to keep both the natural world and the social world in good working order, and it was clear they felt a close kinship with other aspects of the natural and divine worlds. Aryan religion at this time supported a culture that was generally static and relatively peaceful. Innovation was often viewed with suspicion and frequently regarded as sacrilegious because it represented a departure from the primordial acts of the gods.

THE RAIDERS

Despite the conservative forces in Indo-Iranian society, the way of life for these people eventually changed. As they drifted southward from the Central Asian steppes, the Indo-Iranians acquired the knowledge to domesticate the horse and to build and use war chariots. They also learned how to make bronze and

---

5. *The Rig Veda,* 8.48, trans. Wendy Doniger (New York: Penguin, 2005), 134–35.

availed themselves of the rich ore deposits of the area to fashion weapons. The coming of the chariot and the implements of war completely disrupted the once-stable culture. A new form of livelihood now emerged to supplement the passive tending of sheep and cows, and that was *stealing* sheep and cows. Many of the later Indo-Iranians became rustlers. Raiding and pillaging developed into a new way of life, initiating a restless, heroic age, not unlike the cultures of the old Norsemen and pre-Islamic Arabia. A career in raiding brought a fundamental new purpose to those who partook of this new form of living: gaining wealth and glory. Cattle and sheep had long been the measure of prosperity among the Indo-Iranians. Besides providing meat and milk, these animals were the sources of leather for clothing and tents, bones for tools, dung for fire, and even urine for the consecration of sacred utensils.

But raiding not only altered the economy of the Indo-Iranians, it also disrupted moral concerns and respect for the rule of law. These pillaging rustlers showed little regard for the weak and defenseless; whole villages might be wiped out in an afternoon just to enhance another clan's livestock holdings. Might rather than right ruled the day. A third class of individuals thus arose alongside the priests and producers: the warlords and professional warriors. This new class soon became identified with their love for rough living, hard drinking, and gambling, in many ways similar to the Hollywood versions of the old American West, with its outlaws, gunslingers, and saloons. There was excitement and a thrill to living on the edge and outside the restraints of conventional society.

Certainly not all Indo-Iranians adopted the lifestyle of cattle rustling and village pillaging, just as not all denizens of the Old West were cowboys and outlaws. A new kind of nomenclature entered the Aryan lexicon to distinguish between the two kinds of people. The *ashavans* followed the way of order and stability, but the wicked ones (at least so called by the *ashavans*) were the *drujvants*, the devotees of the principle of disorder. And like the guys with white and black hats in the old westerns, the *ashavans* and *drujvants* were depicted differently. The followers of *asha* were believed to have been given a heavenly blessing (*khvarna*), which suggested divine approval. In images, the blessing was represented as golden flames surrounding the head. Similar motifs seen in later images of the Buddha, Christian saints, and Muhammad may have derived from this Iranian influence.

The Religious Transformation

Although not all Indo-Iranians were rustlers and outlaws, the raiding and looting life had ramifications for those who wanted nothing to do with it. These effects were even felt in Indo-Iranian religious life. New gods more acceptable to the emerging warrior caste began to appear and even dominate some forms of religion. Many turned to worship Indra, the brave new deity of the heroic age. In fact, by the time the Aryans reached India, Indra was the ascendant divine being. Over one-quarter of the thousand hymns of praise in the Rig Veda are addressed to him alone.

Indra was a macho god, to be sure. He was valiant in combat, reckless to the point of being foolhardy, nearly amoral, but loyal to those who revered him and made offerings to him. In return, he was a giver of many gifts to his followers. And he loved Soma, the intoxicating beverage that fueled his passion and reckless spirit. Earlier, we observed how Soma was imbibed to allow the Indo-Iranians to commune with the gods, to imagine a new life free of distress, and to inspire poetry. In the heroic age of raiding, Soma seems to have acquired another dimension. Perhaps it had been there all the along, but certainly in these latter days, its potential to produce a frenzy conducive to war and lawlessness was fully exploited:

> This, yes this is my thought: I will win [i.e., steal!] a cow and a horse. Have I not drunk Soma?
>
> Like impetuous winds, the drinks have lifted me up. Have I not drunk Soma?
>
> The drinks have lifted me up, like swift horses bolting with a chariot. Have I not drunk Soma?
>
> . . . .
>
> The five tribes are no more to me than a mote in the eye. Have I not drunk Soma?
>
> . . . .
>
> In my vastness, I surpassed the sky and this vast earth. Have I not drunk Soma?
>
> Yes! I will place the earth here, or perhaps there. Have I not drunk Soma?
>
> . . . .
>
> I am huge, huge! flying to the cloud. Have I not drunk Soma?
>
> I am going to a well-stocked house, carrying oblations to the gods. Have I not drunk Soma?[6]

---

6. *The Rig Veda*, 10.119, trans. Doniger, 131–32.

Where Soma enabled the priests to see visions of the gods and poets to utter great, beautiful words, it now propelled the warriors to feel invincible, powerful, beyond the confines of worldly limits.

In contrast to Indra, worship of many other gods began to decline. For some, Varuna, the venerable *ahura*, seemed a little too tame, sitting up in his palace in heaven, keeping order in the world. For a nomadic people equipped with the horse and chariot, the more adventurous life of the daring Indra was more appealing—or at least that is what the texts suggest by the sheer volume of songs written to him. In time, Varuna and Indra would come to be seen as virtually diametrically opposite gods.

Division

Over time, the Indo-Iranian family began to divide and settle in different lands, where their once-shared religious practices and beliefs underwent significant transformations that ultimately produced the traditions that would much later be known as Zoroastrianism and Hinduism. The split was gradual, of course, and the religious developments were incremental. The actual divergence of the branches may have begun in the third millennium BCE, but it was definitely under way by the mid-second millennium. Dates for nomadic peoples are notoriously difficult to establish with precision, because nomads leave very few archaeological artifacts.

To study the developments initiated by this division, we turn first to West Asia, particularly the land of Iran, and then later trace the movement of the Indo-Aryans into South Asia. We start with an Iranian prophet named Zoroaster, who was not exactly a full-blown axial sage but an individual whose life and thought seem to prefigure much of what was to come in other axial centers. Zoroaster, or Zarathustra, as he is sometimes known,[7] is one of the least understood founding figures in the history of the world's religions. Perhaps best regarded as a transitional figure, he represents an interesting mixture of preaxial and axial religious elements.

---

7. Zoroaster, the name by which he is most commonly known, is a Greek transliteration of Zarathustra.

2

The Life of Zoroaster

Precious little is known about Zoroaster beyond his name. Most scholars agree that a biographical account of him would be tenuous at best, and wildly varying speculations have been put forth as to when and where he lived. Some research puts his birth anywhere between 1500 and 1000 BCE or even earlier. Mary Boyce, one of the leading specialists in this area, dates him to around 1200 BCE. According to tradition, his birth date was 628 BCE, making him an older contemporary of Confucius. Current scholarship places him right at or sometime before the start of Axial Age. According to general consensus, he lived in the eastern area of present-day Iran, but some researchers would place him in Central Asia. We will have to live with these uncertainties. What *is* clear is that Zoroaster came from a modest family living in the seminomadic conditions of Indo-Iranian times, as the rustlers and outlaws were in their prime, and *druj* seemed to be overwhelming *asha*.

Aside from much later traditions and legends, all the information we have about Zoroaster comes from the Gathas, or the "Verses," which are among the oldest parts of the Avesta, the foundational scripture of Zoroaster's religion. There are only seventeen extant gathas, but there may have been more at one time. These verses are believed to have been composed by Zoroaster himself under moments of religious inspiration. They are written in an archaic dialect, very close to the Sanskrit of the Rig Veda, and they resemble spontaneous prayers addressed to god; they are not sermons or didactic proclamations.

The Gathas tell us that Zoroaster was a priest. He called himself a *zaotar*, one of the libation pourers. As an authorized ritual specialist, Zoroaster would have been trained early in the priestly tradition and recognized as a full-fledged priest by age fifteen. His priestly vocation and his commitment to the rituals of his youth may have prompted the transformation that eventually led him to assume the role of "prophet" and inspire the reform movement that became Zoroastrianism. As a prophet, Zoroaster would have played a different religious role from that of priest. A priest usually functions ritually as a mediator between humans and the divine; a prophet, by contrast, is often a critic of religious practices and functions as a mouthpiece for a god. Many think Zoroaster may have been the world's first prophet in this sense.

> "As a prophet, Zoroaster would have played a different religious role from that of priest. A priest usually functions ritually as a mediator between humans and the divine; a prophet, by contrast, is often a critic of religious practices and functions as a mouthpiece for a god. Many think Zoroaster may have been the world's first prophet in this sense."

Zoroaster was acutely aware of and troubled by the violence and lawlessness of the land. It is not difficult to imagine the deep concern he might have felt over the way the old sacred rituals were being pressed into the services of war and thieving. In a later chapter, we will observe how similar social circumstances in China quickened the moral conscience of Confucius, causing him to urge a renewed respect for religious ceremonies.

Zoroaster's moral sensitivities seem to have ultimately led him on a quest for deeper truths, much as the Buddha and many others took to the wandering life to see the world in a clearer and more focused way during the Indian Axial Age. Tradition says that at age thirty, Zoroaster had an impressive visionary experience at a river, in which he was led into the presence of the Ahura Mazda and six other radiant beings, known collectively as the Heptad (that is, the Seven), and received a special revelation. He left this luminous audience with a new sense of purpose, departing with the words, "I shall teach men to seek the right [*asha*]."[1] The revelations did not stop there, though; Zoroaster had several more, but this was clearly the turning point in his life that transformed him from a mere priest to a prophet with a fire in the belly.

The beginning of Zoroaster's career as a prophet parallels a number of initiatory stories in the lives of other sages. Like many of these stories in the prophetic tradition, Zoroaster's calling occurred in the context of water. Indeed, decisive revelations seem to frequently occur by or in streams of water. The Hebrew prophet Ezekiel wrote that while standing "by the river Chebar, the heavens were opened, and I saw visions of God."[2] Jesus was baptized by John at the River Jordan and heard the blessing of God the Father, had a vision of a dove, and began preaching about the kingdom of god. Guru Nanak,

---

1. Yasna 28.4 quoted in Mary Boyce, *Zoroastrians: Their Religious Beliefs and Practices* (New York: Routledge, 2001), 19.

2. Ezek. 1:1.

the founder of the Sikh movement in medieval India, was taken away into heaven for three days while bathing in a stream; he returned after having been commissioned with a new message for Muslims and Hindus. Equally intriguing is the fact that these experiences occurred to these individuals at or around the age of thirty. Zoroaster, Ezekiel, Jesus, Nanak, and perhaps others in the prophetic tradition were at this age when their critical revelations came.

Once he understood that he had received a prophetic call, Zoroaster's response to this new vocation was both conservative and revolutionary. As a traditionalist, he called his fellow Iranians to a simple return to respect for the principles of good, order, and harmony. But he added novel dimensions to this traditional approach that made it an extremely powerful vision of the world.

Zoroaster's Theology

Zoroaster's theology had two chief foci, both movements in the direction of simplification. One focus was a set of ideas that nudged Iranian religion towards monotheism. The other was the notion that spiritual beings could be divided into two categories defining them as forces for either good or evil.

Movement toward Monotheism

Apparently as a result of his vision, Zoroaster became a passionate advocate for the worship of Ahura Mazda as the foremost deity. He wanted Mazda to be seen as superior to Varuna and the other *ahuras*. In his vision of the Heptad, Zoroaster unmistakably saw Mazda as the dominant deity. In later reflection and visions, Zoroaster seems to have refined this idea even further, suggesting that all the other *ahuras* and divinities were actually just emanations from or partial manifestations of Mazda. In Zoroaster's view, Mazda was the only uncreated god and the agent behind the seven-stage creation scheme in the Avesta. It may be too much to say that Zoroaster was a monotheist, but it seems fair to say that his thinking certainly tended in this direction and probably helped contribute to the religious environment that would ultimately champion the monotheistic perspective.

THEISTIC DUALISM

Zoroaster's second innovation was to simplify the pantheon by assigning clear moral qualities to the gods. All the spirits—the *daevas* and the *ahuras*—were now plainly associated with either good or evil. Zoroaster removed any ambiguity. Because the *daevas* like Indra were honored by the rustlers, whom Zoroaster called the Followers of the Lie, he reserved the word *daeva* exclusively for the wicked gods and the word *ahura* for the ethical gods. This usage is still current in the West; our word "devil" derives from the Iranian use of the word *daeva*. (It is important to note that Western practice came down through Iran and not India; in India, the word *deva* does not hold this dichotomized association. The term *deva* refers more to the power and status of divine beings and not specifically to their ethical nature. However, as if to return the favor to Zoroaster, the Indo-Aryans came to consider the *asuras*—the Sanskrit counterparts to the *ahuras*—as *evil* divinities.) Zoroaster also used the term *yazatas* to refer to good spirits or divine assistants—not really gods as such—but beings associated with the principle of good and truth. The *yazatas* were probably the prototype for angels in the other Western religions.

> "Zoroaster's theology had two chief foci, both movements in the direction of simplification: (1) the worship of Ahura Mazda as the foremost deity, and (2) simplification of the pantheon by assigning clear moral qualities to the gods."

Consistent with this theological simplification, Zoroaster also suggested the existence of an independent evil deity, a chief god among the *daevas*. It is not certain, by any means, given the scant evidence, but Zoroaster may in fact have been the first theologian in history to have conceived of an autonomous, wholly evil, supernatural being. In the Zoroastrian texts, this figure is called by various names including Aeshma and Angra Mainyu, but he is more commonly called by the name Ahriman. Zoroaster thus envisioned two superior beings—one completely good, the other completely evil—locked in mortal combat since the beginning of time, each struggling for the triumph of his principles and power.

In one of the ancient gathas, we get a flavor of Zoroaster's worldview in a brief, and rather cryptic, text called "The Two Spirits." The language is archaic, and it is not fully understood by modern scholars, but it does convey a sense of Zoroaster's theological conceptions:

Now, these are the two original Spirits who, as twins, have been perceived (by me) through a vision. In both thought and speech, (and) in deed, these two are what is good and evil. Between these two, the pious, not the impious, will choose rightly.

Furthermore, the two Spirits confronted each other; in the beginning (each) create(d) for himself life and nonlife, so that in the end there will be the worst existence for the drujvants, but the best mind for the Righteous.

Of these two Spirits, the deceitful (drujvant) chose the worst course of action, (while) the most beneficent Spirit who is clothed in hardest stone (chose) Truth, (as) also (do) those who believingly propitiate Ahura Mazda.

Between these two (Spirits) the daewas did not choose rightly at all since, while they were taking counsel among themselves, delusion came upon them, so that they chose the worst Mind. Then, all together, they ran to Wrath with which they infect the life of man.[3]

This passage presents many problems theologically. For instance, if Mazda were the original uncreated and wholly benevolent god, where did the evil spirit come from and why? Of course, that is the very problem of evil that has plagued the Western traditions in religion for eons. Zoroaster does not attempt to solve the issue. What is important for him is not the abstract matter of theological consistency, but the very pragmatic and existentially vital point that the human being has to make a choice between good and evil. Irrespective of the origins of these entities, human beings cannot escape the responsibility of aligning themselves with *asha* or *druj* and must live their lives accordingly. Just as the *daevas* had a choice to make, and ultimately made the wrong one, individual human beings are confronted with the identical decision.

The Rise of Moral Obligation

The need to choose between good and evil is one of the precise points where Zoroaster anticipates and perhaps partly instigates the transformations of the Axial Age. Time and again, as our study proceeds, we will encounter the call to make a choice, to align one's personal existence with the good or the evil, however these are conceived by the axial sages. The Axial Age obligated

---

3. Yasna 30.3-6 from William W. Malandra, *An Introduction to Ancient Iranian Religion: Readings from the Avesta and Achaemenid Inscriptions* (Minneapolis: University of Minnesota Press, 1983), 40.

individuals to accept responsibility for the moral quality of their actions and words.

In the postaxial age, such claims on our lives might seem totally unremarkable; of course we must take moral responsibility for our decisions. But by and large, the call to this kind of personal obligation was novel at this juncture in religious history, because it was connected with new ideas about what it means to be human and divine. Our continuing discussion on Zoroaster's reform and the influences it had will help verify this point. We will see that, for Zoroaster, the individual's moral and religious decision now determined the quality of his or her personal destiny. One's future well-being, especially in the world beyond this one, depended on one's behavior here and now. This idea is both unique at this moment in history and common across the axial centers.

3

Zoroaster's Legacy

Zoroaster was both a zealous prophet calling for a return to old-time religion and a grand visionary with startling new ideas. The result of his teachings was one of the most compelling and influential worldviews in history. In terms of its effects on *other* religions, Zoroastrianism may well have had the greatest impact of any single religion in the world. In this chapter, we will continue to explore the novel aspects of Zoroaster's theology and suggest ways his innovations may have directly and indirectly shaped subsequent religious perspectives.

Zoroaster's Innovations

There were two areas in which Zoroaster's thinking yielded enduring effects. The first was his demand for moral responsibility, and the second was his belief in a final destiny for the cosmos.

Choice, Destiny, and Moral Responsibility

As we noted in Chapter 2, Zoroaster greatly simplified Iranian religion. Everything came down to a straightforward, uncomplicated choice: Are you on the side of *asha* or of *druj*? He had already made clear which powers were good and which were evil. All that remained was for the individual human being to make a choice, the same way the divine beings had.

But to this choice, Zoroaster added profound consequences. Zoroaster believed that the individual's ultimate destiny depended on the choice he or she made. How he arrived at this conclusion is far from clear, but he was convinced that one's final end as a human being depended on whether one sided with the wholly good Mazda or the wholly evil Ahriman. To the modern person, this idea is such a commonplace notion that it seems almost totally unremarkable. Virtually every major religion makes a similar claim. What ultimately becomes of each of us—whether you go to heaven as in Christianity or paradise in Islam, or find *nibbana* in Buddhism or *moksha* in Hinduism—is contingent on the moral and theological choices we make in the here and now.

But in the preaxial age, this *was* a remarkable idea. It was unusual to suggest that the individual human even *has* a destiny beyond this life. Prior to the Axial Age, such a belief was not widely accepted. Some societies may have held that prominent individuals, such as the king, enjoyed a postmortem existence. But even this idea was rarely well defined and thought out. With the advent of the Axial Age, the view that ordinary individuals might have a destiny in a hereafter became more widely accepted.

But even more uncommon was Zoroaster's claim that those prospects were dependent on one's *moral* choices. Even in cultures that held to some kind of belief in an afterlife, almost never was destiny contingent on moral behavior. One's after-death future might be predicated on ritual practices—whether or not one had pleased the gods with sacrifices of sufficient quantity and quality—or perhaps on the performance of great deeds such as heroism in an epic battle. But until the Axial Age, we hardly ever find the claim that individual destiny is determined by moral decisions. This is one of the great themes of the axial transformation, and one to which we will continually return. For convenience, we will refer to this motif as "ethicization," the process whereby certain beliefs and practices are interpreted and understood in moral terms. In the view of Zoroaster, then, we can say the future of the human being has become "ethicized."

Zoroaster believed that individuals would be judged on the fourth day following their death. He imagined that judgment would take place at High Hara, the first and most sacred mountain on earth, where the great *ahuras* had their palaces. Individuals found to be good were led to the heavens across a wide bridge accompanied by a beautiful maiden, who was a reflection of their own inner goodness. In the heavens, they enjoyed the company of Mazda and other *ashavans*. Those who were judged evil had to cross an extremely narrow bridge—the texts say the width of a razor's edge—and were led by an ugly hag. Inevitably, they fell while crossing and landed in the abyss of hell, where they suffered painfully for their sins in the realm ruled by the Evil One.

Cosmological Drama

But the story does not end there. The assignment to heaven or hell was ultimately only temporary. Zoroaster also envisioned a final *cosmic* destiny. As he saw it, history—not just individual people, but history itself—was headed in a particular direction. Zoroaster envisioned time moving in a linear fashion, from a specific beginning to an apocalyptic conclusion. The end of the world, he thought, would come as the universal struggle between good and evil came to a head. He thought this final conflict would end in a spectacular battle called the Frashokereti, "the making glorious." In this war to end all wars, Zoroaster had no doubt that good would prevail and evil would be utterly and forever banished from existence. The Evil One, his minions, hell, and all its human inhabitants would be annihilated, and paradise would be established on earth. Zoroaster may have connected this vision with a bodily resurrection of the dead, in which those who had initially gone to heaven would return to earth to continue life in physical form. If this were Zoroaster's belief, he would have been among the first—if not *the* first—to have conceptualized such a fate.

Zoroaster also seems to have expected a savior figure or apocalyptic judge who would appear at the Frashokereti and play a decisive role in it. The ancient Avestan texts refer to this future redeemer-judge as a *Saoshyant*. According to Zoroastrian prophecy, the *Saoshyant* would be born from a virgin who had become pregnant by bathing in a lake in which Zoroaster's semen had been miraculously preserved.

The Power of Zoroaster's Worldview

These concepts—a grand cosmic struggle between good and evil, history moving toward a final conclusion, the appearance of a redeemer-judge, the resurrection of dead bodies, and the call for humans to choose sides—constitute Zoroaster's novel ideas. We cannot say for certain that these notions all originated with him; perhaps he was in conversation with like-minded individuals or ancient traditions. But we *can* say that it was through Zoroaster's influence and prophetic message that these ideas were widely disseminated among the Iranians.

What made this vision so compelling to many of Zoroaster's contemporaries? First, Zoroaster's vision implied a decisive role for human beings. To Zoroaster, people were *not* the pawns of the gods. The gods did not intervene and fool with the lives of hapless humans. People had a choice to make, and that choice was essential. It determined the individual's future, and it shaped the cosmic drama itself. The gods were at

> "These concepts—a grand cosmic struggle between good and evil, history moving toward a final conclusion, the appearance of a redeemer-judge, the resurrection of dead bodies, and the call for humans to choose sides—constitute Zoroaster's novel ideas."

war, and human beings had to act to ensure that the side of right prevailed. In this way, Zoroaster greatly elevated the importance of human moral responsibility.

But equally important was the way Zoroaster's vision provided meaning to human suffering and promised ultimate compensation for it. Those suffering from an unkind fate, from the thieves and cattle rustlers, or from illness and deprivation, could see their plight in a much larger context. Their anguish and misery were part of a grand drama involving the entire world, not just bad luck or random happenstance. For their suffering, the righteous would be given ample reparations. Immortal life in paradise, free of any and all evil, would suffice to make earthly suffering seem insignificant by comparison. And those who suffered could be satisfied by the sense that evil ones, too, would receive their just deserts.

Despite the compelling nature of Zoroaster's theology, the Gathas say Zoroaster was not well received in his own community, a fate he shared with two other great prophets, Jesus and Muhammad.[1] Soon after his rejection, Zoroaster moved to another location and there obtained some success in gathering followers through the patronage of influential persons in the area. He spent the rest of his life preaching and sending missionaries to spread his message, an uncommon practice in the preaxial world. Since it was taken for granted that different societies worshiped different gods, the idea of proselytizing others simply never occurred until the concept of a universal deity or ultimate reality emerged more definitively in the Axial Age.

Eventually, Zoroaster's message was disseminated throughout West Asia and as far east as China. Along the way, his message met with opposition, and many of his followers were persecuted and killed. The persecutions, however, merely convinced Zoroaster's followers of the truth of their convictions and effectively strengthened the movement. By the sixth century BCE, the Zoroastrian worldview had amassed enough power to function as the state religion of the Achaemenid (Persian) Empire and remained the state religion of two subsequent Iranian empires until the seventh century CE, when it was finally displaced by Islam.

Zoroastrian Practices

The various rituals of Zoroastrianism—prayer, purification, and celebrations—were intended to express and reinforce its basic message and

---

1. "But Jesus, said unto them, 'A prophet is not without honor, but in his own country, and among his own kin, and in his own house'" (Mark 6:4).

theology. A brief survey of some of the more important rites will help complete our picture of this tradition.

Prayer

Zoroaster prescribed one central practice for all of his followers: prayer five times each day. The Indo-Iranians were already accustomed to praying three times a day; Zoroaster added prayer at dawn and midnight to this routine. For the followers of Zoroaster, prayer was to be performed while standing in the presence of fire. The fire might be the sun, if one were outdoors, or the hearth, if in the home. The sun had come to be closely associated with Ahura Mazda. Like their Indo-Aryan relatives, the Iranians maintained the custom of keeping the sacred fires constantly lit. Some Muslims later criticized the Zoroastrians as "fire worshippers," and they are still sometimes called that in places like India, where they are known as Parsis. Zoroastrians, of course, resent the label, since they understand themselves to be worshiping god, not fire.

Purity Practices

Purity was also extremely important to the Iranians, just as it was to the Indo-Aryans. Activities that could cause ritual pollution included contact with dead bodies, body waste, and animals such as snakes, flies, ants, and wolves. Sickness, menstruation, and childbirth were also believed to contaminate. Since it was regarded as a symbol of the sacred, ceremonies involving fire were performed to restore a pristine state following pollution.

According to Zoroaster, the constituent elements of the world—earth, fire, and especially water—needed to be kept clean and uncontaminated. The Zoroastrians even gave up burial of the dead for fear of befouling the soil, and instead placed corpses in "towers of silence," exposed to the air to let birds of prey pick the bones clean. The Zoroastrian purity code also included the penalty of death for anyone polluting a sacred fire. Yet at the same time, it allowed the killing of snakes and scorpions, both believed to be demonic animals in league with the *daevas*.

Celebrations

The Zoroastrians celebrated seven major festivals tied mainly to the rhythms of agricultural life. By far the most important was honoring the new year, which the Iranians called Nowruz, meaning "New Day," and celebrated at the spring equinox. New Day is still widely celebrated by Iranians (and in Pakistan, Afghanistan, and parts of India) and is one of the oldest continuously celebrated festivals on earth. Nowruz is intended to anticipate the overthrow of the evil ones at the end of time and hence is a very joyful occasion.

THE INFLUENCES OF ZOROASTER AND ZOROASTRIANISM

Much of Zoroaster's theology must sound familiar to anyone acquainted with the Abrahamic traditions: Judaism, Christianity, and Islam. Are the parallels among these traditions merely coincidental, or has there been actual historical influence from one tradition to the others? This has been and still is a controversial issue. Many Jews, Christians, and Muslims deny or minimize the significance of the parallels, believing that such comparisons somehow detract from the uniqueness or divine origin of their religion. Nonetheless, many scholars working in this area are convinced that formative Judaism and Christianity, and through them Islam, *were* shaped, directly or indirectly, by the more ancient Zoroastrian beliefs.

> "Many scholars working in this area are convinced that formative Judaism, Christianity, and Islam *were* shaped, directly or indirectly, by the more ancient Zoroastrian beliefs."

This influence, however, is difficult to document and prove conclusively because the case would have to be based largely on circumstantial evidence. There are no passages in the Bible or Qur'an that quote from the Gathas or even paraphrase it. While there *are* examples of such borrowing from other scriptures in West Asia, there is none from Zoroastrianism. Early Jewish and Christian theologians probably never could access any of the Zoroastrian teachings because most of Zoroaster's religion remained in oral tradition for centuries. The infiltration of Zoroastrian ideas most likely occurred in a much less formal way, as Jews encountered Zoroastrian practitioners and engaged them in conversation and observed their practices.

Although circumstantial, the case for Zoroastrian influence remains persuasive. The argument is a simple one: In the sixth century BCE, during the formative period of Judaism, Jews came into contact with the Persian Empire during and after the Exile, or Babylonian Captivity, and thereafter, new ideas—curiously like Zoroaster's—began to appear in Jewish and then later Christian writings. These ideas were significantly different from the theology of earlier Hebrew writings and bear the traces of outside influences.

Time and History

Consider the linear view of time—the idea that cosmic history has a beginning, middle, and end. This concept is often contrasted with the more common ancient view of time as cyclical, as constantly repeating itself but ultimately going nowhere, a view we will encounter when we get to the traditions of India. The key element of the linear understanding of history is the idea of an end-time. Although there were vague intimations of an eschaton, or end-time, in Jewish writings prior to the Exile, it was only afterward that this theme began to dominate Jewish thought and was accepted as mainstream Jewish theology. And it was most often connected with the idea of a final apocalypse, the end of history brought about by a grand showdown between good and evil and ending in the final judgment of human beings according to their deeds.

The Day of Judgment

The notion of a Day of Judgment did not appear in Jewish theology until the postexilic period. The first appearance of this idea in the Bible was in the books of Ecclesiastes and Daniel, both written after the Jewish contact with the Persian world. The book of Ecclesiastes ends with this verse: "For God will bring every deed into judgment, including every secret thing, whether good or evil."[2] The book of Daniel is even more explicit: "There shall be a time of anguish, such as has never occurred since nations came into existence. But at that time your people shall be delivered, everyone who is found written in the book. Many of those who sleep in the dust of the earth shall awake, some to everlasting life, and some to shame and everlasting contempt. Those who are wise shall shine like the brightness of the sky, and those who lead many to righteousness, like the stars forever and ever."[3] We hear in these words of Daniel's vision the same Zoroastrian themes of an apocalyptic end to history, a resurrection of bodies and a day of judgment, and the determination of human destiny based on the moral quality of the individual's life.

Heaven and Hell

After the Exile, we also see for the first time in Jewish thought the ideas of heaven and hell as ultimate human destinations, the belief in angels and demons, and the concepts of a universal savior and the devil. Obviously, the Bible speaks of heaven from the opening of Genesis, but throughout most of the Bible, heaven simply means the realm of the divine, the place Yahweh inhabits. The

---

2. Eccles. 12:14.
3. Dan. 12:1-3.

idea that human beings might attain everlasting life in the heavenly realm was simply foreign to Jewish thinking prior to the Exile. The "shades," or disembodied spirits of individuals, were believed to descend to an underworld known as Sheol, where they continued a shadowy quasi-existence. Descent to Sheol was simply in the nature of things; it did not depend in any way on one's moral character. After Persian contact, however, Jewish thinkers increasingly conceived of an afterlife in either heaven or hell, now understood as a paradise or perdition, respectively. Interestingly, the word *paradise*, which the later books of the Bible use as synonymous with heaven, derives from the ancient Iranian words *pairi-daeza*, meaning an "enclosed garden."

THE DEVIL

The idea of the devil, which came to figure more prominently in Christianity than in Judaism, seems quite clearly to be of Iranian origin. The closest thing to a "devil" in the Hebrew Bible is found in the book of Job. Contrary to common belief, the devil appears nowhere in the story of Adam and Eve, or anywhere else in Genesis. Even in the book of Job, the figure called "the satan" is not really the same character as the one who goes by that name in the New Testament. In the story of Job, "the satan," which is a title rather than a name, is a member of the heavenly court who tries to keep god honest by challenging him to a wager involving a righteous man. In no sense does the satan appear as a wholly malevolent deity or the embodiment of evil. In Job, it appears that god and the satan are on friendly, if somewhat adversarial, terms.

But by the time the New Testament was written, some 500 to 600 years after the Babylonian exile, Satan had come to be regarded as a god of evil, living in hell and constantly assaulting godly people, the way the Zoroastrians thought of Ahriman. Jesus speaks a great deal of the devil, and the New Testament portrays the two confronting one another. Jesus' death and resurrection are even interpreted as breaking the power of the devil over humanity. Some centuries after Jesus, the Christian theologian Augustine argued that Satan was once one of God's spiritual creatures who chose to be evil out of pride.[4] At this point, it is hard to distinguish the Christian view of Satan from Zoroaster's concept of the Evil One, and it is equally hard to resist the conclusion that the latter decisively contributed to the conceptualization of the former.

---

4. Augustine, *The City of God*.

THE SON OF MAN

Zoroaster also advanced a belief in a universal savior or apocalyptic judge who appears at the end of time. The anticipation of a messiah has become an important part of the Jewish tradition, and there are indications that this expectation began to emerge before the Jews had contact with Zoroastrians. The early Jewish hopes for the messiah, however, were far from clear or monolithic. Messiah, which simply means "anointed one," was used to refer to individuals such as King David and even Cyrus, the Persian king who freed the Jews from their Babylonian Captivity. By the time of Jesus, the anticipation of a messiah was rife among the Jews, although there seems to have been no consensus as to whom this figure was supposed be or what he was supposed to do.

Zoroaster's idea of a *Saoshyant*, a universal redeemer who would appear at the end time, may have shaped some of the Jews' expectations. In the postexilic book of Daniel, we read for the first time in the Bible about an apocalyptic figure called the Son of Man. According to Daniel, the Son of Man will descend from heaven at the end of history and play a decisive role in the annihilation of evil and return the world to the path of righteousness. Daniel writes of his vision:

> I saw one like a [Son of Man]
> coming with the clouds of heaven.
> And he came to the Ancient One
> and was presented before him.
> To him was given dominion
> and glory and kingship,
> that all the peoples, nations, and languages
> should serve him.
> His dominion is an everlasting dominion
> that shall not pass away,
> and his kingship is one
> that shall never be destroyed.[5]

Jesus frequently referred to himself as the Son of Man, particularly in Mark, the earliest gospel. There is debate, of course, over what he may have meant in using that title, but it is plausible that he believed his role in ushering in the kingdom of god would be his postcrucifixion appearance as the end-time redeemer and judge. Whether or not many Jews believed Jesus was the one,

---

5. Dan. 7:13-14.

it is clear that many expected a messiah whose role would be like that of the *Saoshyant*.

Finally, it is with respect to Jesus that we have at least one biblical reference to the religion of the Zoroastrians. The Gospel of Matthew mentions that a year or two after Jesus' birth, wise men "from the East," who had been studying the stars, came to visit and pay their respects. These wise men were called Magi, a Greek word based on *magus*, a Persian term for priest. Matthew's story takes on added richness when we consider that these eastern visitors may have been Zoroastrians who were scanning the heavens for signs of their *Saoshyant* and were led to Judea, where Jesus was born.

Although there is much more to be said about Zoroaster, his religion, and the impact he had in world religion, we must draw this discussion to a close. In the next chapter, we will return to the Aryans who chose not to stay in Iran but continued their migration into South Asia.

PART II

South Asia

4

South Asia before the Axial Age

We now direct our attention to South Asia and especially the area we know as the Indian subcontinent. In coming chapters, we will discuss the evolution of Hinduism, Buddhism, and Jainism in this region. But first, we start with a sketch of this location before the axial ferment to help us understand the transformations that led to the birth of these religions.

We are already familiar with a major part of the preaxial Indian world from our discussions of the Indo-Iranian peoples who migrated from the Central Asian steppes. We spent a fair amount of time exploring the religious world of the Indo-Iranians prior to their division. With this chapter, we begin to turn our attention to the development of this tradition through the Indo-Aryans who ultimately settled in India. Just as the tradition that developed in Iran assumed new forms and made significant departures from the ancient religion, so too the Indo-Aryan tradition changed in diverse and novel ways when it entered its new homeland.

The Indus Valley Civilization

Before we take up the Indo-Aryans' migration into India, however, we must first consider another culture that occupied this territory long before their arrival. The Indus Valley Civilization, as it is now called, was situated along the Indus and Saraswati River systems in present-day Pakistan and the northwestern portion of the Republic of India. This extensive culture existed at least 1,500 years before the Indo-Aryans appeared. By the time the Aryans began to settle in this area, around 1600 BCE, the Indus Valley Civilization was in decline. Yet its vestiges were still potent enough to profoundly influence the evolution of Hinduism. Today, scholars generally believe that Hindu traditions emerged out of the confluence of the ancient Indo-Aryan and Indus religions.

Until the middle of the nineteenth century, the Indus Valley Civilization had been completely forgotten by humanity. Not until 1856, when British engineers accidentally uncovered some of the ruins of this culture, did modern humanity have any idea that there had ever been an Indus Valley Civilization. Today, we know this civilization was the largest of the ancient world. So far, archaeologists have discovered more than seventy cities in an area about the size of Texas. These urban centers were remarkably well planned and organized. The largest may have contained as many as fifty thousand inhabitants at one time. We know very little about the way that Indus dwellers governed themselves or structured their society, but the uniformity of their cities suggests some sort of centralized authority and law enforcement. We can infer from the absence of any significant weapons among the archaeological artifacts that the Indus Valley Civilization was relatively peaceful. We also know that agriculture was the basis of their economy, along with trade with other cultures, most notably the Mesopotamians living along the Tigris and Euphrates Rivers.

What we do *not* know is their language. There are numerous examples of what most scholars think is Indus writing, but as yet, linguists have been unable to decipher it. Thus, we have no idea what the citizens of this great society called themselves, and we have no literary sources for understanding Indus religion. Our present knowledge is essentially informed speculation based the material artifacts of the ruins. There is simply no textual evidence to help corroborate or refute scholarly inferences.

We *can* say with some confidence that Indus dwellers were deeply concerned with the functions of sexuality and procreation, and that this preoccupation was reflected in their religious practices. Throughout the region, archaeologists have discovered a large number of terra-cotta figurines of women with exaggerated hips and large breasts. Interestingly, no corresponding portrayals of men as icons of sexuality have been unearthed. Rather, to depict male sexuality, Indus artisans created images of horned animals—such as bulls and buffalo—with very powerful flanks and rather obvious male genitalia. In addition to these representations, excavations have turned up an array of stone and clay phalluses and vulvas whose precise function is not certain but which may symbolize divine powers of reproduction and creativity.

Without written literature, we can only make educated guesses about these artifacts based on similar findings in other societies and in later Hinduism. Female figurines, similar to those of the Indus Valley, have been unearthed in various parts of the world and are thought to symbolize a divine woman or goddess. Some researchers have argued that these images indicate that the earliest humans worshipped a mother goddess long before male gods. If so, perhaps the Indus dwellers were part of this vast goddess religion. But the idea of a pervasive goddess religion is still a controversial one, and not all scholars agree on it. Nevertheless, it does seem evident that—at least in the ancient culture of the Indus Valley—the reproductive powers of women were revered and celebrated, and perhaps women themselves were regarded as sacred. It is certain that worship of the goddess is a prominent part of contemporary Hinduism and has a long, deep-rooted history. It seems entirely reasonable, therefore, to believe that this Hindu tradition may have derived from these Indus practices.

The depiction of horned male animals and stone phalluses also implies a fascination with—and perhaps an anxiety about—sexuality and reproductive functions. But what precisely was the function of these objects? Here, historical and current religious practices may give us clues. Throughout their recorded history, Hindus have revered a god known as Shiva, who has been represented symbolically as the male and female sex organs in an icon called the lingam. The meaning of this representation is very rich, as it alludes to the generative powers of creation and procreation as well as to the importance of balance between male and female. The stone and clay images found in the Indus culture may have functioned in much the same way as the later representations of Shiva, providing a focus for revering these principles of creative power and balance. It is also possible that these sexual images served a magical function. In some cultures, carved phalluses are used as good-luck charms to enhance fertility and conception. It is plausible that dwellers of the Indus Valley may have used such carvings in similar ways to magically facilitate the reproductive process. We moderns often forget that for most of human history, reproduction was an extremely mysterious process.

Throughout the cities of the Indus Valley, in public places and private homes, there were sophisticated bathing facilities, plumbed and lined with ceramic tiles in a relatively modern way. The ubiquity of the baths, their central locations, and the care with which they were constructed all suggest an intense concern with purity and cleanness. Almost certainly, this interest was with more than simple hygiene. Like many premodern cultures, and like Hindus today, the Indus dwellers were probably preoccupied with ritual purity. Ritual purity, as compared with hygienic purity, involves more than removing the sweat and grime that accumulate on the body and avoiding germs that cause disease. In its most basic sense, ritual purity is the state of cleanliness that is necessary for approaching the sacred. It often entails what and how one eats, the kinds of clothes one wears, the persons one may touch or associate with, and a host of similar regulations and restrictions. Such rules, of course, vary from culture to culture, but essentially they all involve maintaining a society's sense of order.

Whenever that order is violated—whether intentionally or unintentionally—it must be restored. We do not know specifically what kinds of things the Indus dwellers regarded as ritually impure. Whatever these things may have been, the bathing ritual most likely served to remove those impurities and reinstate the order of things, just as it does in contemporary Hinduism. In modern India, the first religious act of the day for most Hindus is bathing, a ritual practice that brings the individual into the appropriate bodily and mental state for relating to the gods and other persons.

Perhaps as important as what archaeologists have uncovered in the Indus Valley is what they have failed to find. As yet, no one has discovered a temple or house of worship that can be positively identified as a sacred precinct. It may be that the central location of religion for this culture was the home, as it is in present-day Hinduism. In any event, the absence of clearly recognizable temples underscores an important fact of preaxial existence throughout the world: that sacred and secular, or the holy and the profane, are not sharply distinguished. There was no separate domain of life that could be identified as "religious."

Thus, the Indus culture adds several strokes to our emerging portrait of life in preaxial India. As best we can discern with our current knowledge, many Indians were, before the Axial Age, especially concerned with sexuality and reproduction, and that attentiveness probably encompassed the human, the animal, and the plant realms, as would be customary for an agricultural society. In all likelihood, this fascination and anxiety implicated the divine realm. Perhaps a mother goddess and animals themselves were worshipped to help ensure fertility and fecundity on all levels of life. Finally, the design of cities and the practices of ritual purity indicate a high value on order and restraint.

To the extent that this is an accurate sketch of Indus religion, it suggests that beliefs and practices were oriented toward the present life here on earth and not toward a life hereafter. There is nothing in the ruins to indicate that Indus dwellers thought much about an afterlife or even wondered about what might be in store for the individual on the other side of death. Ritual practices and sacrifices seemed to be chiefly—if not exclusively—for the purpose of maintaining order in the present. Religion served a conservative function in this culture: to keep things as they were, to maintain the world itself by honoring and harnessing its powers and respecting its boundaries. And for a millennium and a half, the Indus religion was quite successful at doing that. Little seems to have changed in this civilization during its 1,500-year life span.

The Aryans

> "Religion served a conservative function in this culture: to keep things as they were, to maintain the world itself by honoring and harnessing its powers and respecting its boundaries."

Possibly due to gradual environmental changes, the Indus Valley Civilization eventually came to an end. The details are still unclear, but by 1900 BCE, the culture was in serious decline. Within a few centuries, around 1600 BCE, members of the "Indo" branch of the Indo-Iranian people began to drift into the Indus Valley and probably coexisted for some time with the remaining inhabitants of the indigenous culture.

For many years, historians believed that the Indo-Aryans invaded the Indus Valley Civilization and conquered its inhabitants. This was not an unreasonable conclusion, given the Aryans' professed love for war and conquest, as disclosed in parts of the Rig Veda. This scholarly belief, in fact, informed Adolf Hitler's appropriation of the myth of Aryan superiority and his adoption of the swastika, an ancient Aryan symbol. Today, however, most students of ancient India think the Aryans' arrival in India was well short of an invasion. The Indo-Aryans probably migrated slowly and relatively peacefully into the Indus region, living alongside the last citizens of Indus culture.

It should be pointed out, however, that the "Aryan question" is the subject of current debate. An important minority of scholars and some traditional Hindus contend that the Aryans were actually indigenous to India, not Central Asia, and migrated from the subcontinent to other locations. According to this perspective, known as the Out-of-India theory, the dwellers of the Indus Valley Civilization and the Indo-Aryans were the same people. Clearly, I have presented a different view of the migration. To pick apart that argument is beyond the scope of this book, though it certainly merits the attention of interested readers.[1] But regardless of *where* the Aryans originated, there can be little doubt about the ancient connections between the "Indo-Aryans" and the Iranians.

As we noted earlier, the Indo-Aryans were initially pastoral nomads rather than settled agriculturalists. By the time they entered India, they were skilled in horsemanship, the use of chariots, and the manufacturing of bronze. They organized themselves into tribes led by chieftains, often calling themselves the "Five Tribes." Their favorite self-designation, however, was the "Noble Ones,"

---

1. An excellent resource is Edwin Bryant, *The Quest for the Origins of Vedic Culture: The Indo-Aryan Migration Debate* (Oxford: Oxford University Press, 2001).

the literal meaning of Aryan. To simplify our discussion, we will now refer to them as just Aryans, rather than Indo-Aryans, unless we need to distinguish them from their Irano-Aryan cousins.

THE VEDAS

The basis of our knowledge of the Aryans is the canonical collections known as the Vedas. Today, orthodox Hindus—who think of themselves as the heirs of the Aryan people—regard the Vedas as their oldest and most sacred scripture. Most Hindus believe that the Vedas are divine knowledge containing the deep secrets of the universe. They call the Vedas *shruti*, a word that means "revelation." According to traditional Hindu belief, the Vedas have no author but were revealed to certain ancient sages by reality itself.

The Vedas are divided into four collections. The oldest and most important of these, is the Rig Veda. The Rig Veda contains over a thousand songs to various gods and goddesses. Some scholars have argued that it may be over thirty thousand years old, but most believe it to have a far more recent origin, between 2300 and 1200 BCE. In any event, it is clearly preaxial. All of the Vedas were kept in oral tradition for centuries and probably not written down until well after the Axial Age.

What the Vedas tell us is that religion in Indo-Aryan life was principally a matter of ritual and sacrifice. As with the Indus culture, Aryan rituals seems to have been very much a this-worldly activity, focused primarily on cosmic maintenance–obtaining the necessary goods for a happy and comfortable existence here and now. The Vedas contain instructions, prayers, and hymns composed for the purpose of performing these rituals. To gain an understanding of the Vedic world, we will look at some of these rituals, why they were performed, and to whom they were addressed. We will begin with this question: Who were the gods for whom Vedic ceremonies were enacted?

THE DEVAS

Tradition says there are thirty-three gods and goddesses in the Vedas, though that number is not exact. These gods, known in Sanskrit as *devas*, were believed to dwell on earth, in heaven, and in the midspace between them, a tripartite view of the world, not unlike the Iranians'. Most *devas* were understood to have specific functions or realms associated with them. Indra was the god of war. He led the Aryans into battle and served as the model soldier. According to Zoroaster, Indra was one of the principal *devas* associated with *druj*, that is, chaos and evil. Like other *devas*, Indra also ruled a province of nature—the waters of heaven that brought the monsoons. Agni was the divine fire, who lived on earth in the domestic hearth and in plants; he also dwelled in midspace as lightning and in heaven as the sun. Because of his versatility, Agni was the mediator between gods and humans and therefore figured prominently in Aryan rituals. The Vedas also mention Surya, the god of the sun; Yama, the king of death; Ushas, the goddess of the dawn; Kubera, the *deva* of wealth and prosperity; Varuna, the guardian of *rita*; and a host of lesser divine beings of different ranks and qualities, including the *asuras* (the Sanskrit term for the Avestan *ahuras*), which the Vedas considered evil.

At various stages in the history of Vedic religion, some *devas* were more prominent than others. Although there were many gods, when the Aryans worshipped, they often treated one god or goddess as the supreme deity. Generally, the Aryans worshipped the *deva* or *devi* whose favors were needed at the moment. As Aryan interests and needs evolved, so did worship practices. We can discern, for instance, that the war *deva* Indra was much more important in early Vedic period than later, when the Aryans were more settled and more concerned with agriculture and ranching.

Humanity

Later we will investigate how the Aryans related to their gods, but first we must understand how these people viewed themselves and their place in the universe. After all, much of what was at stake in the Axial Age was the transformation of human self-understanding.

One of the most telling observations about the Vedic views on human nature and destiny is that the preaxial Vedas had precious little to say on the subject. Very few statements explicitly address this question, so we must rely on inference. It is apparent that the Aryans did not spend much time analyzing themselves and developing a systematic self-understanding. This point becomes even more obvious when we compare the sparse early Vedic speculation on human nature with the incredible energy spent on self-scrutiny in the axial era. The Vedas were much more interested in the praise of the gods and the performance of sacrifices and other rituals than in attempting to understand what it means to be human. It may be even more accurate to say it was primarily *through ritual* that the Aryans understood the meaning of being human.

One place where we can discern some sense of the Aryan perspective on the human self is in the few hymns in the Rig Veda that concern death. We should not be too surprised to discover Aryan reflections on the essence of being human in this context. In the face of death, whether that of our individual selves or that of others, we humans almost reflexively raise questions about the essential nature of who we are and what our lives mean. When it rises to consciousness, the prospect of death has a profound way of prompting us to think about the real significance of our lives.

In this handful of Vedic hymns, we discover fairly wide-ranging speculation about what occurs at death. In one hymn alone,[2] several fates for the human individual are mentioned as possibilities. In one verse, the individual is believed to travel to heaven, carried by the cremation fires, where he or she joins the gods and the ancestors in a pleasant postmortem existence. In another verse in the same hymn, the individual is seen as dissolving into the elements of the natural world. Addressing the dead person, the hymn says: "May your eye go to the sun, your life's breath to the wind. Go to the sky or to the earth, as is your nature; or go to the waters, if that is your fate. Take root in the plants with your limbs."[3] Still later, the same hymn suggests that perhaps the corpse is "cooked" by the funeral pyre to make it a fit sacrifice to be consumed by the gods. Other Vedic hymns suggest that the soul descends to the "house of clay," the underworld ruled by the god of death, Yama. Obviously, the Vedas do not reach agreement about the ultimate destination of human beings.

Furthermore, these hymns reach no consensus about the makeup of the human personality or about what determines one's final destiny. Occasionally, the hymns refer to the *atman*, which is often identified as the self, soul, or even the breath, and to the *manas*, which is a rather vague idea indicating the mind, the heart, or the life-spirit that animates the body. Just as these realities are not well developed as ideas in the Vedas, their relationship to the body is not spelled out. The Vedas are also not clear about what determines one's fate. Sometimes, it appears as if the correct performance of sacrifices and other rituals decides one's destiny; sometimes it seems as if other deeds, such as fighting in battle or giving gifts to the priests, makes this determination; and sometimes it seems as if one's ultimate fate has no relationship at all to how one lived his or her life. One thing is fairly clear: the preaxial Vedas make no unambiguous and certain pronouncements that individual destiny—if there is one—is related to moral choices in the way that Zoroaster linked decision and fate.

The Aryans surely regarded death as an occasion for grief because life on earth is valuable and precious and something to be held onto for as long as possible. Yet, nothing indicates that death was terrifying to the Aryans, and nothing suggests that life after death—if indeed there was thought to be

---

2. *The Rig Veda*, 10.16, trans. Doniger, 46.
3. *The Rig Veda*, 10.16.3, trans. Doniger, 49.

one—might be torturous or unpleasant. We might also observe, anticipating our next chapter, that the Rig Veda says nothing explicitly of what comes to be called reincarnation, the notion that the spiritual essence of the person resumes life in a new body an infinite number of times. The concept of a cyclical existence is an axial development that received widespread acceptance only as the Vedic tradition gave rise to what was later called Hinduism.

Up to this point, our examination of the Aryans has focused on their beliefs: what they thought about the divine world, themselves, and their ultimate destinies. But this picture of Vedic life is still incomplete, because we have not yet explored the very important matter of ritual. When we take up this topic in the next chapter, we will be investigating the dimension of Aryan religion that brings together the divine and human realms. Our turn to ritual will take us into the very heart of preaxial religious life in ancient India and will provide us with the basis for understanding the dramatic transformations that occurred when the Axial Age began.

5

The Start of the Indian Axial Age

Our first look into the religious environment of ancient India revealed a world of gods and goddesses controlling the various aspects of existence that were of particular concern to the inhabitants of the Indus Valley and their Aryan successors. The interest that the Aryans and Indus dwellers had in their gods seemed to focus on the ways these powerful beings could help sustain and improve human life on earth. Gods and goddesses might be called upon to render aid in a battle, stave off disease, or enable reproduction.

The essential means for making these appeals to the divine was through ritual. Ritual was of vital importance in preaxial India, especially to the Aryans, whose entire scripture was dedicated to its proper practice. For the first part of this chapter, we will focus on the nature of these ceremonies, attending especially to the beliefs about how they accomplished their intended purpose. It is important to understand the dynamics of preaxial ritual in order to grasp the impulses that led to the reevaluation and reinterpretation of ritual in the Axial Age. By the end of this chapter, we will have seen how new ideas began to emerge in Indian religion that provided the foundations for Hinduism, Buddhism, and Jainism.

Vedic Ritual

The Vedas reveal that the Aryans did not have a highly developed or consistent self-understanding, and they are rather vague about how the Aryans understood human nature or the ultimate destiny of the individual. However, we should not infer from this that the Aryans were somehow incapable of sophisticated or systematic thinking. When we come to Vedic ritual practices, it becomes abundantly evident that these ancients were

> "Ritual was of vital importance in preaxial India, especially to the Aryans, whose entire scripture was dedicated to its proper practice."

able to think in complex and abstract ways. In fact, the Aryans devoted intense intellectual energy to understanding and practicing their rituals.

To illustrate the complexity of the belief structure supporting their rituals, let us consider an intriguing passage from the Rig Veda that describes the world's creation. This myth is one of a half-dozen creation stories in the Rig Veda alone; obviously, the Aryans were not greatly troubled by having several different cosmogonies.

This well-known story describes the ritual dismemberment of a primordial person. This myth is a late addition to the Vedas, which puts it closer to the start of the Axial Age than other Vedic material. But the narrative clearly echoes a very ancient creation theme: the idea that the world is created by the gods through sacrifice. That theme, we recall, was also part of the Avestan cosmogony. In the Vedic version, the sacrificial victim is called the Purusha, who is described as a massive cosmic man with a "thousand heads, a thousand eyes, [and] a thousand feet," larger than the physical universe itself:

> When the gods spread the sacrifice with the Man as the offering, spring was the clarified butter, summer the fuel, autumn the oblation.
>
> They anointed the Man, the sacrifice born at the beginning, upon the sacred grass. With him the gods . . . sacrificed.
>
> From that sacrifice in which everything was offered, the melted fat was collected, and he[1] made it into those beasts who live in the air, in the forest, and in villages.
>
> From that sacrifice in which everything was offered, the verses and chants were born, the metres were born from it, and from it the formulas were born.
>
> Horses were born from it, and those other animals that have two rows of teeth; cows were born from it, and from it goats and sheep were born.
>
> When they divided the Man, into how many parts did they apportion him? What do they call his mouth, his two arms, and thighs and feet?
>
> His mouth became the [Priest]; his arms were made into the Warrior, his thighs the [Producers], and from his feet the servants were born.
>
> The moon was born from his mind; from his eye the sun was born. Indra and Agni came from his mouth, and from his vital breath the Wind was born.
>
> From his navel the middle realm of space arose; from his head the sky evolved. From his two feet came the earth, and the quarters of the sky from his ear. Thus they set the worlds in order.[2]

---

1. "He" may refer to a creator god or the Purusha himself.
2. *The Rig Veda*, 10.90, trans. Wendy Doniger (New York: Penguin, 2005), 30–31.

One important aspect of this hymn is the way it established reciprocal relationships among the sacrifice, the act of creation, and the elements of the world. Because it was the primordial mode of creation, sacrifice was the method of renewing creation, of recreating and maintaining the world periodically when necessary. Performing sacrifice, as the gods did at the beginning of all time, renewed and invigorated the world. The priests who thus performed sacrifices—and this was clearly the way the Aryans understood it—were reenacting creation itself, making themselves tantamount to gods.

It may be difficult for those of us in the modern world to completely grasp this ancient need to participate actively in the process of cosmic regeneration. We tend to think the world proceeds on its own. We do not perform ceremonies to help the sun come up in the morning or to ensure that the change of seasons is regular and timely. We do not rely on rituals to coax seeds to sprout and produce an abundant crop. But the ancient world often viewed the human relationship to the natural world quite differently. For many ancients, the powers responsible for the well-being of life often needed human assistance. In the Iranian tradition, we noted this belief in the practice of pouring libations of milk into water or animal fat into the fire. The human and divine worlds maintained a symbiotic relationship. Each relied on the other for the maintenance of life.

The formation of the parts of the world out of the ritual dismemberment of the first human also implies a system of relationships between the ritual and the greater world beyond it. If, as the story suggests, the seasons are identified with the components of the sacrifice (and that is the meaning of that very cryptic phrase, "spring was the clarified butter, summer the fuel, autumn the oblation"), then by manipulating these aspects of the ritual, the priests were effectively controlling the seasons themselves. The technical term for this belief is sympathetic magic. Sir James Frazer, one of the early theorists on magic and religion and the author of an influential book entitled *The Golden Bough*, explained it this way: "things which have once been in contact with each other continue to act on each other at a distance after the physical contact has been severed."[3] Because everything that is was once connected to the Purusha and because the Purusha is sympathetically connected to the ritual, the performance of ritual sacrifice was understood to have effects in the world beyond. One might liken this manner of thinking to the way voodoo dolls are supposed to affect the person they represent: a pin stuck in the doll is believed to cause pain to the one it symbolizes.

---

3. James George Frazer, *The Golden Bough*, ch. 3, §1, 15. Available at http://www.sacred-texts.com/pag/frazer/gb00301.htm.

Finally, the myth of the Purusha has implications for the understanding of caste, which is mentioned in the hymn for the first time in the Vedas. In chapter 1, we witnessed the gradual evolution of the caste system among the Aryans, beginning with the simple distinction of priests and producers among the earliest Indo-Iranians. Then we saw the addition of the warrior caste as the cattle-rustling and village-raiding life became more popular, creating a three-tiered society of priests, warriors, and the producers. When the Aryans migrated to the Indian subcontinent, the fourth and lowest tier in the system was added. This caste, designated as the "servants" by the Vedas, probably comprised the remaining indigenous people from the old Indus Valley Civilization.

The story of the Purusha suggests that the stratification of humanity into priests, warriors, producers, and servants is both intended by the gods and embedded in the very fabric of the cosmos. This account of the divine origin of caste is part of the ideological structure that has kept this system in place for over three thousand years. Caste is not regarded as a mere social construction but as a fundamental element in the nature of reality. To challenge the system would be like opposing the gods or defying physical laws, and the consequences would be dire.

These principles were the basis for the Aryans' understanding of the necessity of ritual and its effectiveness. As we might expect, the Aryans performed different kinds of rituals and for different reasons. Like many ancient cultures—and a number of societies still today—Vedic religion prescribed rituals to assist individuals during times of crisis (for example, sickness), through transitions (for example, birth, marriage, or death), and on auspicious days (for example, the new moon or harvest time). Rituals also provided protection from demons and snakes, promoted good luck in gambling, and caused misfortune for one's enemies.

But the most important rituals for Aryan religious life may have been the *shrauta* rites, particularly the fire sacrifice. These rituals were more elaborate than other ceremonies and were performed with less frequency. *Shrauta* rites were conducted for various occasions, such as a coronation. Wealthy persons could also pay to have the ritual performed on their behalf. Only members of the Brahmin, or priestly, class were able to enact these kinds of ceremonies. The *shrauta* ritual required great skill, and only those with training as a Brahmin had the requisite expertise. Indeed, as these rituals grew in importance for the Aryans, the Brahmins grew in power and prestige.

A typical *shrauta* sacrifice involved a team of Brahmins, each charged with different responsibilities. Setting up and performing the sacrifice might take several days or even weeks. Under Brahmin supervision, workers staked out a sacred space outdoors by erecting a temporary canopy, using very precise measurements. Under the canopy, earthen altars were constructed to contain the sacred fires. Each of three altars corresponded to a component of the world: earth, midspace, and heaven. Once the ritual was under way, the gods were invited to attend; Soma, that divine drink prized by the Indo-Iranians, was drunk; an animal such as a goat was sacrificed and cooked; and then the sacred food was offered to the gods and human participants. The most important aspect of the sacrifice, however, was the hymns and prayers sung by the Brahmin priests. These were verses taken from the Vedas, and it was essential that they be chanted correctly. One priest's sole responsibility was to ensure that the sacred words were accurately uttered; he corrected any mistakes made by the others. Errors rendered the ritual ineffective, perhaps even dangerous; hence, the Brahmins placed great importance on exact memorization of the Vedas.

Although the *shrauta* rituals were performed for a variety of reasons, they ordinarily had this-worldly aims. Sacrificers—the ones who paid for the ceremony—sought to improve their relations with the gods in order to achieve greater success in business, breed more and better cattle, produce "manly" sons, and promote health and longevity. The attainment of a pleasant afterlife in heaven might also have been included in this list, but that goal seems to have been secondary to the others.

In the early Vedic period, the Aryans believed the sacrifices persuaded the gods to act on behalf of the sacrificer. Persuasion took the form of flattering songs sung in honor of a *deva* and the offering of delicious foods for the gods to eat and Soma to drink. Over time, however, the ritual itself came to be regarded as the transformative agent. Priests no longer thought they were urging the gods to act in certain ways. By manipulating the objects of the sacrifice, and especially by uttering powerful words they called mantras, the Brahmins believed that they themselves were controlling the cosmic powers. This belief seems to be the logical development of the idea of corresponding relationships between the ritual and the world beyond it.

Eventually, the sacred words used during rituals came to be seen as powerful in themselves. The utterance of these words generated or tapped into the creative power of the sacrifice. The priests called this power *brahman*, a word that means "that which makes great," and they came to regard themselves as the custodians of this *brahman*.

Our study of Vedic ritual has revealed several points that we may summarize as follows. First, ritual was immensely important in Vedic religion. The Aryans, like most preaxial peoples, were not terribly concerned about belief and doctrine. But they were greatly interested in the correct performance of specific religious acts, because these ceremonies and sacrifices were integral to their well-being on earth and perhaps to their destiny after death. Gradually, these ritual practices came to be regarded as the special province of experts, individuals trained to enact these ceremonies in precise ways. As these religious practices were developed and refined, the Aryans grew to believe that the rituals themselves were powerful. It was not so much that the rites persuaded or prompted the gods to act on human behalf; rather, the rite itself—especially the words of the ritual—was increasingly seen as the true agent of control.

> "The Aryans, like most preaxial peoples, were not terribly concerned about belief and doctrine. But they were greatly interested in the correct performance of specific religious acts, because these ceremonies and sacrifices were integral to their well-being on earth and perhaps to their destiny after death."

THE ADVENT OF THE AXIAL AGE

This brief synopsis characterizes the world of Indo-Aryan religion near the end of what we conventionally call the Vedic period of Indian religious history (1600–800 BCE). This era was succeeded by what is known as "classical Hinduism," so designated because during this time, the complex of traditions we refer to as Hinduism began to take its characteristic shape. The rise of classical Hinduism also coincided with the advent of the Axial Age in India.

To say the Vedic period ended and the classical Hindu period began does not imply that one era superseded the other. The rise of classical Hinduism did not mean that Vedic religion was no longer practiced or that it gradually faded into oblivion. On the contrary, the Vedic traditions were retained and still observed. Perhaps a better way of imagining this development is to think that as classical Hinduism arose, Indian religion enlarged. The older Vedic notions and practices were kept intact and to some extent reinterpreted. In addition, a set of new ideas and concerns were added to the mix, and this emerging amalgam resulted in what is now called Hinduism. Perhaps the situation was not so different from the way Christianity developed out of Judaism, retaining many Jewish elements, reinterpreting others, and then adding novel features from other sources. The appearance of classical Hinduism, therefore, did not signal the disappearance of traditional Indo-Aryan religion.

But changes *did* occur, and the changes were motivated by a number of factors, many of which seem to be characteristic of axial changes in other parts of the world. One of the most important of these was the expansion of the Indo-Aryans into the Gangetic Plain of northeastern India, beginning around

1000 BCE. This extension of Aryan culture entailed what some call the "second urbanization" of India. The Aryans began to give up the nomadic life, settle in villages and towns, and take up farming and trade. This development eventually led to a period of greater material progress and put the Aryans in greater contact with non-Aryan peoples.

These basic sociological changes can be coordinated with certain developments in Aryan religion. For instance, the late Vedic period seems to have been marked by increased questioning of the value of ritual. In part, these challenges appear to be associated with the middle castes' resentment of the Brahmin priests' power and their monopoly on ritual performance. But perhaps even deeper was an emerging sense that what the rituals accomplished was not, in the final analysis, all that worthwhile.

We see these doubts arising in a story that appeared in a collection of writings from this time, near the end of the Vedic period and the start of classical Hinduism. This collection, which we will discuss in much greater detail in the next several chapters, is known as the Upanishads. For now, let us simply attend to a particular passage that illustrates the Aryans' axial reevaluation of Vedic practices. This selection is a dialogue between a young Brahmin and Yama, the King of Death. Through an interesting set of circumstances, the young man, whose name is Nachiketas, has found himself sent to the underworld, where he is forced to wait for three days without food because the King of Death is away, doing what the grim reaper does. When Yama returns home to the underworld, he realizes he has committed a grave offense by neglecting his obligations of hospitality to a Brahmin. To atone for his mistake, Yama offers to grant Nachiketas three wishes. For his third and most important wish, Nachiketas asks Yama to explain to him what happens when a person dies, a seemingly simple request to make of the King of Death—or so one would think. Yama is surprisingly reluctant to answer this question. The dialogue proceeds in this manner:

Nachiketas: When a man dies, this doubt arises: some say "he is" and some say "he is not." Teach me the truth.

Death: Even the gods had this doubt in times of old; for mysterious is the law of life and death. Ask for another boon. Release me from this.

Nachiketas: This doubt indeed arose even to the gods, and you say, O Death, that it is difficult to understand; but no greater teacher than you can explain it, and there is no other boon as great as this.

Death: Take horses and gold and cattle and elephants; choose sons and grandsons that shall live a hundred years. Have vast expanses of land, and live as many years as you desire. Or choose another gift that you think equal to this, and enjoy it with wealth and long life. Be a ruler of this vast earth. I will grant you all your desires. Ask for any wishes in the world of mortals, however hard to obtain.... I will give you fair maidens with chariots and musical instruments. But ask me not, Nachiketas, the secrets of death.

Nachiketas: All these pleasures pass away, O End of all! They weaken the power of life. And indeed how short is all life! Keep your horses and dancing and singing. Man cannot be satisfied with wealth. Shall we enjoy wealth with you in sight? Shall we live while you are in power? I can only ask for the boon I have asked.... Solve then the doubt as to the great beyond. Grant me the gift that unveils the mystery.[4]

This brief passage is important to our study for two reasons. We will begin with what may not be so obvious on a casual reading, and that is what Yama offers Nachiketas as alternatives to his request. The King of Death promises the young Brahmin cattle and horses; wealth, power, and land; and children and a long comfortable life. What is significant to observe is that all of these things are precisely what the Vedic rituals were intended to secure. In an earlier age, the Aryans considered these things the highest goods of life. What more could one hope for? Wealth, children, longevity—these were the epitome of mortal success.

Yet now, in this passage from the dawn of the Axial Age, those very things count for little. An important shift has occurred—or has begun to occur—among some practitioners of Indian religion. What was seen as most valuable was now regarded with significantly less favor, and perhaps even with a touch of contempt. As Nachiketas says, these things "weaken the power of life." Here is an implicit criticism of the Vedic ritual system that should not be overlooked. It is not so much that later thinkers were suggesting that the old rituals did not work; rather, they were saying that what the rituals provided was ultimately not so important.

A second point also is significant. For the first time in the early Indian literature, we have begun to hear expressions of anxiety about death. Nachiketas wants to know whether the individual exists or does not exist after death. His question carries a sense of urgency and intensity. He wants to know the answer, and he refuses to let the King of Death off the hook. There is nothing like this

---

4. *Katha Upanishad* in *The Upanishads*, trans. Juan Mascaró (New York: Penguin, 1965), 56–57.

in the earlier Vedic literature. In chapter 4, we looked at some of the passages about death from the Rig Veda, and we noted a good deal of speculation about the ultimate human fate. What we did not encounter was any sense that the afterlife was a pressing issue for the Indo-Aryans. If they gave it much thought at all, some of the Aryans believed that death conferred a pleasant existence in heaven with the ancestors; others imagined a kind of dissolution of the soul and body as they melted into their elemental forms; and some may have thought the corpse was consumed by the gods. What seems to have been lacking was the sense that knowing what lay on the other side of death was a matter of deep concern.

The stage is now set for change. In the next chapter of Indian religious history, questions that are now appearing here and there—questions about the ultimate destiny of human beings, the nature of existence after death, and the absolute reality of the entire cosmos—will become more pressing. These concerns will be addressed as an entirely new cast of characters emerges to consider them.

6

Death and Rebirth

At the end of the previous chapter, we identified a significant period of transition in Indian religious history. The Vedic age was drawing to a close, and the era of classical Hinduism was emerging, a period that coincided with the start of India's Axial Age. Of course, there is no distinct point in time at which we can definitively say the Vedic period has ended and the classical Hindu period has begun. As mentioned previously, the Vedic traditions were largely retained and embraced within emerging Hinduism. What distinguishes the classical Hindu era is the reorientation of religious life toward new concerns and new beliefs. This evolution took place over a two-hundred-year span, between 800 and 600 BCE, according to contemporary Western reckoning.

Is That All There Is?

During these two hundred years, Indian religious life began to change dramatically. The venerable old Vedic ritual system, which had dominated Indian religion for centuries, came under scrutiny. Increasingly, thinkers expressed doubts about the kinds of benefits the Vedic rituals could produce. It was not so much that the Aryans no longer valued long life, health, material prosperity, and children—the sorts of things rituals were intended to provide; rather, these goods were now regarded as less important in the grand scheme of things. Sages were starting to wonder: Is this all there is to life, or does human existence have some meaning or significance that transcends the acquisition of these traditional goods, as valuable as they are?

This question arose with more frequency as the Aryans increasingly enjoyed greater material success and as they settled in villages and became agriculturists and traders. While concerns with subsistence needs receded into the background, other questions—what we might call philosophical or transcendental issues—seem to have come to the fore. The increase in material well-being does not wholly account for this philosophical turn, but it surely played a part. How many of us—particularly in our affluent society—after having attained everything we *thought* we wanted, raised our heads and asked, "Is that all?" For a variety of reasons, growing numbers of individuals throughout northern India in the period we are considering were asking the same question: "Is that all there is? Is there something more to life than simply satisfying our desires, and if so, how do we find it?"

Anxiety about Death

Closely connected with this question was an increasing concern with death and the ultimate fate of the individual person. The Aryans of the Vedic period were not *unconcerned* about death, but neither was their interest a great preoccupation or a matter of deep passion. The face of death was neither terrifying nor the object of intense speculation. Death was a simple reality of life, and the point of existence seemed to be to enjoy what the world had to offer before death comes. There was nothing in Vedic culture to suggest anything like what Ernest Becker called "the denial of death."[1] To be sure, some passages in the Vedas intimated that there *might* be some form of existence for the person beyond his or her individual demise, but this was by no means a consistent or universal belief. The clear emphasis throughout the Vedic period was on the complete enjoyment of the goods of this earthly life.

But as the age of classical Hinduism came into full manifestation, the issue of death arose as a topic of greater attention, and it was approached with an unprecedented energy. In the previous chapter, we saw this exemplified in the tale of Nachiketas and his dialogue with Yama, the King of Death. Rather than accepting the pleasures of the earthly life, the young Brahmin compelled the god of the underworld to reveal to him the secrets of existence beyond death, a demand Yama was reluctant to grant.

As Nachiketas's dialogue with the King of Death demonstrates, the question of death and the afterlife had become a matter of much discussion and speculation among certain groups of Aryans. These were probably the Brahmins and other high-caste members who were acquainted with the Vedas and sufficiently leisured to ponder such matters. At any rate, the evidence that remains comes only from these educated classes, and it suggests that conjectures about death were very diverse and anything but consistent.

Among the many ideas being debated among philosophically minded individuals, one is of particular interest for subsequent Indian thinking. We noted earlier that some Aryans understood death as the transition of the body

---

1. Ernest Becker, *The Denial of Death* (New York: Free Press, 1973).

or the life force to heaven, where the individual would enjoy a pleasant and permanent existence among the gods and ancestors. One of the Vedic hymns promoting this view encourages believers with the promise that "this pasture . . . shall not be taken away."[2] Although this was by no means a universal Aryan view, certainly a significant number believed it, and many thought that performing the appropriate sacrifices and rituals was the way to secure it.

Yet, at the end of the Vedic era and the start of classical Hinduism, doubts began to creep into this picture of the afterlife. Some of the later portions of the Vedas express suspicions about the permanency of existence in heaven once it had been attained. In these later texts, the fear arises that one might initially reach the heavenly goal only to lose it again through death. The word *redeath* now enters the religious lexicon to describe the situation in which the individual dies and ascends to heaven, lives there for a period, and then dies again, this time dissolving into the elements of the natural world. It does not take much imagination to see how this emerging notion of destiny was beginning to take on rather ominous qualities.

The notion of redeath, was probably an intermediate step toward the development of the concept of reincarnation, or what Hindus call the transmigration of the self. This idea—that the individual self endures a continual series of births, deaths, and rebirths—seems to have appeared for the first time in India at the start of the Axial Age.[3]

The Fear of Rebirth

The truth is that we are not altogether sure how the belief in reincarnation appeared and then became widely accepted throughout India. The concept of rebirth is certainly not unique to India. The notion is found among some Native Americans, the Trobriand Islanders, in West Africa, and perhaps most significantly for our study, among some Axial Age philosophers of ancient Greece, including Pythagoras and Socrates. Many scholars of ancient Indian religion believe that the concept of rebirth began in northern India among a small coterie of philosophers and holy persons, just as it did in Greece. These early Indians thinkers taught this idea to growing numbers of ordinary folk, and eventually, it was widely accepted. Interestingly, in ancient Greece it always remained a philosopher's notion and never caught on with the masses of people.

---

2. *The Rig Veda*, 10.14.2, trans. Wendy Doniger (New York: Penguin, 2005), 43.

3. Some have suggested that perhaps the idea of rebirth developed initially within the old Indus Valley Civilization and then reappeared centuries later after a period of suppression by the Aryans. But there is really no evidence to support that conjecture.

But in India, the premise of rebirth was so widely accepted that it became the fundamental assumption of virtually all Indian religions and philosophies, including Hinduism, Buddhism, Jainism, and much later, Sikhism. These traditions understand rebirth in different ways, but the basic sense that existence is characterized by an endless series of births, deaths, and rebirths is common to them all. The term used by these traditions to denote this situation is *samsara*, a word that literally means "wandering," suggesting a kind of aimlessness or pointlessness to the process of moving from one condition to another.

> "In India, the premise of rebirth was so widely accepted that it became the fundamental assumption of virtually all Indian religions and philosophies, including Hinduism, Buddhism, Jainism, and much later, Sikhism. These traditions understand rebirth in different ways, but the basic sense that existence is characterized by an endless series of births, deaths, and rebirths is common to them all. The term used by these traditions to denote this situation is *samsara*, a word that literally means "wandering," suggesting a kind of aimlessness or pointlessness to the process of moving from one condition to another."

THE UPANISHADS

The first place in the ancient Indian texts where we get a clear sense of the idea of transmigration is a collection of writings called the Upanishads. The most important Upanishads were probably composed between 800 and 400 BCE, which places them squarely within the Axial Age. The authors of these works—and there were many of them—are not known to us today, but clearly they were individuals of a philosophical mind-set, seeking answers to the fundamental mysteries of life.

By the time the Upanishads appeared, the concept of rebirth had begun to enjoy widespread acceptance. Even so, no clear or systematic understanding of the nature of this process is found in these writings. Most of the Upanishadic passages dealing with rebirth do so by means of metaphor or analogy. Here is a typical and well-known selection from one of the Upanishads, often called *The Supreme Teaching*, one of the oldest texts in the collection:

> [Rebirth] is like this. As a caterpillar, when it comes to the tip of a blade of grass, reaches out to a new foothold and draws itself onto it, so the self, after it has knocked down this body and rendered it unconscious, reaches out to a new foothold and draws itself onto it.

[Rebirth] is like this. As a weaver, after she has removed the coloured yarn weaves a different design that is newer and more attractive, so the self, after it has knocked down this body and rendered it unconscious, makes for himself a different figure that is newer and more attractive—the figure of a forefather, ... or of a god, ... or else the figure of some other being.[4]

These excerpts imply that continued existence is driven by desire, that the self that is reincarnated *wills* to be reborn. Indeed, as we will see later in the development of Indian philosophy, desire is precisely what propels the process.

But this view of reincarnation was not universally accepted among the sages composing the Upanishads. A different passage from another early Upanishad offers an alternative perspective. Here, the author hypothesizes that the cremation fires convert corpses into smoke, which carries them to heaven on the wind, and there, after other transformations, they become food for the gods. After being consumed by the gods, "they return by the same path they went—first to space, and from space to the wind. And after the wind has formed, it turns into smoke; after the smoke has formed, it turns into a thunder-cloud; after the thunder-cloud has formed, it turns into a rain-cloud; and after a rain-cloud has formed, it rains down. On earth they spring up as rice and barley, plants and trees, sesame and beans . . . . When someone eats that food and deposits the semen, from him one comes into being again."[5] Apparently, this reincarnation theory is a further refinement of the old Vedic view that the corpse is cooked and consumed by the gods. It simply follows that process to its logical end, based on the ancient belief that the male semen actually contains the complete incipient human and the female womb serves as a kind of incubator but does not contribute materially to the embryo. It is quite an ingenious theory. This effort to explain rebirth is, in its own way, empirical in the way it reasons inductively from observable phenomena.

In both selections, we see that although the idea of rebirth gained wide acceptance during this period of Indian history, there was no consensus about how it worked or what it actually meant. It is not even clear *what* these sages believed was reincarnated or what determined the form of one's next life. One of the passages suggests that one gets a newer and more attractive body, such as that of a god, but the later Hindu tradition will come to believe that rebirth

---

4. *Bṛhadāranyaka Upanishad*, 4.4.3-4, in Patrick Olivelle, trans. *Upaniṣads* (New York: Oxford University Press, 1996), 64.
5. *Chandogya Upanishad*, 5.10.5-6, in Olivelle, trans. *Upaniṣads,* 142.

does not always imply progress or improvement. In fact, rebirth might very well mean going from being human to being a dog or an insect.

Karma and the Ethicization of Rebirth

As the Axial Age progressed, and as the Upanishads developed further, many of these issues were addressed and refined. One of the most important developments was the concept of karma. Karma adds a unique dimension to the Indian view of rebirth. Whereas the idea of rebirth is not exclusive to India, the belief that one's future incarnation depends on how one behaves in this life *is* a distinctive Indian contribution. The ethicization of rebirth is the principal upshot of the doctrine of karma. The Upanishads make one's moral behavior the decisive element in human destiny. In the Upanishads, as for the Indian religions generally, karma determines the form and status of one's next birth.

Karma is a term with which most Westerners are now familiar, but many who use it are not completely sure about its meaning. Some treat it as a synonym for luck. On occasion, a person might say "Well, I guess that's just my bad karma" to explain an unfortunate situation. Karma is not luck, if luck is understood as a random or chance occurrence, nor is it technically analogous with fate, if fate is a preordained sequence of events determined by a god or superhuman power. In fact, karma means just the *opposite* of luck and fate in these senses. According to the theory of karma, the events in one's life—good or bad—are not chance occurrences, nor are they foreordained by realities outside of oneself.

> "The Upanishads make one's moral behavior the decisive element in human destiny. In the Upanishads, as for the Indian religions generally, karma determines the form and status of one's next birth."

In its most basic sense, karma refers to the actions that one performs and the consequences of those actions, in a cycle of cause and effect. Just as dropping a pebble into a pond creates ripples that reverberate on the surface of the water, so our every action has reverberating consequences. There is no way to separate action and consequences; the effects of one's act can be considered as part of the act itself, according to most Hindu thinkers. The doctrine of karma maintains that those effects will at some point return to the agent, to the one who performed the act in the first place. So the waves created by a dropped pebble reach the edge of the pond and then continue to ripple back to the point where the pebble was dropped. The return of the consequences of action to the agent is called the "fruiting" of karma.

The fruiting of karma is inevitable, and it always returns to the agent who created it, no matter how long it takes. We sometimes experience the consequences of our actions soon after they are committed. An angry person might quickly reap the fruit of her anger as other people act out of anger in response to her. Or it may take another lifetime or two for karma to come to fruition. But about this you can be sure: "karma is gonna get you," as John Lennon suggested in his popular song "Instant Karma." It is important to remember, however, that *you* are the one who generated the karma in the first place.

Karma can be of two basic kinds: good and evil, or positive and negative. Actually, the philosophical literature on the kinds of karma is quite complex; we are reducing the idea here to its elemental forms. In essence, we can say that by performing good actions, one produces "positive" karma; wicked, immoral, irresponsible actions create "negative" karma. And at some point, whether in this life or another, the karma we have generated returns to us—to our benefit, if good; to our detriment, if evil.

In short, the concept of karma means that every person gets what he or she deserves. Karma is a principle of justice. This process occurs ineluctably and impersonally, just as the law of gravity acts on physical bodies. In the general understanding, there is no divine being meting out justice; in fact, according to Hinduism, even the gods themselves are subject to the law of karma. What Hindus mean by karma is reflected in the Western expression "What goes around comes around." For better or worse, we cannot escape the consequences of our actions.

7

The Quest for Liberation

So far, we have observed the development of two key ideas about the nature and destiny of human beings that arose in India during the early Axial Age. The first was rebirth, the concept that our present earthly existence is only one in a series of lifetimes; and the second was karma, the belief that our deeds have positive or negative consequences that return to the agent according to the nature of the act. These two concepts come together in the notion that the state of one's future existence is determined by how one acts in this present life. Good karma ultimately determines a favorable rebirth; bad karma means an unfavorable rebirth.

To speak of a "good" or "bad" rebirth implies a hierarchy of being. One might be reborn at any place on this hierarchy, ranging from plant life to the various levels of animal life to the human realm, which is stratified from low caste to high caste, and then to various states of divinity. A preponderance of bad karma might take you from human to buzzard; an abundance of good karma might enable the low-caste person to be reborn as a Brahmin.

To have a "high" birth—to be reborn as a god or a Brahmin or, in some senses, as simply a human person—is extremely rare and requires a great deal of karmic merit. For the vast portion of our infinite number of rebirths, most of us have been reborn as insects or other animal forms. That we have achieved a human rebirth in this life is a wondrous—almost miraculous—occurrence, because it is such a difficult feat. An ancient parable from this era makes the point in a vivid way. The parable invites us to imagine that the entire world is covered with water and that floating on the water's surface is a yoke with a single hole, like a collar used to harness an ox. An eastern wind pushes the yoke west; a western wind pushes it east. A wind from the north pushes it south, and a southern wind drives it north, so the yoke is constantly moving. Now, suppose a blind sea turtle lived in this vast ocean and came to the surface once every century. How often do you think that blind sea turtle, coming to the surface once every one hundred years, would stick its neck into the yoke with a single hole? The parable suggests that a human rebirth occurs with the same frequency.

The Tibetans, who adopted one of the Indian views on rebirth, frequently refer to existence as "this precious human birth." What makes it so precious is not just its rarity, but also its great significance. Humans, more than other animals or even the gods, have the ideal opportunity for positively affecting their future existence. One of the reasons that beings spend a great number of lifetimes at the animal level is that animals simply are not capable of generating much karma, good or bad. Those beings are not in a position greatly to affect their rebirth, but humans, by the nature of their very makeup, have almost limitless opportunities to act morally, that is, to produce karmically relevant deeds. To squander this precious human life would be tragic, to say the least.

SAMSARA: THE PROBLEM

The ideas of rebirth and karma may have arisen independently of one another. If so, it is clear they came to be inextricably linked in the Indian imagination during the Axial Age. When that connection was made and widely accepted throughout India, then a completely new attitude toward life came to pervade the Indians' view of the world. In the preaxial era, the Aryans took delight in the pleasures of this life and beseeched their gods for the goods that could make their lives more comfortable and enjoyable. Death was accepted as a fact of life and perhaps as the transition to an agreeable existence in heaven. That perspective changed significantly when the concept of *samsara* was adopted.

THE REEVALUATION OF THE WORLD

One of the first tenets of the theory of rebirth that must be grasped—and this is especially true for many of us living in the West—is that *samsara* is not a desirable situation. Most people who believe in reincarnation do not want to be reborn. Usually, those who look forward to rebirth imagine continual existences much like the current (and probably privileged) life they presently enjoy. They do not think of themselves as living as an aardvark or a cockroach, or imagine themselves as lunch for a tiger in the jungle. But perhaps because the ancient Indians were closer to the natural world than most modern people are, such possibilities were very much on their minds.

Yet no matter how confident one is that his or her good behavior is sufficient to merit better and better rebirths, there comes a point when one realizes that even the best possible life is fraught with suffering, pain, and grief and must eventually end in death. Just reaching the top of the great chain of being, therefore, cannot be the ultimate goal. Even at the summit of the hierarchy of life, rebirth continues without end. The good karma we have acquired will eventually exhaust itself, and reincarnation will be inevitable, along with the suffering that accompanies every life.

It may take a million more lifetimes, but the individual will eventually become convinced of the futility of samsaric existence. In the end, one must seek the ultimate aim of life: liberation from *samsara* altogether. This is *moksha*, complete release, the end of reincarnation. Thus, seeking a favorable rebirth can only be a preliminary or proximate goal. One hopes to maximize one's good karma, steadily improving rebirth, until one is has attained a life in which realizing *moksha* is possible.

From this point of view, existence does not seem so agreeable. To be sure, the worldly life has its pleasures: the warmth of family and children, the joys of eating good food and seeing beautiful sights, the love of friends and companions. Still, from the samsaric standpoint, which assumes an endless number of previous lifetimes and anticipates the prospect of an infinite number more, this world did not carry quite the same attraction for Indians in the Axial Age as it did to the Aryans centuries before. Recall the words of Nachiketas to the King of Death: "All these pleasures pass away, O End of all! They weaken the power of life.... Man cannot be satisfied with wealth. Shall we enjoy wealth with you in sight? Shall we live while you are in power?"[1]

THE QUEST FOR LIBERATING KNOWLEDGE

The idea of *samsara* thus brings with it a new existential problem: how to attain *moksha* and escape the endless round of rebirths altogether. This is the fundamental problem of Indian religion in the Axial Age. Virtually every school of philosophy and religious sect—and there have been very many throughout the history of India—tried to understand and resolve this issue.

> "The idea of *samsara* thus brings with it a new existential problem: how to attain *moksha* and escape the endless round of rebirths altogether. This is the fundamental problem of Indian religion in the Axial Age."

As the idea of *samsara* caught on in the Axial Age, it spurred a widespread movement of individuals who decided that nothing in this world compared to the necessity of ending samsaric existence. So they left their homes and families and jobs to seek a way to escape rebirth. This mass movement included men and some women, of all ages and

---

1. *Katha Upanishad* in Mascaró, trans. *The Upanishads*, 56–57.

castes, but it tended to attract persons from the upper castes especially. For the most part, the principal activity took place in the years 800–400 BCE in the plains area of the Ganges River, in northeastern India, where Aryan culture had expanded many years earlier during the second urbanization of India.

During these years, the Gangetic plains region was marked by economic, social, and religious ferment. Farming and commerce flourished, and more people came to enjoy material prosperity. Over a dozen small republics and kingdoms emerged. Traditional practices and beliefs were no longer taken for granted, and the Brahmin priests lost some of the prestige and power they once enjoyed. Modern historians consider this period to be of such significance that it may have been the "most decisive phase for the development of Indian culture."[2]

It was in this context of great change that the new movement of moksha-seekers arose. Many of those who joined this movement were beginning to experience dissatisfaction with the shape this emerging culture was taking. One individual who left home during this period to join the renouncers described his motivation this way: "I thought: 'Household life is crowded and dusty; life gone forth is wide open. It is not easy, while living in a home, to lead the holy life utterly perfect and pure as a polished shell.'"[3] In these words, we hear a discontent with ordinary domestic existence and a yearning for high adventure, for the quest of the perfect life that very few persons ever dare to try. In other words, those who joined the homeless and ascetic life did so not just to escape a world they found abhorrent, but because they saw in renunciation their only hope for a life of freedom and fulfillment. For this reason, the new axial outlook in India can be characterized as ultimately optimistic, despite its negative assessment of the phenomenal world. Although the world as we know it is indeed a vale of tears, the sages were saying that by perfecting the spiritual life, one might conquer the samsaric realm and enjoy an even greater bliss. That was the conclusion of the individual who left his home because it was cramped and dirty, the man who later became known as the Buddha.

Many of these *shramanas*, or "strivers," as they were commonly known, lived alone in caves or in the forests; some stayed with their families in ascetic communities; more wandered from village to village, carrying only a change of clothes and a begging bowl for food (a pattern still very much in evidence in India today). The householders—those who did not leave their homes and places in society—were well-aware of these ascetics and wandering sages. They

---

2. Kulke, Hermann and Dietmar Rothermund, *A History of India*, 3rd ed. (New York: Routledge), 49.

3. *The Great Discourse to Saccaka* in Bhikkhu Ñāṇamoli and Bhikkhu Bodhi, trans. *The Middle Length Discourses of the Buddha: A New Translation of the* Majjhima Nikāya, (Somerville, MA: Wisdom, 1995), 335.

were common sights in the villages and towns, and often the householders sought them out for advice and lessons for living. So large and familiar was this countercultural movement that the *shramanas* were virtually regarded as a fifth caste, alongside the priests, the warriors, the producers, and the servants.

The relationship between these ascetics and the ordinary householders became symbiotic, since the holy men and women needed the support of the ordinary folk to make their quest for liberation possible. Supporting the ascetics and renouncers by giving them food, clothing, and shelter came to be seen as meritorious, as a way of gaining good karma necessary for better rebirth. The ordinary householder might help the *shramanas* now, in this life, knowing that in a future lifetime, others would help him in his effort to attain *moksha*. This emerging relationship between the *shramanas* and the householders established an important difference in the respective religious orientations of these two groups. The *shramanas* sought *moksha* in this lifetime. The householders—those who retained their roles in society, living a conventional life involving work and family—could not afford to devote their time and energies to the pursuit of *moksha*, so they chose to postpone that endeavor until a later lifetime when circumstances would favor it. In the meantime, the householder's goal was to improve his rebirth through the accumulation of positive karma. So while liberation from *samsara* was the ultimate goal, not everyone sought it in this life.

This period in Indian religious history had an intensely experimental quality. Individuals often wandered from place to place, seeking this guru or that holy man, trying now one form of discipline and now another, adopting this doctrine and then that. Many of the practices we have come to associate with Indian religion were developed and refined at this time—disciplines such as meditation, asana yoga, and the countless varieties of self-denial and self-mortification, from fasting and celibacy to standing on one leg and lying on beds of nails. Teachers competed with one another for the allegiance of students and lay followers. Debates were held; conversations became heated; rivalries were common. Oftentimes, this competitiveness seemed to contain little of the spiritual or enlightened perspective in it, but the intensity and antagonistic energy of these times also pointed to the profound importance and urgency of the quest.

The lifestyles and beliefs of this fifth caste of ascetics varied widely, but they were united in their quest for relief from the acute sense of suffering implied by their understanding of *samsara*. They were united in another way as well: in the belief that the way to freedom lay in acquiring knowledge. Their renunciation of the world is perhaps best seen in this light, as a necessary course of action for removing the impediments that might prevent them from gaining the extraordinary understanding that would win *moksha*. The search for the knowledge that would lead to freedom was so important and so demanding that all worldly concerns had to be set aside.

Knowledge had always played an important role in Vedic religion. It was central to the success of Aryan rituals for the priests to know what needed to be done and spoken without error or misstep. Practitioners of Vedic rituals had to study for more than a dozen years to gain the understanding necessary to function as priests. So it is not surprising that knowledge was initially emphasized in this growing movement.

In the Axial Age, the quest for understanding took a different turn, urged on by the new goal of liberation from *samsara*. *Shramanas* sought more than the knowledge of ritual action and sacred words. Such learning could only be useful in acquiring worldly goods or a brief respite in heaven. Now the sages wanted to know the deep reality that was the basis of ritual practice—and the foundation for the whole of life.

This was different from the forms of knowing stressed in earlier manifestations of Indian religion. The Axial Age quest was for a knowledge that was comprehensive and fundamental. It was no longer enough simply to chant the correct mantras and perform the right ritual actions; the *shramanas* wanted to understand the whole of reality by knowing its deepest principles. The composer of the *Mundaka Upanishad* wonders, "What is that which, being known, illuminates everything else?"[4]

The desire to grasp reality's elemental nature that we see in the Upanishads is not unlike the hope of modern physics to discover a unified field theory, which physicists sometimes call the Theory of Everything. For decades, physicists have worked to reconcile the four basic forces in the cosmos and understand them by a single mathematical formula, in essence reducing them to a singular principle. The goal of a unified field theory has been the Holy Grail for many physicists, who believe that finding it will unlock some of the deepest mysteries of the universe. In their own ways, the sages of the Upanishads and other axial thinkers were trying to develop their own Theory of Everything. They wanted to understand it all, not because they valued knowledge for knowledge's sake, but because knowing the fundamental basis of existence, they believed, could bring genuine freedom and fulfillment. This was a knowledge that conferred liberation.

The knowledge sought by the north Indian *shramanas* was an extraordinary sort, to be gained by rigorous methods of asceticism and introspection and

---

4. *Mundaka Upanishad* in Mascaró, trans. *The Upanishads*, 75.

not merely transmitted by lectures or gained from reading books. The Sanskrit word for this form of knowledge is *jñana*, which is closely related to the Greek word *gnōsis*. Many will recognize *gnōsis* as the word for an esoteric understanding that was sought by some early Christians and others called, aptly enough, Gnostics. In the same way, the Indian *shramanas* pursued a supermundane kind of knowing, one that was in principle accessible to everyone but gained only by those willing to make the sacrifices required to get it. Despite the difficulty, and despite the costs—or perhaps because of them—many of these ascetic seekers claimed to have found what they were looking for: the way to final liberation, the answer to life's deepest questions, the knowledge of the secrets of the universe itself.

Having now set out the basic existential predicament of Indian religion, we are in a position to begin our study of some answers proposed by these ancient *shramanas*. The religious excitement of the early Axial Age was marked by a wide variety of competing beliefs and practices, teachers, and schools of thought. Although we have no record of many of these teachings, we know a considerable amount about three of the most prominent. The first solution was known as the Vedanta, which was the view offered by the Upanishads themselves. Vedanta was so influential that it provided the principal theological foundation for the development of subsequent Hindu traditions. Other solutions were offered by two rival schools, Buddhism and Jainism. To appreciate the Buddhist and Jain perspectives, however, it is essential to understand Vedanta.

8

The Vedantic Solution

The Upanishads were composed by sages seeking to unlock the deepest mysteries of existence. Essentially, they wanted to know two things: the nature of ultimate reality and the true nature of the self. Apprehending these, they believed, would confer the liberating knowledge that would halt the samsaric cycle and bring about a state of utter bliss.

The Upanishads thus take two seemingly opposite trajectories. One is in the direction of comprehending the universe in its greatest possible sense, that is, in knowing the fundamental power or principle underlying the totality of all there is. The other direction is that of discovering what lies deep within the individual as his or her essence. The Upanishads have much to say about both lines of inquiry.

THE CONCEPT OF THE SELF

An acerbic bumper sticker once admonished its readers, "Never forget that you are unique—just like everyone else!" Of course, we are all unique, but then there is nothing unique about being unique. We human beings do like to think we are special, whether as individuals or as a species. We want to believe there is something about us that sets us apart from everything else. In the book of Genesis, for instance, the god creates all the animals simply by calling them into existence, but when it comes to the human, he personally fashions a body made of dust and breathes into it the breath of life. God's animating breath and particular attention differentiate humans from the other animals and make us special.

This example from Genesis is not unique, either. Almost all creation narratives reserve special treatment for humans. Other animals do not seem to be as obsessed with themselves as humans are. In fact, there are no other creatures that dwell so much on what they are and what they should be. For millennia, we human beings have wondered about ourselves and about what gives us life and determines our qualities. We have spent enormous amounts of intellectual energy trying to determine the essence of being human—what it is that makes us different from other beings and different from each other. Maybe that drive in itself is part of our essential natures: we are the animals who must interpret ourselves.

The vast majority of religions and philosophies over the past three thousand years have said the human essence is something more than our material bodies. They have given various names to this essence, such as "self," "spirit," "mind," "heart," and perhaps the most common, "soul." There has rarely been much precision about what this essence actually is, but these terms and others like them are what religions and philosophies have used to indicate that aspect of being, whatever it might be, that animates and gives life to our bodies and signifies what we truly are.

The sages who composed the Upanishads used the word *atman* to designate the true human essence. Like the idea of karma, *atman* was an ancient Vedic term that was reinterpreted and redefined in the Axial Age. In the early Vedas, the *atman* was closely associated with breath. (The German verb meaning "to breathe" is *atmen*, spelled almost the same way as the Sanskrit.) The Vedic notion that the breath might be the human essence was based on the rather commonsensical view that since breathing stops at death, breath must be the animating force of life. But by the time the Upanishads had begun to be composed, the identification of *atman* with breath was unsatisfying to most thinkers. The breath was seen as too physical, too closely associated with the body. In one of the Upanishads, the great god Indra is even depicted as worried about this association. In response to a *shramana* who claims that body and self are identical, Indra reasons, "If our self, our *atman*, is the body, and is dressed in clothes of beauty when the body is, then when the body is blind, the *atman* is blind, and when the body is lame, the *atman* is lame; and when the body dies, the *atman* dies. I cannot find any joy in this doctrine."[1] What the sages of the Upanishads sought as the human essence was something that transcends the body and survives death, an immortal substance. Part of the context of this passage, of course, was the increasing anxiety about the fate of the individual at death, one of the major themes of the axial transformation.

If not the body or the breath, what does constitute the human essence? What is the *atman*? Some contributors to the Upanishads suggested it was the mind.[2] The mind seems for many of us to be the center of our experience of

---

1. *Chandogya Upanishad* in Mascaró, trans. *The Upanishads*, 123.
2. *Maitri Upanishad* in Mascaró, trans. *The Upanishads*, 99.

the world, the seat of our personality. But almost all of the Upanishadic sages were reluctant to identify the human essence as synonymous with the mind. They asked: How can anything as capricious and as unsettled as the mind be our immortal self? One of the earlier Upanishads says, "It is not the mind that we should want to know; we should want to know the thinker."[3] What was of greatest interest was not the content or the activity of the mind but what exists beneath or beyond it. Some of the sages concluded that what transcends the senses and the mind could not be sensed or thought about. From this insight, the Upanishads derived the unique qualities of the *atman*: it is imperceptible, beyond the categories of thinking, and beyond comprehension. Although the *atman* dwells within the body, it is different from the body and all its parts. Because it transmigrates from body to body through rebirth, the *atman* must also be immortal. The *Chandogya Upanishad* puts it this way: "Ātman, the spirit of vision, is never born and never dies. Before him there was nothing, and he is one for evermore. Never born, eternal, beyond times gone or times to come, he does not die when the body dies. If the slayer thinks that he kills and if the slain thinks that he dies, neither knows the ways of truth. The Eternal in humanity cannot kill; the Eternal in humanity cannot die."[4] The *atman* does not come into being at a specifiable moment. It is not created; it simply always has been.

We might contrast this view with the position of many Western religions that have recently dealt with the question of the soul's creation while struggling with the issue of abortion. Roman Catholicism contends that the soul is created at conception; some Protestant groups have said it starts fourteen days after conception; a Jewish tradition says forty days after conception for boys and ninety days after for girls; and Islam maintains that an angel breathes the life force into the fetus 120 days into pregnancy.[5] Though they disagree on the exact moment of ensoulment, the Abrahamic traditions are fundamentally together in saying the soul comes into being at a particular moment in time.

Although the Upanishadic thinkers are not of one accord in the specific details of their views on the human self, they all subscribe to a general understanding that distinguishes a higher self from a lower self. The lower, or phenomenal, self comprises the body, the senses, and the mind. These aspects are all transitory and mortal. The *atman*, or higher self, is distinguishable from these other elements by virtue of its eternal and spiritual nature. Confusing the higher with the lower self brings anguish to the human condition.

---

3. *Kaushitaki Upanishad* in Mascaró, trans. *The Upanishads*, 107.
4. *Katha Upanishad*, Mascaró, trans. *The Upanishads*, 59.
5. *Science and Theology News*, May 2006, 19.

Brahman

Just as Indian thinkers sought to understand the nature of the true self, they also wanted to comprehend the ultimate reality, the fundamental power or principle supporting all there is. Like the quest for the *atman*, the sages' pursuit of ultimate reality was founded on an idea from the Vedas, which was reinterpreted during the axial period. This particular notion was rooted in the Brahmins' speculation about what made their rituals effective. As we recall from Chapter 5, the Vedas used a specific technical term to refer to the mysterious power that lies hidden inside of the ritual; they called that power *brahman*, and the priestly caste—the Brahmins—believed their principal function was to ensure its proper application.

In the Axial Age, the quest for liberating knowledge came to center on discovering the true nature of this *brahman*. The focus on *brahman* actually follows a very logical development in Indo-Aryan religion. The ritual and its sacred words had always been understood to correspond to greater cosmological and moral realities beyond the simple ceremony itself. The story of the sacrifice of the Purusha that we discussed in chapter 5 suggested that society, the various elements of the world, the ritual practices, and the Sanskrit language itself were all intrinsically and mystically connected to one another. Understanding the hidden *brahman* would therefore reveal the mystery of these connections and the deeper meaning of the whole of existence. By the Axial Age, *brahman* had come to mean more than the power of ritual; it now designated ultimate reality itself. To indicate this transformation of usage, we will use the term Brahman (capitalized) to refer to ultimate reality and *brahman* (lowercase) to denote the ritual power.

The authors of the Upanishads, however, did not reach complete consensus about the exact nature of Brahman. Yet there was at least one thing on which there seemed to be fundamental agreement: throughout the Upanishads, we are told that Brahman is one—a singular, undifferentiated unity. There are no parts or divisions to Brahman. In various passages, Brahman is also credited with creating and sustaining the world and all life. It is sometimes called the 'thread' that strings together all creatures. Brahman is said to permeate all things but cannot be perceived. It embraces good and evil yet transcends both. It is beyond morality altogether. In short, Brahman encompasses the whole of reality yet surpasses it. There is nothing beyond the scope of Brahman.

At this level, it would be misleading to identify Brahman with god, if by god we mean a supreme being. Brahman is not a being, certainly not a personal being; hence, it is referred to with impersonal pronouns such as *it*, rather than as he or she. Brahman would be more aptly described as the Absolute or Being-itself. These words obviously do not tell us much or give us concrete images with which to conceive of Brahman, but that is precisely the point.

This excerpt from the *Isha Upanishad* captures the sense of the magnificence and elusiveness of Brahman:

> "Throughout the Upanishads, we are told that Brahman is one—a singular, undifferentiated unity. There are no parts or divisions to Brahman. In various passages, Brahman is credited with creating and sustaining the world and all life. It is sometimes called the 'thread' that strings together all creatures. Brahman is said to permeate all things but cannot be perceived. It embraces good and evil yet transcends both. It is beyond morality altogether. In short, Brahman encompasses the whole of reality yet surpasses it. There is nothing beyond the scope of Brahman."

> [Brahman], without moving, is swifter than the mind; the senses cannot reach it: It is ever beyond them. Standing still, it overtakes those who run. To the ocean of its being, the spirit of life leads the streams of action. It moves, and it moves not. It is far, and it is near. It is within all, and it is outside all. [Brahman] filled all with its radiance. It is incorporeal and invulnerable, pure and untouched by evil. It is . . . immanent and transcendent. It placed all things in the path of Eternity.[6]

Through the use of paradox and negation, this passage asserts that Brahman transcends all human categories and images. In claiming that it moves and it moves not, for instance, the author demonstrates how Brahman exhausts and depletes our categories for understanding it. How can it both move and not move? What kind of sense does that make? Well, it makes no sense according to our conventional forms of logic. The very point of such a phrase is to confound our thinking. Hindu theologians eventually said of Brahman that it was *nirguna*, meaning "without qualities." To try to describe it in anything

---

6. *Isha Upanishad* in Mascaró, trans. *The Upanishads*, 49. I have replaced Mascaró's misleading use of the masculine pronoun with the neuter "it."

other than a paradoxical or negative way makes it into something that can be comprehended, which by definition, it cannot be.

Gradually, the Upanishadic sages began to realize that Brahman was ultimately unknowable, or at least not knowable in the conventional sense of that word. Brahman, they believed, eluded conceptualization and perception, and so these faculties were ineffective in discovering the absolute reality. What the sages sought was the deepest kind of knowing, a grasp of reality that we can best call "mystical" or "ineffable." An excerpt from the *Kena Upanishad*, one of the shortest of the principal Upanishads, describes the mystical features of this knowledge:

What cannot be spoken with words, but that whereby words are spoken: Know that alone to be Brahman, the spirit, and not what people here adore.

What cannot be thought with the mind, but that whereby the mind can think: Know that alone to be Brahman, the spirit, and not what people here adore.

What cannot be seen with the eye, but that whereby the eye can see: Know that alone to be Brahman, the spirit, and not what people here adore.

What cannot be heard with the ear, but that whereby the ear can hear: Know that alone to be Brahman, the spirit, and not what people here adore.

What cannot be indrawn with the breath, but that whereby breath is indrawn: Know that alone to be Brahman, the spirit, and not what people here adore.[7]

Sight does not reach there; neither does thinking or speech.
We don't know, we can't perceive how one would point it out.
It is far different from what's known.
And it is farther than the unknown.[8]

The Identity of *Atman* and Brahman

As the sages of the Upanishads continued their search to discover the human essence and the ultimate reality, a new insight began to emerge into awareness, an epiphany that came to full expression in the later Upanishads. As they increasingly appreciated the incomprehensible and unutterable nature of both *atman* and Brahman, these two concepts converged. The sages concluded that

---

7. *Kena Upanishad* in Mascaró, trans. *The Upanishads*, 51. The masculine pronoun has been replaced by "it."
8. *Kena Upanishad*, 1.3, in Olivelle, trans. *Upaniṣads*, 227.

what is called the *atman*, or the true self, is identical with ultimate reality. They are the selfsame reality.

The Upanishads express this insight in a variety of ways. One text asserts, "Who[ever] denies [Brahman], denies himself. Who[ever] affirms [Brahman], affirms himself."[9] The *Chandogya Upanishad* puts it this way: "This is the Spirit that is in my heart, smaller than a grain of rice, or a grain of barley, or a grain of mustard-seed, or a grain of canary-seed, or the kernel of a grain of canary-seed. This is the Spirit that is in my heart, greater than the earth, greater than the sky, greater than heaven itself, greater than all these worlds."[10] Another celebrated passage tells how a father named Uddalaka teaches this revelation to his son Svetaketu, a young man who has just completed his formal schooling but who apparently has missed the most important lesson of all. Uddalaka creates an object lesson by asking Svetaketu to take a fruit from the great banyan tree, break it open, and dissect one of the seeds. Svetaketu does as he is told. When he tells his father he finds nothing within, Uddalaka makes his point: "My son from the very essence in the seed which you cannot see comes in truth this vast banyan tree. Believe me, my son, an invisible and subtle essence is the Spirit of the whole universe. That is Reality. That is *Ātman*. THOU ART THAT."[11] These passages are not merely claiming that the true human essence is a *part* of god or carries a divine spark or is created in the *image* of god. Rather, the identity of *atman* and Brahman means they are consubstantial, two names for the same reality. The true self *is* ultimate reality.

> "The Upanishads do not merely claim that the true human essence is a *part* of god or carries a divine spark or is created in the *image* of god. Rather, the identity of *atman* and Brahman means they are consubstantial, two names for the same reality. The true self *is* ultimate reality."

It is hard to imagine a more exalted view of humanity. This assessment of the self seems almost diametrically opposite to that of mainstream Western monotheism, in which god is viewed as "wholly other" than humanity, to use a phrase popular among early-twentieth-century Protestant theologians. Or to cite the Christian theologian Søren Kierkegaard, there is an "infinite qualitative difference" between god and humanity.

---

9. *Taittiriya Upanishad* in Mascaró, trans. *The Upanishads*, 110.
10. *Chandogya Upanishad* in Mascaró, trans. *The Upanishads*, 114.
11. *Chandogya Upanishad* in Mascaró, trans. *The Upanishads*, 117.

Despite the Upanishads' lofty view, the self nonetheless finds itself in an endless cycle of birth, death, and rebirth. Like many religious traditions West and East, the classical Hindu view understands that the embodied self is not at rest, is not in its true home. It continues in this restless state, seeking ever-new manifestations until it finds, as Augustine would say, its rest in god.[12] So how do we reconcile these two seemingly contradictory claims? On the one hand, our true selves are identical with ultimate reality, absolutely the same; on the other, we suffer the rounds of incessant rebirth. How can this be?

According to the Upanishads, *samsara* is a consequence of our ignorance, our misperception and misunderstanding of reality. The Vedantic sages speak of *maya*, a veil over reality that accounts for our ignorance. *Maya* causes us to perceive plurality when in reality there is unity. We think of the world as comprising many different things rather than the one reality that it is. *Maya* deceives us into thinking of ourselves as separate entities, as individuals, separate from one another, separate from ultimate reality. It causes us to forget who we truly are and prompts us to identify with our lower selves. But our lower selves, because they are transitory and inconstant, are ultimately not real. Until we fully recognize the truth about Brahman and *atman*, we continue to suffer on the wheel of *samsara*, because we continue to generate the karma that binds us to the phenomenal world. Believing ourselves to be individuals, we tend to think and act in self-centered ways, creating the desires and deeds that perpetuate the illusion of our separateness from Brahman. And it is this sense of separateness that engenders fear and hatred of others, the greed for material goods and power, and ultimately the fear of death. The *Maitri Upanishad* says, "Whenever the soul has thoughts of 'I' and 'mine,' it binds itself with its lower self, as a bird with the net of a snare."[13] Paradoxically, the very desire to "be special" that we spoke of earlier is the source of our misery.

Describing the Indescribable

Ironically, we have been discussing a reality that by definition cannot be discussed. Whether we call it Brahman or *atman*, the referent of our terms is defined as something beyond mind, concept, and language. Yet without concept and language, this "discussion" of ultimate reality in Hinduism would have been a sheaf of empty pages. Though we must try to speak of these subjects, the most lucid possible essay on Brahman and *atman* will never suffice

---

12. See Augustine, *Confessions*, trans. R. S. Pine-Coffin (London: Penguin, 1961), 21.
13. *Maitri Upanishad* in Mascaró, trans. *The Upanishads*, 101.

to engender the kind of knowledge required for liberation, and until one attains such liberating knowledge, one has not realized ultimate reality.

But if not through language, how is it that one comes to such an understanding? How does one penetrate the *maya* that deceives our minds and causes our unhappiness? This will be the subject of our next chapter.

9

The One and the Many

According to the Upanishads, it is not enough for the mind to grasp the concepts of *atman* and Brahman. Merely knowing the identity of self and ultimate reality in a theoretical or conceptual way does little good unless it is apprehended by the core of one's being. Only then does it become the liberating knowledge that leads to *moksha*. Without this deep, existential understanding, one continues to live a life of self-centeredness and desire, generating the karma that binds us to *samsara*. In this chapter, we will explore what the sages of the Axial Age thought it took to gain this extraordinary kind of understanding and what alternatives there were for those who found this approach too difficult or simply unappealing.

THE KNOWING THAT LEADS TO MOKSHA

GOING WITHIN

Attaining the complete awareness of Brahman and *atman* involves, first of all, a reorientation to the discovery of truth. Whereas many religions encourage their followers to look for truth in a book or creed or rituals, the Vedantic perspective insists that the truth is not "out there," but within, within one's deepest self. To discover one's self is to discover the highest reality. "He who has found and knows his Soul," says the *Chandogya Upanishad*, "has found all the worlds."[1]

The discovery of the divine within is one of the aims of the introspective disciplines of Hinduism, particularly meditation. Meditation was probably practiced in India long before the Axial Age. Some of the artifacts discovered in the ruins of the Indus Valley Civilization depict individuals in what appears to be a traditional meditative pose. The Vedas, as well, suggest that the Indo-

---

1. *Chandogya Upanishad* in Mascaró, trans. *The Upanishads*, 121.

Aryans may have used a form of meditation. By the Axial Age, meditation had come to eclipse ritual as the chief discipline for *shramanas* seeking *moksha*.

The various Upanishads recommended different methods for engaging in meditation, but there were characteristics common to all of them. Of prime importance was restraining the body and mind to achieve a state of inner stillness. Ordinarily, this objective involved sitting in an upright posture in a quiet place, free from distractions. Then the mind was focused on a particular object, such as the breath, an external or internal image, or a mantra, a special word intoned silently to oneself. This focus helped the mind concentrate and avoid thoughts and sensations that distracted from the aim of the practice. Over time, serious and regular meditation was said to bring about an array of experiences, including visions, ecstasy, the intensification of awareness, and transcendence of thoughts and imaginings. One of the Upanishads also promised "health . . . lightness of body, a pleasant scent, and sweet voice; and an absence of greedy desires."[2] By the steady engagement of meditative techniques, one gained access to the higher self, to the *atman*.

Disciplining the Lower Self

The practice of meditation was complemented by the *shramanas'* efforts to dissociate from the lower self that is habitually mistaken for the genuine self. Some of the techniques were intended to close off avenues that led seekers astray, keeping them trapped in the net of *maya*. Some ascetics took vows of silence to eliminate words, since the knowledge of Brahman was beyond language. Some tried to overcome their attachments to the material world by poverty, fasting, and celibacy. Others took more extreme measures that involved mortifying the body, literally putting the flesh to death. Mortification techniques comprised a wide range of observances, including standing immobile for long periods of time, often years; piercing the flesh with sharp objects; lying on beds of nails or thorns; and self-flagellation.

The point of all these practices, from the mild to the harsh, was to train the ascetic to give up all attachments that encouraged a sense of individuality or separateness from the rest of reality. To realize the higher self and its identity with Brahman, one had to relinquish all selfish desires. *The Supreme Teaching* says, "When all desires that cling to the heart disappear, then a mortal becomes immortal, and even in this life attains Liberation."[3] Since desire creates karma, and karma binds one to *samsara,* giving up desire is freedom from *samsara*.

---

2. *Svetasvatara Upanishad* in Mascaró, trans. *The Upanishads*, 88.
3. *The Supreme Teaching* in Mascaró, trans. *The Upanishads*, 140.

MOKSHA

For the Upanishadic sages, to see the true self meant to see there was nothing to desire and nothing to fear. If the *atman* were immortal and consubstantial with ultimate reality itself, what reason would there be to want or fear anything? Because one lacked for nothing and feared nothing, taking this path to its end brought about a deep sense of serenity and indescribable joy beyond all earthly pleasures. "The Spirit of man," says *The Supreme Teaching*, "has crossed the lands of good and evil, and has passed beyond the sorrows of the heart."[4] There would be no rebirth, because there would be no clinging to life, no dread of dying, just a state of equanimity toward the world. This was *moksha*. It was a goal that could be realized in one's lifetime, and those who did were called *jivanmuktas*—living, liberated souls.

Some texts refer to the experience of *moksha* as "merging with" or "returning to" Brahman, but those images may be somewhat misleading. The true self does not need to unite with Brahman because it already *is* Brahman; it merely fails to recognize that. *Moksha*, then, is less an achievement than the simple apprehension of truth. And here we encounter another paradox of this spiritual pathway. Although the *jivanmukta* must strive to reach liberation, it is not the effort that accomplishes unity with Brahman. This remarkable insight was beautifully expressed by a mystic from another tradition similar in many ways to Vedanta. Bayazid al-Bistami (804–874 CE), a medieval Sufi *shaykh*, or master, told his followers, "This thing we tell of can never be found by seeking, yet only seekers find it." So it was with the path of Vedanta.

THE PHILOSOPHICAL PROBLEMS OF VEDANTA

Although the identity of Brahman and *atman* is a lofty conception, it is not without problems as theology. For instance, how does one account for *maya*? If Brahman-*atman* is the only reality there is, why does the illusion of *maya* exist, and how is it created? An even more vexing question is this: If there are no individuals, then there are no selves in the plural. But if there are no selves, only *atman*-Brahman, in what sense is reincarnation real? Is *samsara* itself an illusion? In an intriguing passage, one Upanishad comes very close to making this claim: "Samsara, the transmigration of life, takes place in one's own mind. Let one therefore keep the mind pure, for what a man thinks, that he becomes: this is the mystery of Eternity."[5] The Upanishads blended

---

4. *The Supreme Teaching* in Mascaró, trans. *The Upanishads*, 136.
5. *Maitri Upanishad* in Mascaró, trans. *The Upanishads*, 103.

tantalizing and provocative ideas with just enough vagueness and uncertainty to inspire successive generations to continue to work through and reinterpret their essential features. No less than three subschools of Hindu philosophy were based on Vedanta, and they each developed different perspectives on the issues we have been discussing. Two of Hinduism's greatest philosophers, Shankara and Ramanuja, both postaxial sages, were founders of Vedantic schools.

But the Upanishads' significance goes well beyond providing grist for the philosopher's mill; their importance to the overall Hindu traditions was more a matter of establishing the key elements that provided Hinduism with many of its characteristic features: the belief in the unity and incomprehensible nature of the ultimate reality; the conceptions of *samsara*, karma, *atman*, and *moksha*; and the sense that the world and our selves are not really the way they appear.

Worship of the Gods and Goddesses

Despite the profound importance of the Vedantic perspective in the development of the Hindu tradition, though, not everyone found Vedanta congenial to his or her religious sensibilities. As Hinduism evolved through the Axial Age, it continued to add new perspectives and practices to accommodate individual beliefs and tastes. Ultimately, Hinduism became a family of religions without a creed or core of beliefs that every Hindu was expected to accept. Unlike some other religions in which doctrinal purity is essential and dissidents are excommunicated, Hinduism has embraced differences rather than excluded them. Early on, Hinduism recognized that people were at various stages in their spiritual lives and the practices and beliefs for one person might not be suitable for another. In its most quoted passage, the Rig Veda declares, "Truth is One, but the sages refer to it in different ways."[6] Rather than impose a single set of doctrines and rituals, Hinduism has given wide latitude for persons to appropriate its vast resources in the way most meaningful and enriching for the individual.

---

6. Rig Veda 1.164.46. My translation.

> "Hinduism became a family of religions without a creed or core of beliefs that every Hindu was expected to accept. Unlike some other religions in which doctrinal purity is essential and dissidents are excommunicated, Hinduism has embraced differences rather than excluded them.... Rather than impose a single set of doctrines and rituals, Hinduism has given wide latitude for persons to appropriate its vast resources in the way most meaningful and enriching for the individual."

As one might expect, many Indians found the Upanishads' path of knowledge simply too demanding and unappealing as a way of life. The mystical tradition of imageless silence may attract some, but by far most religious people need symbols and words to guide their spirits. Aristotle wrote, "The soul never thinks without an image,"[7] and most people need to think about and conceptualize the object of their devotion. Consequently, most Hindus preferred a more traditional piety focused on worshiping a personal god or goddess rather than the highly abstract, impersonal Brahman. That there are no temples in India dedicated to Brahman is evidence that conventional religious practices such as prayer and ceremonies are not conducive to this concept of ultimate reality. How does one pray to an inconceivable principle? How does one ask for healing or favors from Brahman? How does one celebrate or tell stories about Brahman? An ultimate reality without qualities simply did not satisfy the religious needs of many. But because emerging Hinduism did not insist on uniformity of practice and belief, preexisting customs could be incorporated into the developing faith. The worship of personal deities thus continued unabated in the Axial Age and became even more popular near its end. This point is reflected in the fact that today the most popular religious literature among Hindus is not the philosophical Upanishads but the postaxial stories about the gods—the *Ramayana*, the Puranas, and the *Bhagavad Gita*, perhaps the most frequently read Hindu scripture.

The historical coexistence of these two paths—one of devotion to the gods and goddesses and the other of seeking the realization of Brahman—naturally invites us to ask about the relationship between these very different religious outlooks. Although the way of knowledge emphasizes that ultimate reality is inconceivable and beyond words and images, anyone who knows much about India knows that Hindus are anything but silent about god. India as a land is home to an astounding array of divine icons. There are pictures and statues of

---

7. Aristotle, *On the Soul*, Bk 3, Ch.7 in *The Basic Works of Aristotle*, ed. Richard McKeon (New York: Random House, 1941), 594.

members of the Hindu pantheon everywhere you go. In public buildings, on buses, in taxis and rickshaws, at the tea stalls and shops, and on the sides of roads, the gods and goddesses cast a watchful eye over everything. The casual observer could hardly guess that the ultimate reality of Hinduism was incomprehensible and beyond imagination.

SAGUNA BRAHMAN

To incorporate the vast numbers of anthropomorphic gods and goddesses who are venerated all throughout India, Hinduism refined the theology of Brahman. By introducing another dimension to the theory of Brahman, Hindu theologians provided a way for the devotees of the gods and the seekers of Brahman to understand themselves as relating to the same ultimate reality. In so doing, Hinduism provided the theoretical foundations for its broad tolerance and inclusive outlook.

The Upanishads clearly emphasize the incomprehensible nature of Brahman, but later thinkers would say there is a sense in which Brahman *is* knowable and can be represented and comprehended, at least partially. Thus, in addition to the claim that Brahman was *nirguna*, without qualities and beyond the mind's grasp, later theologians argued that Brahman was also *saguna*, with qualities and characteristics, and therefore able to be conceived and perceived. The formless and the infinite could take form and finitude. On this belief, the many gods and goddesses of popular piety became so many manifestations of the one inconceivable reality. Through devotion to any manifestation, the individual relates to Brahman. Each god or goddess functions as a portal or conduit to the ultimate reality, mediating the sacred to the believer.

HINDU ICONOGRAPHY

The idea of *saguna* Brahman recognizes that most people require a concrete focus for the religious life, a symbol or image towards which they can orient their devotion, direct their prayers, and grasp something of the nature of the ultimate. Even those on the mystical path to *nirguna* Brahman needed, at some point on their journey, symbols of the divine, although they must ultimately strive to relinquish them. Throughout their history, Hindus have fashioned physical representations of gods and goddesses to provide these focal points for faith. Since the great majority of Hindus of the past–and many still today–have not been able to read, these physical images were a principal source of their theology.

Hindu images of the divine can be anthropomorphic or nonanthropomorphic. Since Brahman pervades all there is, in principle anything can manifest divine reality and yield access to the sacred for those who have eyes to see. The countless array of nonanthropomorphic symbols include natural phenomena such as stones, trees, rivers, and celestial bodies. Other prominent nonanthropomorphic representations are the lingam that symbolizes the presence of Shiva and the footprints of Vishnu.

The anthropomorphic images are those that appear humanlike. To imagine ultimate reality as in some measure like us—with intelligence, will, emotions, and perhaps even a body—helps us to imagine mystery and to relate to it in ways not possible with nonanthropomorphic representations. Anthropomorphic images allow devotees to feel close to the highest reality and believe that whoever or whatever is in charge of this world is concerned about human well-being.

The danger in personalizing the divine, however, is making it seem so human that it appears utterly finite and unworthy of devotion. The recent furor over several fictional accounts of the life of Jesus—*The Last Temptation of Christ*, *The Da Vinci Code*, and Mel Gibson's *The Passion of the Christ*—all concern this very issue. Among other things, critics argue that these stories so strongly emphasize Jesus' humanity that his divinity is virtually lost.

Hindu images of the gods are designed to avert this danger by incorporating elements that bluntly remind devotees that the gods are *not* like us and cannot be reduced to finite status. The Hindu gods thus appear simultaneously human and nonhuman. Ganesha, the remover of obstacles, has a very human body but the head of an elephant. Lord Rama, a manifestation of the god Vishnu, appears to be completely human, but his blue skin reminds Hindus of his divinity. The goddess Durga looks like a woman, but her eight arms tell us she is not. Each of these instances gives shape to the unseen and allows Hindus to glimpse some salient aspect of the divine. Durga's many arms, for example, indicate immense power, just as Brahma's many heads suggest omniscience. The androgynous image known as Ardhanarishvara is half the god Shiva and half the goddess Parvati, expressing the ideal of balance between the male and female principles. At the same time, the unusual qualities such as the multiple arms and heads or bisexual bodies remind devotees that the divine always transcends ordinary experience.

IMAGES AS INCARNATIONS

These unearthly characteristics serve to point beyond the human-made image to ultimate, infinite reality. As symbols, no one would confuse the images with that to which they refer. Yet there is a special sense in which they *are* understood to embody the divine reality, allowing the images to function as incarnations of the god.

When a craftsperson completes an image, elaborate rituals of consecration may be used to invite the god or goddess it represents to inhabit it. In a temple, the consecrated image is then treated as if it were a god in living form. In the morning, it is gently wakened from sleep, bathed and clothed, decorated with flower garlands and cosmetics, and offered food. During the day, the image is offered gifts such as flowers, fruit, water, and coconuts. At specific times during the day, the temple image is made available to worshippers for *darshan*, a special viewing of the divine image. Seeing the god and being seen by the god is a transaction of great importance in Hinduism. At night, the image is affectionately put to bed.

Ordinarily, the incarnation lasts for a specific period of time, perhaps for a weeklong festival in honor of the *deva* or *devi*. When the designated time is up, the physical image is destroyed, often by burning or immersion in water, in what amounts to a funeral. This practice reminds devotees that although the god may indeed incarnate the image, the image is not the god. It is still the product of human creation. The image is like an impermanent body, temporarily housing divine reality, just as the *atman* briefly inhabits a human body.

Even though the Hindu pantheon is immense, individual Hindus do not worship all the gods. Each devotee has an *ishta-devata*, a personal deity of choice. Often this personal *deva* is the god venerated by one's family or village, but it is not uncommon for family members to be devoted to other gods. One's decision to worship a specific god is uniquely one's own and may be based on a special affinity one feels for a particular god. Devotees worship their chosen deity as the supreme god but do not feel compelled to deny the reality of other gods or their supremacy for their followers. In a land of 330 million gods—the traditional number of the pantheon—this is how Hindus can understand themselves as monotheists.

IMAGES AND IDOLATRY

Many in the Western world consider the religious use of images blasphemous and accordingly refer to images used in this way as "idols." Often, those who level such criticism against the use of physical images fail to realize that their own beliefs and theologies are full of images of the divine, albeit linguistic rather than material images. To call god "father" or "king" and to carve a statue of Vishnu are both human efforts to give form to that which is ultimately formless. Unless one is absolutely silent about ultimate reality, it is not possible to avoid human-made images and concepts. And all images—physical and linguistic—are subject to the dangers of idolatry. Idolatry is not creating physical symbols or representations of god, as such, but confusing and identifying transcendent divine reality with what is merely the product of our minds and hands. Idolatry means to believe that god *really is* a father or *really has* four heads, rather than to recognize that these images and metaphors are merely our limited human efforts to grasp an elusive mystery.

Here is where *nirguna* Brahman is of immense theological value. The idea of *nirguna* Brahman reminds the devotee that the ultimate reality always transcends any image. *Nirguna* Brahman means that no single representation of a god or goddess could ever exhaust the limitlessness of Brahman, or for that matter neither could 330 million images. The very number of gods in Hinduism and their complex manifestations, so outrageous in their extravagance, serves to astound and overwhelm the human mind. And that, in a fashion, reminds Hindus of the ultimate reality's unspeakable nature. Thus, *nirguna* Brahman provides a safeguard against absolutist claims about god and promotes epistemological humility, the recognition of the limited capacities of the human mind in the face of universal mystery.

Liberation through Devotion

The best resource within Hinduism for understanding the dynamics of worship of the gods is probably the *Bhagavad Gita*, the popular scripture that was written down at the end of the Axial Age or just shortly afterward. Primarily a dialogue between a warrior named Arjuna and the god Krishna, the *Gita* is a veritable tour through the many practices of Hinduism, including Vedic rituals, karma and morality, meditation and yoga, and devotion to the gods. One of its central points is that all of these disciplines are spiritually beneficial. But the *Gita* also suggests that devotion to god is the best of all. Toward the book's end, Krishna encourages Arjuna to focus his mind, will, and heart on god and to let go of all else. In so doing, Arjuna—and any devotee—will find liberation from *samsara*. Krishna says:

"*Nirguna* Brahman means that no single representation of a god or goddess could ever exhaust the limitlessness of Brahman, or for that matter neither could 330 million images. The very number of gods in Hinduism and their complex manifestations, so outrageous in their extravagance, serves to astound and overwhelm the human mind.... Thus, *nirguna* Brahman provides a safeguard against absolutist claims about god and promotes epistemological humility, the recognition of the limited capacities of the human mind in the face of universal mystery."

> Whatever you do—what you take,
> what you offer, what you give,
> what penances you perform—
> do as an offering to me ...!
> You will be freed from the bonds of action [karma],
> from the fruit of fortune and misfortune;
> armed with the discipline of renunciation,
> your self liberated, you will join me.[8]

All that matters is to do all things with faith in and dedication to the god. According to the *Gita*, faith can be so potent it does not even matter whether one is devoted to the god Krishna by name:

> When devoted men sacrifice
> to other deities with faith,

---

8. *Bhagavad Gita*, 9.27-28, trans. Barbara S. Miller (New York: Bantam, 1986), 86–87.

they sacrifice to me . . . ,
however aberrant the rites.[9]

What matters is not faith's object but its quality and sincerity.

The Inexpressible and Its Expressions

We have observed two fundamentally different theologies and practices emerging in the Indian axial period: the first, a mystical theology asserting that ultimate reality is beyond the reach of the mind and ordinary consciousness; the second, a theistic view in which the divine can be represented by symbols and images, allowing the devotee to draw close through acts of reverence and veneration. While followers of each path may claim superiority for their particular way, both approaches have been embraced in the greater tradition of Hinduism. Neither can claim to be more authentically Hindu than the other.

---

9. *Bhagavad Gita,* 9.23, trans. Miller, 86.

10

The Life of Siddhattha Gotama

Among the thousands of intrepid individuals who sought to end *samsara* in the forests of northeastern India in the Axial Age was a young man by the name of Siddhattha Gotama. Like many others, Gotama had been convinced that conquering the anguish of samsaric existence was life's highest aspiration. Nothing else could be more important, and he was willing to give up everything to attain that goal. Yet his pursuit of the spiritual options available at the time brought him no satisfaction. He quickly mastered the ascetic disciplines for realizing Brahman but found that they did not bring what he was looking for. The way of devotion to the gods held little interest for him; he thought the gods themselves were in need of the solution he sought. After many years of frustration, he departed from these well-trodden paths and on his own discovered the object of his search. His discovery finally brought him happiness and relief from the suffering that appeared to be inherent in life itself. Siddhattha Gotama had become the Buddha.

We will begin our study of this remarkable individual with special attention to the early experiences that led him to discover a new perspective. In later chapters, we will compare the teachings and practices he espoused and relate them to the other Axial Age philosophies we have already examined. For the first time in our study of the Indian Axial Age, we have an actual historical individual to whom we can connect specific teachings. It is important to study the Buddha's teachings in the context of his life, because the two are so closely intertwined. The Buddha was not an armchair philosopher; his view was the direct result of his attentive engagement with his own experience, a habit of being he encouraged in his followers.

The Historical Buddha

Like other founders of religious movements, we can distinguish the historical Buddha from the Buddha of myth and legend. By "the historical Buddha," we mean the actual individual who lived in human history and what we can say about him with reasonable certainty using modern methods of historiography. By "the Buddha of myth and legend," we mean the aspects of his life story that are later embellishments added by his followers after his death. In many cases, the line between history and myth is not always easy to draw, and scholars constantly debate what belongs on one side or the other.

> "For the first time in our study of the Indian Axial Age, we have an actual historical individual to whom we can connect specific teachings. It is important to study the Buddha's teachings in the context of his life, because the two are so closely intertwined. The Buddha was not an armchair philosopher; his view was the direct result of his attentive engagement with his own experience, a habit of being he encouraged in his followers."

The Sources

Part of the difficulty in recovering the historical Buddha resides in the nature of our sources. The earliest Buddhist scriptures first existed in oral form and were not written down until three to four hundred years after the Buddha's death. Furthermore, as the Buddhist tradition continued to develop and spread to different regions of Asia, new scriptures were added to reflect the philosophical emphases of emerging new sects. As Buddhism evolved, followers' views of the Buddha's life and its significance also changed.

The Pali Canon, the Buddhist texts closest in time to the life of the Buddha, are the most reliable sources for constructing the life of the historical Buddha. There are also collections of scriptures in Tibetan, Sanskrit, and Chinese, which were written later and are less historically dependable than the Pali Canon.[1] The Pali collection comprises a large number of volumes, enough to occupy a couple of feet on a library shelf. The most important part of the canon for our purposes is the set of writings called the Suttas, or discourses, which the Buddhist tradition considers the direct words of the Buddha himself.

---

1. "Pali" refers to the language of the text. The Buddha probably did not speak Pali himself but a Sanskritic language close to it. Pali is also a Sanskritic language, but a vernacular spoken by ordinary people, not the formal Sanskrit used by the Brahmin priests.

HISTORICAL FACTS OF GOTAMA'S LIFE

Interestingly, the Pali Suttas tell us very little about the Buddha's life prior to his awakening experience. The focus of these writings is his teachings. If we adhere to the standards of modern historical scholarship, we can construct only a bare-bones outline of his life using these scriptures.

Based on those standards, we can say with fairly high confidence that there was in fact an individual named Gotama who was born into privileged circumstances in the area near the current border between India and Nepal. At the time, this region was occupied by Aryans known as the Sakyas. According to traditions based on the Pali texts, Gotama was born in the year 563 BCE. As with Zoroaster, however, scholars are not in complete agreement about when Gotama actually lived, but the range of dates is not nearly as broad as Zoroaster's. The majority of scholars today would place Gotama's date of birth near 490 BCE. In any event, the Indian sage lived well within the Axial Age.

Historical scholarship also tells us that Gotama underwent a profound life-changing experience near the age of thirty that eventually led him to new insights into the human condition and to a new spiritual movement based on his discoveries. He taught his ideas to a growing body of followers throughout northeastern India during a period of great social change and religious ferment. There is good reason to believe that the Suttas of the Pali Canon accurately reflect the essential core of his teachings, though almost certainly some ideas of later interpreters have been included. Following the Buddha's awakening, his teaching ministry lasted for several decades until he died. Tradition says he lived until the age of eighty.

EMBELLISHMENTS TO THE STORY

Beyond these sparse statements, little else can be said about the historical Buddha with much certainty. This meager outline, however, leaves out much of the Buddha's life story that has provided inspiration and meaning to Buddhists for over two millennia. For this reason, we must risk leaving the historically verifiable facts and venture into the realm of myth and legend. It is precisely in this realm, however, that we ascertain so much of what made the Buddha such a compelling figure for millions. The life of the Buddha as told in these traditions—whether historically true or not—is the very embodiment of Buddhist teachings, so we dare not neglect the legendary literature.

There are several versions of the early life of Gotama and how he came to claim the title the Buddha, but most of them are variations on a basic story line that begins with Siddhattha Gotama being born to the king and queen of the realm of the Sakyan peoples. Modern historiography places doubt on this royal lineage. While it is probably true that Gotama's family was privileged and members of the warrior caste, it is unlikely that his parents were monarchs, since the small states of this area were tribal republics ruled by councils of elders. But again, to remain strictly on the side of history eliminates the deeper significance of the story.

One late addition to the narrative suggests that Siddhattha was conceived by his mother, Queen Maya, during a dream in which she was impregnated by a white godlike King Elephant, implying that the conception was divinely ordained and supernaturally accomplished. This variation goes on to say that ten lunar months later, the child Siddhattha was born while his mother was on a journey to the home of her parents. Along the way, she gave birth in a grove of trees near the town of Lumbini. The child came forth from his mother's side while she stood upright, holding the branch of a tree. Immediately, the newborn took seven steps and confidently declared that he was born for the good of the world and this would be his last birth in the samsaric realm. Clearly, this tale is mythic, but it serves to foreground the universal significance of Siddhattha's life.

Not all versions include this miraculous birth story, but most of them contain the account of how King Suddhodana—Prince Siddhattha's father—consulted with court astrologers after his son's birth. The soothsayers all agreed: the king's firstborn would become a *cakravartin*, a "wheel turner," one whose existence would decisively change the lives of others. The court sages, however, were not clear about the specific domain of Siddhattha's accomplishments. He might pursue the way of the world and become a great monarch, or he might forsake the world and follow the path of the spiritual pioneer. Determined to see his son follow in his own footsteps, King Suddhodana asked how he might ensure that his son would take the road to kingship. Again, the court sages were unanimous: At all costs, the boy must be shielded from any unpleasantness and raised in a wholly delightful environment. He must enjoy only the best food, wear the best clothes, and engage in constant diversions and entertainments. He must never be exposed to the brutal realities of existence until he firmly committed himself to being king.

Suddhodana followed the sages' recommendations zealously and to the letter. The accounts offer various and differing details. Some say Siddhattha was never permitted to leave the palace; others suggest he made occasional excursions beyond the palace confines, but only after his father had arranged to have the young man's route carefully planned and purged of potentially upsetting sights. Thus, beggars, old men and women, and the sick and disabled were rounded up and kept out of view until the prince's entourage had passed.

By all accounts, Siddhattha lived only the most pleasant sort of life, unaware that there was any other way to live. In a rare self-revelation in the Pali Canon, the Buddha describes his early years in a way that confirms the essence of the legend, although it does not verify all the details. Many years after his awakening, the Buddha tells his followers,

> I was delicately brought up, O monks, highly delicate, exceedingly delicate was my upbringing. At my father's house, lotus ponds were made: in one of them blue lotuses bloomed, in another white lotuses, and in a third red lotuses, just for my enjoyment. I used only sandal unguent from [the city of] Benares and my head dress, my jacket, my undergarment and my tunic were made of Benares muslin. By day and by night a white canopy was held over me, lest cold and heat, dust, chaff or dew should trouble me.[2]

At age sixteen, Siddhattha married his beautiful cousin, Yashodhara, who eventually gave birth to his son. Everything seemed right with the world. And so it was, for Siddhattha's first twenty-nine years.

Again, whether historical or not, the story of his father's royal status, wealth, power, and overprotectiveness is rich with meaning. It suggests that, without even lifting a finger, the individual who would become the Buddha had already received everything other people spend their lives trying to acquire. Simply by virtue of birth, he had riches, power, celebrity, and every imaginable creature comfort. Even according to the Pali accounts, Siddhattha was uncommonly handsome, athletically endowed, and blessed with deep blue eyes, robust health, the love of family, and a deeply compassionate nature. It is hard even to imagine what more could be added to such a life. This young Gotama epitomized the fulfillment of humanity's greatest dreams, the embodiment of what almost all of us think we want. Who could possibly desire more? But this is the very point of the legend of Siddhattha's extravagant early life: having it all is still not enough.

In a crucial moment, at the age of twenty-nine, the young prince arrived at this insight. Whether by accident or design (various texts say different things), the shell of his sheltered existence was cracked, and Siddhattha came face-to-face with suffering for the very first time. In short order, he encountered a person in the throes of illness, another ravaged by age, and a corpse en route to the charnel ground. The narrative claims that up until that moment, the prince

---

2. *Numerical Discourses of the Buddha: An Anthology of Suttas from the* Anguttara Nikāya, 3:38, ed. and trans. Nyanaponika Thera and Bhikkhu Bodhi, (Walnut Creek, CA: AltaMira, 1999), 53–54.

had never witnessed any of these things nor even heard of sickness, old age, and death. Learning about these realities of life and discovering that all beings were subject to them caused Siddhattha great distress. On his return home, he saw another impressive sight: a wandering *shramana* who had renounced everything and who nonetheless appeared happy in the midst of a suffering world. Distraught by the first three spectacles and intrigued by the fourth, the young man decided to give up the comforts of the privileged life to seek a way to soothe his now-troubled mind. The Buddhist traditions refer to this episode as The Four Sights.

Siddhattha took immediate action. In the dark of night, he quietly kissed his wife and young son good-bye and left palace life forever. With the help of a close friend, he slipped out of his father's house, cut off his hair, and took up the robes and begging bowl of the *shramanas*.

Demythologizing the Narrative

Much in this story makes it difficult to accept as historically true, which is why most scholars assign it to the category of myth. It is hard to believe that, as zealous as his father was to shield Siddhattha from life's harsh realities, he could have actually managed to do so for three decades. It is equally difficult to accept that, for so many years, the young man was totally oblivious to suffering, old age, and death. Clearly, the legend needs to be demythologized to uncover its real depth.

Rather than being the story of a father's overprotectiveness, let us consider that the account is really about youthful naïveté. While obviously something of great significance happened to Siddhattha at age twenty-nine, one may seriously doubt that it was merely learning that people get sick, grow old, and die. Surely, he already knew these things. The real epiphany for Siddhattha came when he recognized that *he himself*, the one who had it all, and everyone he cared about were all subject to these realities of life. Until this moment, Siddhattha's knowledge of these truths was merely abstract and conceptual. We all know from a fairly young age that living things die, yet for much of our lives, especially in our youth, we do not *really* believe death will come to us.

Leo Tolstoy's novella, *The Death of Ivan Ilyich*, is a disturbing study of the psychological mechanisms by which we prevent our own personal demise from coming into full consciousness. When word of Ivan Ilyich's death reaches his associates, his close friend Pyotr Ivanovich momentarily lets the news upset him and then quickly, but only half-consciously, reasons it away:

> Pyotr Ivanovich was overcome with horror as he thought of the suffering of someone he had known so well, first as a carefree boy, then as a schoolmate, later as a grown man, his colleague.... "Three days of terrible suffering and death. Why, the same thing could happen to me at any time now," he thought and for a moment felt panic-stricken. But at once, he himself did not know how, he was rescued by the customary reflection that all this happened to Ivan Ilyich, not to him, that it could not and should not happen to him; and that if he were to grant such a possibility, he would succumb to depression.... With this line of reasoning, Pyotr Ivanovich set his mind at rest and began to press for details about Ivan Ilyich's death, as though death were a chance experience that could only happen to Ivan Ilyich, never to himself.[3]

The kind of forgetfulness that overcame Pyotr Ivanovich like a narcotic was not possible for Siddhattha Gotama. At this critical moment, Siddhattha truly understood: "I, too, will die; I too will lose everything I hold dear." His illusion had shattered, and there was simply no returning to life as if suffering and death were not real.

Significantly, this insight comes to Siddhattha near the age of thirty, the same age, we observed earlier, at which the lives of Jesus, Zoroaster, Ezekiel, Mahavira, and Guru Nanak took dramatic turns. Why thirty? I can only offer speculation based largely on my own experience. It was at thirty that I became personally acquainted with the aging of my body, and I suspect that this begins to happen to others around this age. I began seeing the little signs that my youth was becoming a thing of the past—a tiny wrinkle here, a little sagging there, more hair in the shower drain. It was not much that anyone else could detect, but to someone as self-absorbed as I am, these things caused me much anxiety. It took me a long time to come to terms with this fact of life. I simply did not believe these things were happening to me; like Pyotr Ivanovich, I assumed that an exception would be made in my case.

With these reflections, I am suggesting that that one way to read the story of "The Four Sights" is as Siddhattha's complete acceptance that aging and death would indeed come to him, and not just to others. It hardly matters whether Siddhattha grasped this by stealthily observing his father's kingdom or by looking in a mirror or just calmly contemplating the natural course of life. In whatever way it happened, this recognition, I believe, was the Buddha's first awakening. Without this experience, there would have been no second

---

3. Leo Tolstoy, *The Death of Ivan Ilyich*, trans. Lynn Solotaroff (New York: Bantam, 1981), 44.

awakening, no illumination while quietly sitting under a tree several years later. Unlike his subsequent and ultimate awakening, this first epiphany brought no serenity of mind, but profound agitation and restiveness. It meant dropping the pretense of uniqueness and accepting wholeheartedly his common share with everyone else. It was enough to cause him to walk away from his incomparable life of ease and comfort. Presumably, he might have stayed right within the walls of his prison of pleasure. He might have done what most of us do when the recognition of our frailties comes upon us—that is, denying and forgetting. We are constantly seeking new ways to put our vulnerabilities out of mind. As T. S. Eliot once said, "Humankind cannot bear very much reality."[4] But for the young Gotama, returning to naïveté was not an option. Reality was just too real.

Renunciation

So Gotama left and took up the homeless life of a wandering ascetic, as so many others had done. From his home in the Himalayan foothills, he traveled on foot toward the urban centers of the Ganges River basin and spent the rest of his life in this rapidly developing area. As a novice *shramana*, Gotama sought someone who could serve as a teacher, introducing him to the disciplines necessary to find the end to suffering and rebirth. His first teacher was Alara Kalama, a renowned master of yogic meditation. Gotama soon mastered his teacher's doctrine and the meditative states on which they were based. Alara Kalama's instruction was able to take the aspiring renunciant to what he called the state of "nothingness," but no further.

Siddhattha found that this state did not bring him the freedom he sought, so he left in search of someone who could take him further. His second instructor, Uddaka Ramaputta, was also a famous practitioner of meditative yoga. Under his tutelage, Siddhattha was able to reach the level of "neither perception nor nonperception," but this meditative state did not satisfy young Gotama either. So he left Ramaputta.

These practices brought extraordinary—but only temporary—experiences. As long as he was absorbed in meditation, Siddhattha's experience was quite pleasant, but after the meditation ended, so did the pleasant state. Siddhattha wanted to attain permanent freedom from suffering and *samsara*. He continued to find value in meditation, but he rejected his teachers' claims that their yogic states were the highest realization of the spiritual life.

---

4. T. S. Eliot, "Burnt Norton," in *Four Quartets* (San Diego, CA: Harcourt Brace Jovanovich, 1943, 1971), 14.

The young *shramana* next took his quest to a more extreme level involving self-mortification. When he engaged in the practice of intense asceticism, Siddhattha did so with the same zeal that had characterized his work with his yoga teachers. He deprived his body of food and subsisted on a paltry diet of a few grains of rice or beans. In the Pali Canon, he describes his appearance after many months of this kind of self-torture: "My body reached a state of extreme emaciation. Because of eating so little my limbs became like the jointed segments of vine stems or bamboo stems . . . my backside became like a camel's hoof . . . the projections on my spine stood forth like corded beads . . . my ribs jutted out as gaunt as the crazy rafters of an old roofless barn . . . the gleam of my eyes sank far down in their sockets . . . my belly skin adhered to my backbone; thus if I touched my belly skin I encountered my backbone."[5] To passers-by, the contemplative ascetic looked like a decaying corpse.

Gotama was so dedicated to his task and committed to this discipline that a small group of five disciples gathered around him, hoping to follow him to *moksha*. But eventually, Gotama concluded that this path was a dead end. Far from terminating suffering, self-mortification only intensified it, and its ultimate destination could only be death. Surely there had to be some other way to conquer *samsara*.

---

5. *The Greater Discourse to Saccaka* 26.28, in Bhikkhu Ñānamoli and Bhikkhu Bodhi, trans. *The Middle Length Discourses of the Buddha: A New Translation of the* Majjhima Nikaya, (Somerville, MA: Wisdom, 1995), 339.

11

"I Am Awake"

For six years following his departure from palace life, Siddhattha Gotama fervently practiced the contemplative and ascetic arts. At last, he concluded that he was no closer to liberation than when he had begun. It occurred to him that all his life, he had been an extremist. As a youth in his father's house, he knew nothing but pleasure and delight. Following his renunciation, he knew nothing but self-denial and mortification. He now realized that neither extreme was the path to what he sought, and he surmised that steering a course between them, avoiding the pitfalls of both, was the more promising approach. He called this method the Middle Way and decided to follow it.

THE AWAKENING

The legends tell us that shortly after making this decision, Gotama went to a nearby river and washed off the dust that had accumulated on his body for many months. A local village girl gave him a bowl of milk-rice to eat. With this new approach, he would have to care for his body, not as an end in itself but because physical well-being was necessary to pursue liberation. The harsh forms of self-mortification had to be relinquished. Gradually, he returned to health. When his five students witnessed his change, they concluded that he was simply not up to the demands of the ascetic life, so they left, just as he had left his teachers years before.

A short time later, sitting beneath a tree near the village of Gaya in the present Indian state of Bihar, Gotama began to contemplate his next steps. Resting in the shade revived an old memory of sitting under a rose-apple tree as a child, during a Sakyan agricultural festival. He recalled that as his father was engaged in ceremonial plowing, he became bored and restless and, with nothing else to do, began to pay close attention to his breath. In those moments, he discovered a heightened sense of awareness and a pervasive calm that dissolved his boredom and restlessness. Remembering that time, Gotama thought that this gentle practice of meditation might provide the wisdom he was looking for. What distinguished this form of meditation from the practices of his teachers was its emphasis on the quality of mindfulness. Whereas the goal of other forms of meditation was to become absorbed in extraordinary states of mind, mindfulness meditation aimed at reaching a sharpened awareness of the immediate moment, so that one became attentive to what was happening in the mind, body, and external environment and witnessed these processes without judgment. Without trying to force particular states of mind, the mindfulness meditator simply observed without controlling. By letting go of goals and releasing preconceptions and judgments, Gotama believed, the mind would become more receptive to insight into the true nature of the world and the self.

Buddhist tradition says that on the evening of the full moon in the month of Vesakha (April–May according to Western calendars), Siddhattha Gotama sat beneath a huge tree—which later became known as the "bodhi," or wisdom, tree—and vowed not to leave the spot until he had realized the liberating knowledge that he had sought for so many years. He said, "Let only my skin, sinew, and bones remain, let the flesh and blood dry up in my body, but I will not give up this seat without attaining complete awakening." Thus Gotama began his meditation.

In the course of the night, his contemplations took him deeper than he had ever gone before. One tradition says he was even able to recall over 100,000 of his previous lives. But far more important was the deeper insights into the human condition that he attained. This was the liberating knowledge he had been searching for. As he made these advancements, he was approached by Mara, the demonic tempter, who tried to lure him away from his objective by offering him the pleasures of the world and taunting him with threats and doubts, much as Satan tried to do to Jesus in the New Testament. But Gotama was undeterred. At dawn, as the morning star first appeared in the sky, he knew he had won the understanding that liberates and conquers *samsara*. Later he told his followers that in that instant, "The knowledge and the vision arose in me: 'Unshakable is the liberation of my mind. This is my last birth. Now there is no more renewed existence.'"[1] At that moment and not before, Gotama earned the title of the Buddha, "the Awakened One."

---

1. *Setting in Motion the Wheel of Dhamma* in Bhikkhu Bodhi, trans. *The Connected Discourses of the Buddha: A Translation of the* Samyutta Nikaya (Boston: Wisdom, 2000), 1846.

Setting in Motion the Wheel of Dhamma

What does one do after attaining permanent, unconditional happiness? For forty-nine days, according to tradition, the Buddha enjoyed his liberation and pondered whether it would be worthwhile to teach his insights to others. But could others realize the truths that he saw? He ultimately concluded that while not everyone would understand, many would be receptive and might benefit from his new awareness. He decided to begin with his two teachers, but discovered that they had recently died. He next thought of his former disciples, the five who ridiculed him for giving up the ascetic path. He traveled on foot to the holy city of Banaras, the most sacred city in India, to find them. He learned they were staying at the nearby Deer Park, a refuge for *shramanas*. The Buddha exuded such serenity and happiness that on the way he was accosted by an individual who wanted to know whether he was a god. The Buddha said, "I am no god; I am awake."

When the five ascetics saw their former mentor approaching, they too were astounded by his demeanor and recognized that something of profound significance had transpired in him. His calm appearance melted the resentment they still felt toward him, and they welcomed him into their company and invited him to speak. The Buddha's formal talk consisted of a concise formulation of the insights he had received under the bodhi tree. This speech contained what the Buddhist tradition now calls the Four Noble Truths. The talk is sometimes called the Buddha's first discourse or "Turning the Wheel of Dhamma." The Pali word Dhamma, or the Sanskrit word Dharma in the Buddhist sense, refers to the Buddha's teachings. It might be translated simply as "the truth that leads to liberation."

> "The Four Noble Truths are considered by many to be the essence of Buddhism. Most of the Buddha's subsequent teachings might be thought of as explanations and amplifications of these basic points."

The Four Noble Truths are considered by many to be the essence of Buddhism. Most of the Buddha's subsequent teachings might be thought of as explanations and amplifications of these basic points. As recorded in the Pali Canon, his first discourse seems rather terse for those unfamiliar with his ideas. As we discuss these teachings, we will use the Noble Truths as a basic framework for convenience, but we will also draw upon other locations in the Pali scripture to assist in clarifying the Buddha's insights. The Buddha was a masterful teacher and was skilled in addressing his audiences in ways that suited their intellectual capacities and temperaments, so drawing upon these later teaching contexts will enrich our understanding of the fundamental principles.

The Buddha never expected his teachings to be accepted on his authority. In fact, he positively discouraged it. In his travels, the Buddha once came to a community of people known as the Kalamas, who were confused about what or whom to believe in this age of innumerable gurus and doctrines. The Buddha gave the Kalamas the following advice on how to assess the many teachings and teachers they were encountering:

> Do not accept anything simply because it is said to be revelation;
> Do not accept it merely because it is traditional;
> Do not accept anything that is hearsay;
> Do not accept anything because it comes from sacred texts;
> Do not accept it only on the grounds of pure logic
> or because it seems rational;
> Do not accept it because you
> agree with it after reflecting on it;
> Do not accept it on the grounds
> that the teacher is competent or simply because he is regarded
> as "our teacher";
> But when you know *for yourselves* that these
> things are wholesome; that these things are blameless;
> that these things are praised by the wise; and that these things,
> if undertaken and practiced, lead to benefit and happiness, then
> you should accept them and abide in them.[2]

This advice has a very modern tone. It concisely characterizes the Buddha's ideal for practicing his teachings. It encourages individuals to take responsibility for their own convictions and rejects many of the common reasons for which people accept religious and philosophical beliefs.

But the Buddha's advice is misunderstood if it is taken as an endorsement of mere subjectivity, of accepting something as right or wrong on the basis of a "gut feeling" or even because it accords with one's conscience or reasoning faculty. One might be surprised to hear the Buddha rejecting pure logic and reasoning as sufficient grounds for accepting a viewpoint. But he believed that reasoning may be no more reliable than judgments based on texts or charismatic individuals. Postmodern thinkers, especially, have come to appreciate the way what we call "reason" is itself a cultural construction and not the universal and self-evident function of the mind many philosophers have considered it to be.

---

2. *Kalama Sutta* in *Anguttara Nikaya* 3.65, my italics, my translation.

Because the Buddha viewed truth as liberating, it is not enough for a belief or idea to be "merely" reasonable. According to him, a view or belief must be tested by the results it yields when put into practice. The Buddha would have us ask: Does this belief accord with reality, and is it conducive to one's own and others' happiness and freedom? This is a form of what philosophers call the pragmatic criterion of truth. The Buddha further maintained that for a person to guard against the possibility of bias or limitations in his or her understanding, one must check acceptable views against the experience of those who are wise. Of course, these criteria still leave us with other questions: How do we know who is wise? How do we recognize happiness and freedom? The Buddha addresses these issues in other places. At this point, it is necessary only to underscore that a fundamental aspect of Buddhist methodology is the principle of criticism. The Buddha encouraged his followers to subject their beliefs and ideas to rigorous personal testing and not to accept anything—even the Buddha's own teaching—on the mere basis of authority, antiquity, or rationality.

One can imagine what the principle of criticism did when held against the traditions of emerging Hinduism. In effect, the Buddha's teaching implicitly undermined the authority of the Brahmins and their sacred Vedic texts. Throughout its history, Hinduism has regarded the Buddha's teaching as a major Hindu philosophy but always considered it "heterodox," or nonorthodox, because the Buddha and Buddhists did not recognize the authority of the Vedas.

First Noble Truth

In his discourse to his five former disciples, whom he calls *bhikkhus*, the Pali word for monks, the Buddha declares the first of his Noble Truths, essentially setting out the primary issue for his worldview: "Now this, bhikkhus, is the noble truth of suffering: birth is suffering, aging is suffering, illness is suffering, death is suffering; union with what is displeasing is suffering; separation from what is pleasing is suffering; not to get what one wants is suffering; in brief, the five aggregates subject to clinging are suffering."[3] Later in his life, the Buddha stated that he taught only one thing: suffering and the end of suffering. He was not interested in abstract philosophical questions or dealing with many of the speculative matters that had exercised other teachers of his day. Obviously, it will be necessary to know what the Buddha means by suffering.

---

3. *Setting in Motion the Wheel of Dhamma* in *The Connected Discourses of the Buddha: A Translation of the Samyutta Nikaya*, trans. Bhikkhu Bodhi (Boston: Wisdom, 2000), 1844.

The word that has been translated as "suffering" is the Pali term *dukkha*. Most scholars of Buddhism think "suffering" is probably the best English term we have to translate *dukkha*, yet almost all of them agree that it is still an inadequate word. Suffering simply does not effectively convey what the Buddha meant by *dukkha*. Accordingly, there are a host of alternative or additional translations such as pain, illness, unsatisfactoriness, stress, boredom, discontentment, and discomfort. The problem with "suffering" as the basic translation of *dukkha* is that it is sometimes too strong and too limited to express the Buddha's intent. The word *suffering* conjures images of physical pain and agony or tremendous grief and other forms of emotional distress. Certainly, these connotations are carried by the term *dukkha*.

But these images represent only what the Buddha called "ordinary" *dukkha*, the suffering that accompanies injury, sickness, old age, and death. There is also the *dukkha* of change, the kind of suffering caused by loss and being associated with things one finds unpleasant. The *dukkha* of change means the Buddha did not deny that there are moments of real pleasure, but even such delightful times are subject to *dukkha* because they do not last. Friends and family members die or move away; disagreements break up relationships; money comes and goes; our prized possessions are lost, broken, or they decay; happy times come to an end. The Buddha took seriously the impermanent nature of reality and applied it in a thoroughgoing fashion in his Dhamma. Impermanence, or *anicca*, the Pali term, is a salient aspect of the Buddha's vision. He sees the entire world in constant flux, changing from moment to moment, and nothing is exempt from this process. Impermanence is not a cause of *dukkha*, but our unwise and unskillful response to the world of change is.

Dukkha, however, is not limited to these kinds of experiences. When the Buddha refers to *dukkha*, he is describing the fundamental quality of the whole of existence and not merely pointing out that life has moments of tragedy and sorrow. For the Buddha, *dukkha* is insidious and pervasive. Our whole lives, not simply certain occasions or episodes, are saturated with the quality of *dukkha*. This is one of the implications of the Buddha's statement "The five aggregates subject to clinging are suffering." As we will discover in chapter 12, the aggregates refer to the constituent elements of human life. The Buddha suggests that the very makeup of human existence is entangled in *dukkha*.

When we think of *dukkha* in these terms, as comprehensive and constant and not simply as episodes in human life, it becomes clear that understanding *dukkha* is not just a problem of translation; it is an experiential problem as well. We might ask: Why did the Buddha even think it was necessary to say that life is suffering? What kind of insight is that? Perhaps what makes *dukkha* a noble truth, and possibly why the Buddha felt it essential to articulate it, is our failure to fully appreciate the extent to which we suffer or feel the unsatisfactoriness of existence. The First Noble Truth is not the Buddha's statement of a self-evident fact of life but a challenge for individuals to discover for themselves the depth and breadth of *dukkha* by means of introspection and observation. The Buddha himself hinted at such when he said, "This Dhamma that I have attained is profound, hard to see and hard to understand, peaceful and sublime, unattainable by mere reasoning, subtle, to be experienced by the wise."[4] One cannot fully realize the nature and extent of *dukkha* until the moment of complete awakening, as the Buddha himself did on the full moon of Vesakha. The true depth of suffering can be seen only from the perspective of the enlightened mind.

These aspects of *dukkha* invite us to use a word other than or in addition to *suffering*. The word *disappointment* works well. Disappointment, like *dukkha*, is a pervasive feature of our lives though we are not always aware of it. We condition ourselves to ignore many—maybe most—of our disappointments. But consider how often during the course of a day we are disappointed or frustrated. We learn to ignore these disappointments, but they soon add up and begin to affect our mood and disposition toward others and ourselves.

Besides their insidious and pervasive quality, disappointment and *dukkha* are both the consequence of our own habits of mind. Disappointment is the result of one thing: the failure of reality to conform to our desires and expectations. To call this phenomenon a "failure" of reality is an odd way to put it, but we often experience it that way. Reality, of course, is not to blame. Reality just is what it is; the problem is with our desires and expectations. It would be more accurate to say that our desires and expectations often do not conform to reality, and when they don't, we are liable to suffer. So when the Buddha characterizes *dukkha* as not getting what you want, and getting what you don't want, he is implicitly putting the onus on us, not on the thing we want or don't want.

Elsewhere, the Buddha mentions another element that contributes to *dukkha*. No doubt, not getting what you want causes disappointment, but so does getting what you want. Both the frustration of desire and the fulfillment of desire contribute to human suffering. In contemporary American society, in which the way to happiness is virtually *defined* as the fulfillment of wishes,

---

4. *The Noble Search* 19 in Bhikkhu Ñāṇamoli and Bhikkhu Bodhi, trans. *The Middle Length Discourses of the Buddha: A New Translation of the* Majjhima Nikaya (Somerville, MA: Wisdom, 1995), 260.

such a claim must sound odd. For the Buddha, the problem with achieving our desires is that it does not really satisfy us in the way we had hoped, and we end up desiring more and more to try to attain the kind of satisfaction we so badly want. "Were there a mountain all made of gold," said the Buddha, "doubled that would not be enough to satisfy a single man."[5]

Comparing *dukkha* to disappointment emphasizes the role of desire in creating unhappiness. The Buddha also made this connection. But his analysis did not stop there. Desire itself has antecedents, basic causes that urge us to want and crave for things. In the Second Noble Truth, the Buddha explained the factors that lead us to desire in the first place. In the next chapter, we will examine his view on the deeper sources of *dukkha*. Once we have considered those sources, we will be prepared for understanding his prescription for the end of suffering.

---

5. *Kilesavagga* 3.19 in Ven. Dhammika, trans. "Gemstones of the Good Dhamma." Available at http://www.accesstoinsight.org/lib/authors/dhammika/wheel342.html.

12

Why We Suffer

The Four Noble Truths have often been compared to the way a physician might treat a disease. The Buddha thought of himself more as a healer with specific remedies for specific problems than as a philosopher with opinions about metaphysical questions. In the First Noble Truth, the Buddha determined the illness and its symptoms. In the Second Truth, he provided an etiology, a description of the cause of the disease. Once the source of the malady had been understood, he could say whether or not it could be treated. In the Third, he proclaimed that, indeed, a cure is possible. Finally, in the Fourth Noble Truth, he offered a prescription, a regimen for treating the ailment and curing the patient.

In the First Noble Truth, the Buddha identified the disease as *dukkha*, manifesting as a wide range of human experiences from the ordinary events of becoming sick, growing old, and dying to not getting what we want and getting what we do not want. The Buddha also suggested that *dukkha* manifests not only in particular experiences but in the whole of existence; recognizing *dukkha* on this level, however, requires persistent and attentive awareness.

> "In the First Noble Truth, the Buddha determined the illness and its symptoms. In the Second Truth, he provided an etiology, a description of the cause of the disease. Once the source of the malady had been understood, he could say whether or not it could be treated. In the Third, he proclaimed that, indeed, a cure is possible. Finally, in the Fourth Noble Truth, he offered a prescription, a regimen for treating the ailment and curing the patient."

THE SECOND NOBLE TRUTH

In the Second Noble Truth, the Buddha declared that the root of *dukkha* is self-centered desire, or craving. He told the five monks, "Now this, bhikkhus, is the noble truth of the origin of suffering: it is this craving which leads to renewed existence, accompanied by delight and lust, seeking delight here and there; that is, craving for sensual pleasures, craving for existence, craving for extinction."[1] This very compact statement requires a good bit of elaboration. It is important that we do so, because the second truth is at the heart of the Buddha's vision and is the aspect of his teaching that most distinguishes it from other religious perspectives.

THIRST

Let us begin with the word *craving*, since the Buddha connects it so closely with the experience of suffering. The Pali word is *tanha*, which generally is translated as "desire," but it carries an even richer significance when we realize that its literal meaning is "thirst." In this context, of course, thirst is used metaphorically to denote certain qualities in the experience of desire. Thirst conveys an intensity that the word *desire* does not always express. Desire can range in meaning from a simple wish to raging lust. The meaning of thirst is more limited. Because water is essential to our lives, thirst connotes urgency and necessity. Yet the difference between desire as wish and desire as thirst is really only an issue of degree. A desire first conceived as a faint hope can easily and imperceptibly take on the quality of intense craving.

Two aspects of the concept of *tanha* will help us grasp its significance in the Buddha's thought. The first is the nature of the experience that arises out of it—in other words, the state of being conditioned by thirst. The second is the prior states of being that foster thirst in the first place. Exploring the first aspect helps to explain why *tanha* makes us prone to suffering, and the second helps us understand how to alleviate it.

ATTACHMENT AND DUKKHA

Why is the Buddha so concerned with desire? What is wrong with what seems to be such a natural human experience? The answer is that there is nothing wrong with wishing for and wanting things, per se. The problem arises when desires become self-centered and take on the intensity of craving. At that point, what begins as an object of wishing becomes a matter of necessity. We confuse want and need. Our beliefs about the world and ourselves convince us that this item—whatever it is—is something that we *must* have. "I must have this job"; "I must win this award"; "I must marry this person." These beliefs might even make us think our well-being depends on acquiring or doing this or that

---

1. *Setting in Motion the Wheel of Dhamma* in *The Connected Discourses of the Buddha: A Translation of the Samyutta Nikaya*, trans. Bhikkhu Bodhi (Boston: Wisdom, 2000), 1844.

thing. Or it may be that this item is something we already possess and that losing it would be devastating to our existence. Hence, we hold on to it with a white-knuckled grip. What was once mere wish has now become thirst, and our relationship to what we want or what we have is now a form of attachment.

Attachment, or clinging, is an important concept in both Buddhism and Hinduism. Both traditions recognize it as part of the driving mechanism of *samsara* and as a source of suffering. Attachment essentially refers to the nature of the relationship we have to things, and by things, the Buddha meant not just material objects but also people, values, beliefs, ideas, power, status, experiences, and sensations. Although the Buddha does not say so explicitly in his first discourse, *anything* can become the object of attachment, including, as he well knew, his own teachings. The problem the Buddha saw was not with the objects of attachment, but with the nature of our relationships to them. Perhaps a good modern word to help us grasp the idea of attachment is *addiction*. In a very simple sense, an addiction is a situation in which our mind and body convince us that we cannot live without a certain thing we really do not need.

The way that clinging gives rise to *dukkha* should be coming into clear view. In a world of constant change, there is nothing—nothing whatsoever—that can sustain our attachments. Anything we cling to is subject to change. When the objects of attachment are lost or extend beyond reach, we feel disappointment, grief, and tremendous insecurity. The Buddha said, "If one, longing for sensual pleasure, achieves it, yes, he's enraptured at heart. The mortal gets what he wants. But if for that person—longing, desiring—the pleasures diminish, he's shattered, as if shot with an arrow.[2] Having been conditioned to "desire and acquire" to allay this shattered feeling, we seek for something else to cling to, so the process continues. How many of us, when feeling sad or out of sorts, take to the shopping mall to buy something for ourselves? When the good feeling dissipates, we look for something else to restore it. The irony is that the more we try to attain security and happiness through acquisition, the more we suffer.

AVERSION

The Buddha included in this concept of acquisition what might appear to be its opposite: aversion or repugnance. Feeling repelled by anything is effectively the same as attachment. Aversion is attachment of a different sort. It is a relationship to an object—albeit a negative relationship—that is difficult to

---

2. *Kama Sutta: Sensual Pleasure*, trans. Thanissaro Bhikkhu. Available at http://www.what-buddha-taught.net/accesstoinsight/html/tipitaka/kn/snp/snp.4.01.than.html.

relinquish. Aversion to anything depends on clinging to certain beliefs about it. In the children's classic *Green Eggs and Ham* by Dr. Seuss, one of the two central characters, Sam-I-Am, hounds the other character with a platter of green eggs and ham, insisting that he eat them. As Sam-I-Am pursues, the other fellow desperately tries to avoid him and the food, and in so doing, he ends up in a number of unpleasant and perilous situations. Finally, we learn that the guy who hates green eggs and ham has never even tasted them, and when he does, he decides he really likes them. His aversion, in this case, is based on an attachment to the belief that he does not like green eggs and ham, a belief that has no basis in experience, and it causes him to suffer just as much as clinging would.

THE BASIS OF ATTACHMENT

The Buddha's answer to the dual dangers of clinging and aversion was equanimity, the Middle Way between the two extremes. To realize this state of equanimity requires that we inquire further into the dynamics of attachment and antipathy. What drives craving in the first place?

The simplest and most precise answer to this question is this: we misapprehend the nature of the world and ourselves. Many Buddhists writing in English and many translators of Buddhist texts call this "ignorance," to render the Pali word *avijja*. Ignorance suggests a lack of knowledge, and certainly that is part of the problem. But in addition to not knowing, *avijja* suggests the further imposition of wrong ideas and beliefs onto reality. Not only do we fail to know reality, we also misknow it.

Fundamentally, our misknowledge is the attribution of permanence and substantiality to impermanence, to view as a *thing* a reality that is, in fact, a *process*. For the Buddha, change is constant and persistent. Even an object that seems solid and enduring is subject to moment-to-moment change. We would all agree that in a hundred or so years, the object may be reduced to dust, and we grant it impermanence in that way. But the Buddha would contend that from one moment to the next, this so-called solid structure is in continuous flux, no matter how permanent it may seem to be. With the advent of quantum physics, the Buddha's view of the physical universe seems to be confirmed. Current research suggests that the basic units of the physical universe are vibrating strings of energy. While not all scientists agree with this particular theory, there does seem to be consensus that the foundational elements of the world are more like energy fluctuations than solid, substantial things. If we had the capacity, we might perceive all objects as masses of vibrating energies. Like modern physicists, the Buddha viewed the cosmos as a complex array of processes rather than a set of things. So the Buddha is not just saying that things change; he is saying that change is the only thing there is.

Of course, many people will acknowledge the reality of change and will wonder what is so terribly insightful about this claim. The Buddha's innovation is in the thoroughgoing way he applies this concept. Many persons who acknowledge the world's transience still declare part of existence to be exempt from change. The concept of god is one such effort; the concept of the *atman*, as we saw in the Vedanta tradition of Hinduism, is another.

Not-Self

Perhaps the Buddha's most distinctive contribution to the world's religious thought is his rejection of this belief. According to his Dhamma, there is no permanent, immortal, substantial soul or self. It is nowhere to be found. This feature of the Buddha's thought is called *anatta* in Pali, but the Sanskrit term makes a clearer impression. The Sanskrit *anatman* makes evident that the Buddha is denying the *atman*, the Hindu idea of the true self. Both *anatta* and *anatman* are translated as no-self or not-self.

> "According to his Dhamma, there is no permanent, immortal, substantial soul or self. This feature of the Buddha's thought is called *anatta* in Pali, but the Sanskrit term makes a clearer impression. The Sanskrit *anatman* makes evident that the Buddha is denying the *atman*, the Hindu idea of the true self. Both *anatta* and *anatman* are translated as no-self or not-self."

Of all the intriguing aspects of the Buddha's vision, *anatta* must surely be the most difficult to understand, even for Buddhists. What the Buddha meant by this term has been greatly debated throughout the history of Buddhist philosophy. It should help to remember that fully realizing the truth of *anatta*, according to the Buddha, depends on gaining the insights disclosed in enlightenment. Like the idea of *dukkha*, *anatta* cannot be completely understood until one is awakened as the Buddha was.

Most interpreters of Buddhism refer to *anatta* as a doctrine, but it is better understood as a practice. By using the term *practice* rather than *doctrine*, we can more easily see *anatta* as the systematic denial of any effort to conceptually pin down the nature of the self. It is not a concept, but an anti-concept. *Anatta* is a denial of a belief rather than a belief itself. It does not set forth anything positive. The moment we conceive of *anatta* as a concept, we have placed an obstacle in the way of its realization.

In one of his discourses, the Buddha discusses how the concept of self can lead to fruitless speculation and contribute to our suffering. Here he explains why he does not advance an alternative view of the self, rather than merely denying others. This passage also indicates the variety of perspectives circulating in the Indian Axial Age.

> "This is how [the unawakened person] attends unwisely: 'Was I in the past? Was I not in the past? What was I in the past? How was I in the past? Having been what, what did I become in the past? Shall I be in the future? Shall I not be in the future? What shall I be in the future? How shall I be in the future? Having been what, what shall I become in the future?' Or else he is inwardly perplexed about the present thus: 'Am I? Am I not? What am I? How am I? Where has this being come from? Where will it go?'
>
> "When he attends unwisely in this way, one of six views arises in him. The view 'self exists for me' arises in him as true and established; or the view 'no self exists for me' arises in him as true and established; or the view 'I perceive self with self' arises in him as true and established; or the view 'I perceive not-self with self' arises in him as true and established; or the view 'I perceive self with not-self' arises in him as true and established; or else he has some such view as this: 'It is this self of mine that speaks and feels and experiences here and there the result of good and bad actions; but this self of mine is permanent, everlasting, eternal, not subject to change, and it will endure as long as eternity.' This speculative view, bhikkhus, is called the thicket of views . . . the fetter of views. . . . Fettered by the fetter of views, the untaught ordinary person is not freed from birth, ageing, and death, from sorrow, lamentation, pain, grief, and despair; he is not freed from suffering, I say."[3]

Rather than put forward another view of self, the Buddha simply indicates that the concept of self is an unskillful and unwholesome way of thinking about human beings. We might use the word *self* for linguistic convenience—such as the reflexive myself or yourself—but we should never believe that it refers to anything substantial or permanent. But neither should we think that *anatta* means that the Buddha denies our existence or suggests that human life is an

---

3. *All the Taints* 7, from Bhikkhu Ñānamoli and Bhikkhu Bodhi, trans. *The Middle Length Discourses of the Buddha: A New Translation of the* Majjhima Nikaya (Somerville, MA: Wisdom, 1995), 92.

illusion or unreal. We are real, but not in the way we think. The Buddha's denial of self suggests that no *concept* whatsoever is capable of expressing the reality of who we are.

The Buddha's understanding of the profound impermanence of reality is the basis of *anatta* and is much of the reason why who we are eludes conceptualization. Unlike many other thinkers, he applied the idea of change to every aspect of the human person. Thus, the Buddha's description of the human, at least initially, sounds extremely negative. The so-called self is not a thing; it is no-thing, nothing. It is insubstantial; it lacks permanence and immortality. But on further inspection, it is clear that the Buddha's view was not negative. He was merely attempting to disrupt our old habits of thinking about who we are.

THE FIVE AGGREGATES OF BEING

Rather than viewing the person as an immortal self housed in a perishable body, the Buddha saw the human as a complex of interconnected and ever-changing energies or forces. He called these the Five Aggregates of Being. Together, these five processes wholly constitute what we call the human being. They are, first, the aggregate of matter, which refers to our physical makeup, changing by the moment as cells die and are replaced. The second aggregate is sensations or feelings. By this, the Buddha meant the tonal quality of our experiences, the way we automatically judge experiences as pleasant, unpleasant, or neutral. These judgments condition our tendencies of attachment and aversion. Like all beings, we seek out the pleasant and try to avoid the unpleasant. The third aggregate is perception, which means not only what we sense but also what we understand it as, what is known as apperception. The fourth aggregate is mental formations, which are the sources of desires, craving, and intentions. This component is the source of karma for the Buddha. Hence, as long as there is craving, there will be rebirth. Finally, there is the aggregate of consciousness, which is the process of awareness.

Nothing about any of these components endures. At any given moment, whether we are aware of it or not, our perceptions, our thoughts, our bodies, our consciousness are all in flux. Most importantly, there is no permanent subject or agent underlying these processes. An old Buddhist quip captures the idea exactly: "There is thought but no thinker; there is feeling but no feeler." Thinking is real, feeling is real, but there is no subject or self who experiences them.

The soul or self is simply an illusion, an unsubstantiated belief. Yet it certainly *seems* real, and most of the time we act as if it were real. We can compare the Buddha's view of self to the appearance of a rainbow. A rainbow is not a substantial reality in the way it appears. It is an optical illusion, created by the convergence of various conditions including sunlight, moisture in the air, and the physical position of the observer. When these conditions change, the rainbow disappears. No one can ever reach the end of a rainbow, because the observer's position will change, and the illusion will dissipate. To the Buddha, the *atman* is the same thing: an illusion supported by various changing conditions. This is why no one is able to identify or pinpoint the essential self.

But we certainly develop the habit of ascribing reality to this illusion. And therein, the Buddha says, our problems arise. Believing in a permanent, substantial self is not a harmless misperception; it is actually the root of what causes us to suffer. To believe in a real self sets in motion a series of thoughts, words, and deeds that precipitate anguish, misery, and disappointment. When I think this "self" is ultimately real, rather than a habitual construct of the imagination, I begin to identify with it and make it the center of the universe. I do my best to protect it, to make it more secure, to ensure its existence. I develop beliefs that relieve my anxieties about my possible nonexistence and feel threatened if anyone challenges those beliefs. I may seek to enhance the status, prestige, and power of this self. I try to maximize its pleasurable experiences and minimize its painful ones. I develop the qualities of pride and conceit. I feel lonely and separated from others. When unwanted and undesirable things come my way, I feel cheated and unfairly treated: "Why me? I don't deserve this!" And on it goes. Taking the belief in self seriously leads to desire and aversion, which condition attachment and clinging to an impermanent world. And that is why we suffer.

13

The Noble Path

In a chapter of *Thus Spoke Zarathustra* entitled "The Preachers of Death," Friedrich Nietzsche wrote about the Buddha: "There are those with consumption of the soul: hardly are they born when they begin to die and to long for doctrines of weariness and renunciation. They would like to be dead, and we should welcome their wish. Let us beware of waking the dead and disturbing these living coffins! They encounter a sick man or an old man or a corpse and immediately they say, 'Life is refuted.' But only they themselves are refuted, and their eyes, which see only this one face of existence."[1] Nietzsche was far from alone in his assessment. When Westerners first began to study Buddhism, they had difficulty overcoming the impression that the religion was nihilistic. They were, however, wrong. To be fair to Nietzsche and the others, there is much in the Buddha's teaching that on the surface seems rather gloomy. Yet the West's negative evaluation failed to penetrate the Buddha's teaching deeply enough to recognize its ultimately optimistic outlook. Like Jesus, the Buddha proclaimed a "gospel," that is, good news for humanity. These glad tidings are found in the Third and Fourth Noble Truths.

The Third Noble Truth

The Buddha's good news was straightforward and simple: You do not have to suffer. Genuine, enduring happiness is possible. In the first discourse offered to the five monks in the Deer Park, the Buddha explains the Third Noble Truth: "Now this, bhikkhus, is the noble truth of the cessation of suffering: it is the remainderless fading away and cessation of that same craving, the giving up and relinquishing of it, freedom from it, non-reliance on it."[2] If *tanha*—thirst or

---

1. Friedrich Nietzsche, *Thus Spoke Zarathustra* in *The Portable Nietzsche*, trans. Walter Kaufmann (New York: Penguin, 1982), 157.

2. *Setting in Motion the Wheel of Dhamma* in Bhikkhu Bodhi, trans. *The Connected Discourses of the Buddha: A Translation of the* Samyutta Nikaya (Boston: Wisdom, 2000), 1844.

craving—is the cause of *dukkha*, then the solution is clear: stop craving! If we cease craving, we end attachments; if we end attachments, we end suffering and rebirth. Once the problem is properly analyzed, the resolution is obvious.

The difficulty, of course, is giving up craving. The phenomenon of craving has many contributing factors, as we have seen. We have mentioned the insidious way that mere desire can turn into thirst and addiction, the way the belief in a permanent self generates desire and fear, and the way our misapprehension of reality causes us to perceive permanence where there is only change. All of these—and other things—contribute to craving. Because of the many factors involved, and because it is a deeply ingrained pattern of experience, ending craving requires a multifaceted and incremental approach. That method for quenching thirst is detailed for us in the Fourth Noble Truth.

But before we discuss the way to that goal, we must discuss the goal itself. Understanding the objective will help us see why the Buddha formulates the path in the way he does. The objective is *nibbana*, or nirvana, the Sanskrit term more familiar to Westerners.

Nirvana, like karma, is now common in the English language but is often greatly misunderstood. Some think of it as a place one goes, like heaven. Others conceive of it as a state of intense pleasure. Many—like Nietzsche—thought of nirvana as self-annihilation. To distance this concept from these misapprehensions, we will use the Pali term *nibbana* rather than the more familiar form.

Simply stated, *nibbana* is the end of *dukkha*. It is the point at which one stops craving for reality to be other than it is. It is the radical acceptance of the way things are.

> "Simply stated, *nibbana* is the end of suffering. It is the point at which one stops craving for reality to be other than it is. It is the radical acceptance of the way things are."

The principal language about *nibbana* is negative. The Buddha called it the eradication of desire, the cessation of thirst, and the destruction of illusion. It may be even valid to say that *nibbana* is self-annihilation, if we bear in mind that the annihilated self is not real; what is annihilated is the *illusion* of a separate substantial self. *Nibbana* is usually described in negative terms but not because it is a negative state. Like Brahman in the Hindu traditions, *nibbana* refers to a reality beyond ordinary experience and hence beyond the limitations of language. To avoid misleading ideas, the Buddha preferred to use the *via negativa*, the strategy of negation commonly used in mystical traditions when ultimate reality is regarded as beyond conception.

Like *moksha* in Hinduism, *nibbana* can be realized in life. The Buddha, however, distinguished between the *nibbana* in life and the final *nibbana* realized at death. A person who completely "sees" *nibbana* (to use a traditional expression) in this life is known as an *arahant*. An *arahant* has fully realized the Dhamma, the truth of the Buddha's vision, and is free of craving, aversion, and misknowing. As a living person, the *arahant* may still experience physical pain and other forms of karma that come as the consequences of actions prior to awakening. Yet even with physical pain, one does not suffer. In Buddhism, suffering is distinguished from pain; pain is a bodily sensation, but suffering pertains to the mental anguish that comes from resisting pain or merely resisting the way things are. The *arahant* does not generate new karmas but still must experience the effects of old ones; this is called *nibbana* with remainder. At the final *nibbana*, or *parinibbana*, all karmic energies sustaining existence are dissipated, and the *arahant* is released from rebirth. This is *nibbana* without remainder. The image often associated with final *nibbana* is a candle whose flame has gone out because the fuel and oxygen have been exhausted. Similarly, without karma to perpetuate rebirth, the *arahant* "goes out."

Quite naturally, the Buddha's disciples were interested in what happens at *parinibbana*. One of the central issues of the Axial Age, as we have noted, was the individual's destiny after death. The Buddha's response to this concern was deliberately elusive. On one occasion, the monk Malunkyaputta complained that the Master had never explained final nibbana. Specifically, Malunkyaputta wanted to know if an *arahant* exists after death or does not exist after death; or both exists and does not exist after death; or neither exists nor does not exist after death. The Buddha deftly but firmly refused to answer the question, saying that knowing the answer was not essential to seeing *nibbana*, and dwelling on such questions was a hindrance to the goal.[3] The Buddha was reticent about issues—no matter how interesting or important to the questioner—that were not essential to the termination of suffering.

On the whole, the Buddha was suspicious of language. He seemed to think language could be deceptive because words have a tendency to reify or ossify an impermanent, interrelated reality. We can easily become entangled in our concepts and "views," as he called them. Zen, a later form of Buddhism,

---

3. See *The Shorter Discourse to Malunkyaputta* in Bhikkhu Ñānamoli and Bhikkhu Bodhi, trans. *The Middle Length Discourses of the Buddha: A New Translation of the* Majjhima Nikaya (Somerville, MA: Wisdom, 1995), 533–36.

traces its origins back to this theme in the Buddha's teaching. In Zen, words and concepts are obstacles in the pursuit of enlightenment. The goal of Zen is awakening to reality without the imposition of our beliefs and preconceptions. A Zen proverb epitomizes this philosophy: "Open mouth, already a mistake."

THE FOURTH NOBLE TRUTH

Although the Buddha, like Jesus, proclaimed "good news," his message of freedom from suffering was not about grace or a gift from god. Like the path of knowledge in Hinduism, the Buddha's Middle Way requires discipline and effort. Because we are the cause of our own suffering, only we can free ourselves from it. The Buddha admonished his followers to "strive with diligence," because "the Buddha only shows the way."

THE NOBLE EIGHTFOLD PATH

In the Fourth Noble Truth, the Buddha shows the way with an outline of this discipline. In later discourses, he explains each component: "Now this, bhikkhus, is the noble truth of the way leading to the cessation of suffering: it is this Noble Eightfold Path; that is, right understanding, right intention, right speech, right action, right livelihood, right effort, right mindfulness and right concentration."[4] The Pali word *samma* is correctly translated in this passage as "right," but it means more than just true as opposed to false. It also suggests that which promotes the end of suffering. Each element of the path is intended to contribute to the end of suffering and, short of the realization of *nibbana*, a favorable rebirth.

These eight parts are interrelated, so the practice of one supports the practice of the others. The Noble Path is not a program in which the practitioner completes one step before moving to the next. Rather, all eight elements are pursued concurrently. The symbol of the Noble Path is a wheel of eight spokes, which suggests that traversing each spoke simultaneously from the outer circle to the inner hub leads to the same goal: *nibbana*. The Buddha's strategy is to address all the factors contributing to *dukkha*: the illusion of self, misknowing reality, desire, craving, attachment, and self-centered behavior.

---

4. *Setting in Motion the Wheel of Dhamma* in Bhikkhu Bodhi, trans. *The Connected Discourses of the Buddha: A Translation of the* Samyutta Nikaya, 1844.

The Triple Practice

The eight components of the Buddha's discipline have traditionally been divided into three sections: study, conduct, and concentration. For this reason, the Noble Path is sometimes called the Triple Practice. Let us give these divisions somewhat more descriptive designations and call them, respectively, cultivating wisdom, developing moral conduct, and disciplining the mind. Each will be discussed in turn.

Cultivating Wisdom

It seems almost counterintuitive for the first part of the practice to be called cultivating wisdom, since wisdom is actually the aim of the eightfold path. Yet, the Buddha recognized that some measure of understanding is necessary to start the practice of Dhamma in the first place. For this reason, he begins with what he called "skillful understanding." The word *skillful* translates the Pali term *kusala*, which can also mean "wholesome" or "correct." At the outset of the Noble Path, skillful understanding entails becoming acquainted with the basic principles of the Buddha's teaching by study, discussion, and reflection. Eventually, however, the Dhamma must be understood in a deep way that comes only with complete awakening. We can, therefore, think of two kinds of skillful understanding. The first is the result of study and reflection on the Buddha's teaching, the glimmer of truth the practitioner sees that prompts her to take the path at the beginning. The second we will call "awakened understanding" to indicate the wisdom one attains at the end of the path. After discussing all the components of the path, we will return to the idea of awakened understanding.

Skillful intention bridges right understanding and the next division of the Triple Practice, developing moral conduct. Essentially, skillful intention is the determination to follow specific virtues to neutralize our conditioned tendencies toward greed, hatred, and harming by aspiring to the countervailing virtues, which are nonattachment, goodwill, and harmlessness, respectively. To aid in practicing these virtues, one might follow any number of specific techniques that the Buddha prescribed in his teaching. For example, contemplating the suffering connected with worldly pleasures or recognizing the impermanence of reality assists in establishing nonattachment; reflecting on the desire of all beings to be happy helps generate a feeling of goodwill; and wishing for all beings to be free from suffering helps to keep us from causing suffering to others.

DEVELOPING MORAL CONDUCT

Developing moral conduct is a major part of the Buddha's path. Unlike other religions, moral behavior in Buddhism is not commanded by a god who issues specific orders for human beings. Nor is it commanded by the Buddha. The Buddha understood morality to be rooted in our very natures as persons. We ought to act morally because it is our nature to be compassionate. In this respect, the Buddha's teaching approaches that of his Chinese contemporary, Confucius, who encouraged people to be good because goodness is the fundamental goal of human life. Furthermore, observing moral conduct is necessary to alleviate our own suffering. The basic principle of karma, which the Buddha, like other Indians of the Axial Age, accepted, meant that causing others to suffer would eventually result in suffering oneself and would perpetuate the cycle of rebirth. The Buddha did modify the prevailing view of karma, however, by insisting that karma is generated only by *intentional* acts; this difference is grounded in his view that the source of karma is the Aggregate of Mental Formations.

Perhaps the best way to discuss the moral dimension of the Buddha's teaching is to start with what he called wholesome action. Wholesome action is epitomized in the Five Precepts, some of the most important practices for all Buddhists, no matter the sect or whether one is a monk, nun, or layperson. In many Asian countries, learning the Five Precepts is one of the first introductions to Buddhism for children, and they recite these principles throughout their lives. The Five Precepts are aspirations, not commandments. They are ideals that one vows to live by. When practitioners fail to live up to these ideals, they simply acknowledge failure and promise to do better next time. Reciting the precepts regularly, often in schools or other assemblies, recognizing failure, and endeavoring to try harder helps one cultivate the necessary qualities to live a moral life.

These foundational precepts essentially follow the principle of nonharming, or *ahimsa*. The first precept states this principle as a simple promise: "I will refrain from harming sentient beings." Sentient beings are those with feeling and consciousness. Some Buddhists interpret this precept strictly and practice vegetarianism and refuse to kill any form of sentient life. Others, realizing the great difficulty of living in this world without taking life, strive to minimize the amount of harm they do. If they eat meat, as many Buddhists do, they allow others to do the slaughtering, so as not to reap the negative karma.

The remaining precepts devolve from the practice of nonharming. The second precept intends to minimize injury by respecting the possessions of others. The practitioner vows, "I will refrain from taking what is not offered." In other words, one promises not to steal or even covet. The third precept concerns the potential hurt one might cause in the area of sexuality. The aspirant promises, "I will refrain from sexual misconduct."

The fourth precept concerns the misuse of language: "I will refrain from false speech." In the Buddha's teaching, false speech is not only lying and slandering but also gossiping, cursing, loud talk, idle chatter, and meaningless babble. As part of a course I teach in comparative spiritual practices, I require my students to participate in several disciplines from various religions, including a day of abstaining from false speech. Invariably, they tell me that abstaining from false speech is the hardest of all. It is even harder, they say, than being totally silent for a day. Try it for yourself. Take a day and refrain from lying, exaggerating, gossiping, and pointless conversation, and note how often you are unsuccessful.

The fifth precept regards the abuse of intoxicants and other substances: "I will refrain from stupefying drink." Not only does alcohol and substance use often result in addiction, it can dull the senses, hindering the capacity to see the world and oneself clearly. To see the world as it truly is, the Buddha maintained, is essential to liberation.

The other aspects of moral practice in Buddhist spirituality follow the basic principles of right action. Right speech means communicating in the most generous and beneficial ways possible. While the Five Precepts enjoin the practitioner to refrain from false speaking, right speech encourages kind, gentle, and edifying speech. Harsh and bitter language, sarcasm, and meaningless chatter do not promote the habits of compassion. Right livelihood means one should earn a living in ways that foster the well-being of others, rather than their harm. The Buddha specifically named military service, trading in intoxicants or poisons, and selling animals for slavery or slaughter as particularly unwholesome occupations. He obviously believed the spiritual life extended to every aspect of one's life, including the workaday world.

DISCIPLINING THE MIND

Skillful moral behavior is essential to the holy life, but the Buddha considered it equally important to cultivate the mind. Just as self-centered habits obscure the basic compassion of the human heart, deluded patterns of thinking hinder the ability to understand the world. To appreciate the importance of mental discipline, we will briefly discuss how the Buddha understood the mind. Then we will consider the specific techniques he offered for guiding the mind in the quest to end suffering.

Like all else, the Buddha did not think of the mind as a static reality, nor did he identify it with the brain. For the Buddha, the mind meant the totality of thoughts, sensations, feelings, and consciousness that in each moment arise and fall away. The phrase "stream of consciousness" comes close to capturing this sense of mind, though the Buddhist sense is much broader than the literary or psychological use of the term.

The mind has great power and potential, but in its unawakened state, it is out of control. It is unruly and undisciplined. The Buddha likened it to an untamed horse. Until it is tamed, a horse is more likely to cause harm than do good. To bring it under control requires patience, skill, and persistent training.

The characteristics of the undisciplined mind may sound familiar. It has a hard time staying attentive to one thing; it lacks the ability to concentrate for more than a few minutes, if that long. It craves stimulation, particularly the kind of things that will bring it pleasure or help it avoid uncomfortable thoughts and sensations. It tends to move from place to place, idea to idea, seeking new pleasures or stimuli. The conditioned mind has an inordinate love of thoughts, which is part of its attachment to stimulation. It constantly generates ideas and images, the vast majority of which are pure rubbish. Most of these thoughts pertain to either the past or the future, which means not much attention is given to the present. Dwelling in the past, we often regret what we did or did not do. Dwelling in the future, we become fearful and anxious about things that rarely come to pass. Ralph Waldo Emerson put it this way in a poem he translated from the French:

> Some of your hurts you have cured,
> And the sharpest you still have survived,
> But what torments of grief you endured
> From evils which never arrived![5]

The mind spends a great deal of time pondering things over which we have no control. When the undisciplined mind does pay attention to the present, it is constantly passing judgments and generating opinions so that it is really more absorbed with itself than with the present situation. It is as if the mind produces a constant commentary as we experience life. Finally, the mind is a creature of habit. It easily finds itself returning to the same old patterns of thinking. This is how it gets conditioned in the first place. But the good thing about this tendency is that the mind can be trained to develop wholesome habits, and this is what the Buddha's discipline of mental cultivation intends to do.

---

5. Elon Foster, *Cyclopaedia of Poetry*, 1st series (New York: Funk and Wagnalls, 1872), 281.

The three disciplines of skillful effort, skillful concentration, and skillful mindfulness are ways of training the mind and harnessing its considerable powers for the benefit of others and ourselves.

Skillful effort means giving deliberate attention to developing positive qualities and thoughts and to letting go of negative ones. What counts as positive here are those states that promote the alleviation of suffering. These characteristics include generosity, friendliness, equanimity, and patience.

> "The three disciplines of skillful effort, skillful concentration, and skillful mindfulness are ways of training the mind and harnessing its considerable powers for the benefit of others and ourselves."

Skillful concentration is the discipline of meditation; skillful mindfulness is the practice of meditative awareness undertaken in daily life. The Buddha advocated taking time each day to practice meditation to strengthen attentiveness and nonattachment. These and other Buddhist virtues were regarded as skills that anyone could develop and reinforce. As with learning the piano, it is essential to set aside time for practice regularly.

The Buddhist practice of meditation is not intended to create extraordinary or mystical experiences, although that may happen. Rather, the Buddha meant meditation to be used to sharpen awareness of the world and ourselves by attending to the features of ordinary life in the present moment. The basic meditation practice taught by the Buddha was based on his own experiences under the rose-apple and bodhi trees. It involved simply attending to the breath and observing without judgment the rise and fall of thoughts, sensations, feelings, and perceptions. As these phenomena rise to awareness, the meditator notes them and allows them to fall away, without grasping or dwelling on them. The Buddha thought that by merely observing the mind, the body, and the world around, it is possible to gain insight into the true nature of the world and self and learn how to act and think accordingly. He believed this practice would reveal the illusory nature of the self and the source of suffering in the mind's tendencies to grasp for new pleasures and avoid unpleasant experiences. He also thought meditation could restrain the mind's inclination to make knee-jerk judgments and to become absorbed in thoughts about the future and the past, all of which are unwholesome habits.

AWAKENED UNDERSTANDING

As suggested earlier, we can distinguish between two kinds of right understanding. The second form is awakened understanding, the content of the enlightenment experience. It means directly seeing reality the way it is, unencumbered by expectations, beliefs, or defilements of any kind. In the Buddha's view, this form of comprehension meant to know for certain the authenticity of the Four Noble Truths without reliance on authorities other than one's own experience. To realize the Dhamma at this level means to live one's life in accord with its truth. One no longer aspires to *nibbana*. *Nibbana* has been seen.

14

From Buddha to Buddhism

The five *bhikkhus* who first heard the Buddha expound his Dhamma were duly impressed by their former teacher's new insights. According to myth, even the cosmos itself and the vast pantheon of *devas* recognized the supreme significance of this teaching: "And when the Wheel of the Dhamma had been set in motion by the Blessed One, the earth-dwelling devas raised a cry: '[I]n the Deer Park . . . this unsurpassed Wheel of the Dhamma has been set in motion by the Blessed One.' . . . Thus at that moment . . . the cry spread as far as the brahma-world, and this ten thousandfold world system shook, quaked, and trembled, and an immeasurable glorious radiance appeared in the world surpassing the divine majesty of the devas."[1] Kondanna, one of the five, instantly understood the Buddha's message and realized *nibbana* shortly afterward. After a second discourse, the other four gained enlightenment. These five became the first *arahants* of Buddhism.

THE DEVELOPMENT AND FUNCTION OF THE SANGHA

Not long after, the number of *arahants* grew to sixty-one. These individuals were the first members of the Sangha, the monastic community. The Buddha commissioned these enlightened disciples to tour the Gangetic plains and preach the Dhamma, as the scriptures say, "for the welfare of the many, out of compassion for the world, for the good . . . of gods and men."[2] The Buddha told his followers to teach in the language of their listeners, in contrast to the Brahmins, who still taught in Sanskrit, a language understood only by the upper castes.

---

1. *Setting in Motion the Wheel of Dhamma* in Bhikkhu Bodhi, trans. *The Connected Discourses of the Buddha: A Translation of the* Samyutta Nikaya, (Boston: Wisdom Publications, 2000), 1846.

2. *Vinaya Pitaka, Mahavagga, First Khandhaka*, 11.1., trans. T. W. Rhys Davids and Hermann Oldenberg (Oxford: Clarendon, 1881). Available at http://www.sacred-texts.com/bud/sbe13/sbe1312.htm.

These missionaries found a receptive audience among many of the inhabitants of the burgeoning cities in the region. At a time when so many of the traditional political, social, and economic institutions were rapidly changing, the Buddha's message of the impermanency of existence certainly had the ring of truth. With populations increasingly concentrating in urban areas, the suffering and frustration that the Buddha spoke of were probably more and more evident to the city dwellers. The Buddha's emphasis on spiritual independence rather than reliance on tradition or the Brahmin priests appealed to citizens who were becoming accustomed to accepting individual responsibility for their daily well-being and ultimate destiny.

The Buddha and his disciples spoke to people from all walks of life, without discrimination: men, women, and children, aristocrats and peasants, rich and poor, ascetics and priests, thieves and murderers, high castes and low castes. The Buddha's openness to all was inspired by his conviction that spiritual attainment was not limited by caste or social status, as many believed. Awakening was possible for anyone. He subverted the word *Aryan*—a noble one—which customarily indicated a member of the upper castes, by using it to refer to anyone who lived a wise and holy life. One need not be of high caste or social standing to follow the Buddha's Noble Truths.

As the Buddhist Dhamma spread, local monastic communities were established throughout the area. The Sangha served many purposes for the emerging new religion. First, it was intended to provide an ideal setting for individuals seeking to follow the Buddha's way. It was never essential that one join the Sangha in order to find enlightenment and realize *nibbana*. The Suttas report that many ordinary householders attained the end of suffering even as they maintained their home and work lives, but the demands of social and domestic life often made the quest difficult for others. Joining the Sangha relieved one of obligations and responsibilities that might hinder progress toward the ultimate goal; with a simpler life, the monastic could focus on the pursuit of liberation.

> "The Buddha and his disciples spoke to people from all walks of life, without discrimination: men, women, and children, aristocrats and peasants, rich and poor, ascetics and priests, thieves and murderers, high castes and low castes. The Buddha's openness to all was inspired by his conviction that spiritual attainment was not limited by caste or social status, as many believed. Awakening was possible for anyone."

The Sangha also furnished a structure that assisted many in maintaining the discipline necessary to practice the Dhamma. If monastic life was simpler, it was also more restricted, in some senses, than domestic life. Members of the Sangha were expected to adhere to five additional precepts. These extra precepts included not eating after midday; not watching secular entertainment such as dancing, singing, or theater; not using perfume or jewelry; not using a luxurious couch or sleeping on a soft bed; and not handling money. The intent of these precepts was to keep practitioners within the Middle Way by disallowing luxuries or distractions. Beyond these additional precepts, the monastics followed a daily routine of meditation, study and discussion, and begging for food. Other rules of communal life were added as the Sangha grew and new situations arose that demanded guidelines to maintain order. Eventually, the Pali scriptures came to include well over two hundred regulations for monastic life.

The Sangha was also the principal means by which the Buddha's message was disseminated. As Buddhism became more firmly established and as the Sangha became more settled, the role of the monastic as missionary gave way to that of teacher and custodian of the Dhamma. Accordingly, the members of the Sangha were responsible for preserving the Buddha's teachings and interpreting them to the laity. After the Buddha's death, the Sangha met on occasion to discuss and settle doctrinal and polity disputes. At times, these quarrels led to actual schisms within the community, which eventually gave rise to the different varieties of Buddhism. But despite the disagreements and divisions, the Buddhist Sangha has endured for 2,500 years and is the longest-continuing institution of its kind in history.

Five years after the founding of the Sangha, women were admitted as ordained members of the order, at the request of the Buddha's stepmother, Queen Prajapati, and the *bhikkhu* Ananda, the Buddha's personal attendant and close disciple. Queen Prajapati had raised Siddhattha after his natural mother and Prajapati's sister, Queen Maya, died seven days after the child's birth. Prajapati became the first Buddhist nun, or *bhikkhuni*. Later, Yashodhara, the Buddha's wife from his palace years, and his son Rahula also joined the community. The Buddha's consent to accept women into the Sangha was a radical step for the time. Many believed that women, like members of the lower castes, simply did not have the necessary intellectual abilities and were too vain to achieve enlightenment. The Buddha rejected that belief.

The Buddhist texts record many examples of women overcoming particular hardships to follow the Buddha's teaching and become members of the *bhikkhuni* order. One particularly poignant story is that of Kisagotami, a young woman of wealth and high status. After she was married, Kisagotami gave birth to a son, who died as a toddler. She was devastated. In her grief, she began carrying the lifeless body of her son from house to house and village to village, asking for medicine to bring the boy back to life. One wise man advised her to see the Buddha, who, he said, had the medicine she needed. The Buddha told her to get some mustard seeds from a household that had not been touched by death. Thinking the mustard seeds would be used to make the remedy, Kisagotami, still carrying her dead child, went from house to house to make her request. Everyone was willing to help, but she could not find a single family untouched by death. Soon she realized that hers was not the only family that had faced death. Her attitude toward her deceased son immediately changed. She left the corpse in the forest and returned to the Buddha to report her experience. Then the Buddha said, "Gotami, you thought that you were the only one who had lost a son. As you have now realized, death comes to all beings; before their desires are satisfied death takes them away." On hearing this, Kisagotami fully realized the impermanence, unsatisfactoriness, and insubstantiality of life. She was accepted into the Sangha and went on to become one of hundreds of female *arahants* in the Buddha's time.

PARINIBBANA

In his eightieth year, as the Buddha was on one of his teaching expeditions, he became mortally ill near the village of Kushinagara. When he became aware of his impending death, he told his attendant Ananda to prepare an outdoor bed situated between two sala trees. (Once again, notice the appearance of trees at key moments of the Buddha's life.) Ananda had served him for decades and was greatly upset. But the Buddha made even his own death a lesson for his followers. He told Ananda, "Enough . . . do not weep and wail! Have I not already told you that all things that are pleasant and delightful are changeable, subject to separation and becoming other? So how could it be, Ananda—since whatever is born, become, compounded is subject to decay—how could it be that it should not pass away?"[3] The Buddha had grown tired. As his death approached, he asked his disciples three times if there were any doubts about the teachings or the disciplines. The *bhikkhus and bhikkhunis* all stood silent. The Buddha then uttered his final words: "All conditioned things are of a nature to decay—strive on untiringly!"[4] Then he passed into a deep meditative state and entered *mahaparinibbana*, the great final release.

---

3. *The Great Passing* in Maurice Walshe, trans. *The Long Discourses of the Buddha: A Translation of the Digha Nikaya* (Boston: Wisdom, 1987, 1995), 265.

It was on the full moon of the month of Vesakha when this occurred, and the year was around 410 BCE, according to modern reckoning. Tradition says it was also on the full moon day in Vesakha when he was born and was enlightened. Today, the chief Buddhist holiday is Vesak, which celebrates on a single day the birth, awakening, and *parinibbana* of the Buddha.

STUPAS

After his death, the Buddha's body lay in state for the next six days. On the seventh day, the remains were consumed on a funeral pyre of fragrant wood. When the cremation was completed, the ashes and unburned remains were collected as relics. The relics were then divided into eight portions and distributed to representatives of eight city-states that were connected in some way to his life, including Lumbini, his birthplace; Gaya, the site of his awakening; Banaras, the location of his first discourse; and Kushinagara, the place where he realized *parinibbana*.

The relics were interred in *stupas*, the burial sites of royalty from pre-Buddhist times. The earliest *stupas* were essentially great mounds of earth, shaped into hemispheres or domes and faced with brick or stone. Atop the *stupas* were poles with a series of disks, a stylized representation of a parasol, an object associated with royalty. For Buddhists, the parasol-shaped structure also represented the bodhi tree.

Almost immediately after their establishment, the *stupas* became pilgrimage sites. Both laypersons and monastics began to travel great distances just to glimpse these reliquaries and to come into physical proximity to them. The *stupa* came to be regarded as a physical representation of the Dhamma. For some, coming to the *stupa* and walking around it was meritorious and could help ensure a favorable rebirth. For others, the *stupa* was the Buddha himself, containing his bodily relics that perhaps could confer release from suffering or actual healing. Eventually, *stupas* were built all over South and East Asia as Buddhism migrated throughout the continent. With the spread of Buddhism, the *stupa*'s design assimilated the aesthetics and architectural features of its host cultures but retained its basic structure and function. *Stupas* also took on new names in different parts of Asia. In Sri Lanka they were known as *dagobas* and in East Asia as *pagodas*.

---

4. *The Great Passing* in Maurice Walshe, trans. *The Long Discourses of the Buddha: A Translation of the Dīgha Nikāya* (Boston: Wisdom, 1987, 1995), 270.

Interestingly, the Buddha was never represented in human form until several centuries after his death. Now, his likeness is one of the most common images in the world. In early Buddhist history, the Buddha was represented by such things as an empty throne, footprints, the bodhi tree, the wheel of Dhamma, and the parasol. Because he was regarded as transcending the physical world and as superior to the gods, who of course *were* represented by images, any anthropomorphic icon of him was considered profane. It was not until after the Axial Age, between 200 and 100 BCE, that images of the Buddha as a person began to be created in the region of Gandhara, now occupied by the nation of Afghanistan. This area had been conquered by Alexander the Great in the fourth century, so it was under the influence of Greek artistic ideals that the first sculptures of the Buddha took shape. To anyone familiar with Hellenistic art, the influence is unmistakable. Several of the Gandharan Buddha images recall ancient Greek representations of Apollo.

Many will recall the uproar created in 2001 by the Taliban's demolition of two ancient, massive Buddha statues in Afghanistan. Ironically, this destruction occurred in the very vicinity where the icons of the Buddha were first produced. Although many in the world were horrified by this act, the destruction actually bore witness to the Buddha's Dhamma in the way that it graphically portrayed the impermanence of all things.

Institutionalization

In addition to the creation of the *stupa* reliquaries, one of the first acts of the Sangha after the Buddha's *parinibbana* was to gather to discuss the future of the movement. The First Buddhist Council was held shortly after the Buddha's death. The Buddha did not name a successor as leader of the Sangha but recommended a representative form of governance, with the Dhamma itself as guide and teacher. The main item of business for the first council, therefore, was to agree on exactly what the Buddha taught as the Dhamma. Ananda, the Buddha's personal attendant, reputedly stood before the council and recited word for word all the Buddha's discourses, since he had memorized them all. His recollections became the basis for the Suttas in the Pali Canon. Each of the discourses begins with the words "Thus have I heard." Another disciple, Upali, recited all the rules of monastic discipline. Others committed these words to memory, and they were kept in oral tradition until they were finally written down three or four centuries later in Sri Lanka.

A second council was convened approximately seventy years after the first, and a third was held around 250 BCE. These Sangha gatherings were intended to discuss and settle numerous doctrinal and practical disagreements. Since the Buddha did not name a successor and left governance and interpretation of the Dhamma in the hands of the Sangha, such disputes were virtually inevitable.

In some respects, the Buddha's teachings did not furnish an especially good foundation on which to build a religion, as it is ordinarily understood. He neither encouraged nor discouraged belief in god or the gods. The cessation of suffering and rebirth simply did not involve the divine realm. Similarly, the Buddha offered little in the way of worship or ritual practice. He certainly did not suggest that his followers worship or pray to him as a god. Ritual and worship, he believed, could not secure liberation. Although the monks and nuns lived in communities, the practice of the Noble Eightfold Path was essentially solitary. There were no congregational meetings or weekly services. Gatherings of the Sangha were to conduct business or discuss Dhamma, not to encounter the sacred.

Over time, more conventional religious elements were incorporated into the tradition. A creed of sorts was developed and became a declaration of one's Buddhist identity. This statement, known as the Triple Refuge, says "I take refuge in the Buddha, I take refuge in the Dhamma, and I take refuge in the Sangha." Pilgrimages to the *stupas* associated with the Buddha's life helped satisfy the needs of some followers for tangible symbols for the spiritual life. Since the Buddha had little to say about belief in gods, many lay Buddhists (and some ordained monastics) simply retained their worship of the *devas*, which was practiced by virtually all Indians. Divine worship, however, was geared toward asking for particular favors from the gods—for healing, for protection, for success—and not for the ultimate goal of *nibbana*. Thus, veneration of the gods coexisted quite comfortably alongside Buddhist practices, as it still does today in Buddhist cultures. Buddhists who worship the gods do not think of themselves as compromising their Buddhism in any way. Interestingly, the Buddha himself would later become part of the Hindu pantheon as one of the ten principal manifestations of the god Vishnu. Thus, we observe the intriguing situation of many Hindus venerating the Buddha as a god and many Buddhists venerating the gods associated with Hinduism.

Ashoka

Under the patronage of one of India's greatest rulers, King Ashoka, the Buddhist presence became more keenly felt in India and other parts of Asia. Ashoka, who reigned from 273 until 232 BCE, a little more than a century after the Buddha's death, was at first a ruthless monarch, intent on expanding the borders of his Mauryan Empire at any cost. But following a campaign against the state of Kalinga (modern day Orissa), he toured a battlefield in which over 100,000 soldiers and civilians died. He was stunned by the carnage and in anguish asked himself, "What have I done?" Shortly thereafter, he fully embraced the Buddha's Dhamma, to which he had been exposed by one of his wives who was a lay supporter of the Sangha. Ashoka himself had become a nominal Buddhist a year prior to the war with Kalinga, but the significance of the Dhamma seems not to have had an impact on him until afterward.

The stories say he then renounced war and pursued peace. He outlawed animal sacrifices in the capital and took pilgrimages. He built hospitals and schools to improve the well-being of his subjects. He had the original *stupas* opened to retrieve the relics of the Buddha and then redivided them to establish 84,000 new *stupas*, according to legend. Most importantly, he sent missionaries all throughout India and to Southeast Asia, the Greek kingdoms in Afghanistan, and Central Asia to spread the Buddha's Dhamma. His own son Mahinda and daughter Sanghamitta joined the monastic order and took Buddhism to Sri Lanka. Ashoka also did much to cultivate a widespread interest in Buddhist philosophy. It was he who called the third council in 250 BCE to deal with doctrinal issues that were troubling the community.

With Ashoka's influence, Buddhism eventually became a predominant presence in India, until it finally died out between the twelfth and fourteenth centuries CE. Today, the number of Buddhists in the land of its birth is very small, and ironically, missionaries from other Asian countries are sometimes sent to India to try to reinvigorate the religion. But due in large measure to Ashoka's sponsorship, what started as an obscure Hindu sect was soon elevated to the status of an international religion. Today, over half of the world's population lives in an area where Buddhism was or is a principal cultural force.

Theravada and Mahayana

The early centuries of Buddhism were marked by a number of doctrinal disputes and disagreements concerning practice and monastic polity. These debates often led to actual divisions within the community. At one time, there were at least eighteen different schools that regarded the Pali Canon as authoritative. Of these, only the Theravada school remains, making it the oldest extant Buddhist tradition. This heritage is reflected in the name Theravada, which means "the way of the elders." Theravada is also known as Southern Buddhism, because it is found mainly in Sri Lanka, Burma, Cambodia, Laos, and Thailand. Of the major varieties of Buddhism today, Theravada probably represents the form closest to the way Buddhism was practiced at the time of the Buddha.

Around the first century CE, near the time Christianity started, another Buddhist movement known as the Mahayana began to take shape in northwestern India. The Mahayana added a substantially different dimension to the earlier forms of Buddhism: new views about the Buddha and his role in making salvation available to humanity. New mythologies about the Buddha's life appeared that gave him a more divine, godlike status. Mahayana developed the idea of the Bodhisattva, an enlightened being who remained in the samsaric realm to help others attain awakening. With this new cosmology and view of the Buddha, the Mahayana began to take on the qualities of a savior religion. This form of Buddhism was exported to China and other parts of East Asia in the early centuries of the current era; hence, the Mahayana is sometimes called Eastern Buddhism. The Mahayana gradually became the most popular variety of Buddhism and has since remained so. Of course, it too fragmented over time as new schools developed from within it.

Out of the Mahayana also emerged another major form of Buddhism, Vajrayana, which was practiced for centuries in Tibet and Mongolia. Vajrayana is the Buddhism of the Dalai Lama. Both the Mahayana and Vajrayana make for fascinating study, but because they developed outside the time period we are considering in this book, we will have to let these few comments suffice.

With these remarks about the evolution of Buddhism beyond the Axial Age, we leave our study of this tradition for the time being. In the next chapter, we take up the last of the Indian traditions from the Axial Age: Jainism.

15

Jainism

With the transition from Buddhism to Jainism, we move from one of the world's largest religions to one of the smallest. A recent estimate puts the number of Buddhists in the world today at around 535 million[1] and the number of Jains at just over 4 million, almost all of them in India.[2] To put this in other terms, Buddhists make up about 8 percent of the world's population, and Jains compose less than one-half of 1 percent of *India's* population. Although there is a vast disparity in the number of practitioners of each, the two traditions share remarkably similar histories, beliefs, and practices. Both accept the concepts of rebirth and karma and seek release from *samsara*. And both reject the authority of the Vedas and Upanishads, making them heterodox schools of Hindu philosophy. As we explore the Axial Age roots of Jainism, these common features will become evident, and so will the many differences.

In spite of its small size, Jainism has had a tremendous influence on Indian history and religions, an impact disproportionate to the actual number of Jains past and present. The most significant contribution of Jainism has been its practice of *ahimsa*, not harming living beings. No other religion has devoted more attention to the theory, practice, and promotion of nonviolence than Jainism. Some scholars have suggested that the Buddha may have adopted this practice from the Jains when he made it the first of his Five Precepts. Likewise, some have suggested that cow protection and vegetarianism, now prominent features of Hinduism, may have originated with the Jains. The historical data are not clear enough to settle these issues conclusively, but the Jain influence on Mohandas Gandhi is beyond doubt. Gandhi, who grew up in an area with a significant Jain population, acknowledged in his writings that the Jain doctrines

---

1. Peter Harvey, *An Introduction to Buddhism*, 2nd. Edition (Cambridge: Cambridge University Press, 2013.), 5.

2. http://www.adherents.com/Religions_By_Adherents.html. Accessed 26 April 2013.

of *ahimsa* and *satya*, or truth telling, were instrumental in formulating his program of nonviolent resistance.³

The Tirthankaras

Although modern history locates the origins of Jainism in the same cultural environment that gave rise to classical Hinduism and Buddhism, devout Jains do not. According to the faithful, Jainism is an eternal religion, propounding truths that have no beginning in time. At certain moments in the universal life cycle, these truths must be rediscovered

> "In spite of its small size, Jainism has had a tremendous influence on Indian history and religions, an impact disproportionate to the actual number of Jains past and present. The most significant contribution of Jainism has been its practice of *ahimsa*, not harming living beings."

and reintroduced to humanity because they have become forgotten and lost. When an Axial Age sage named Vardhamana Mahavira began to teach the doctrines of Jainism, he was only transmitting a religion that had been taught many times before by others. Each of these previous teachers, says Jain tradition, was a Tirthankara, a word that means a "bridge builder," one who makes it possible to traverse a river or stream.

Like the Buddhists, the Jains frequently speak of gaining liberation from *samsara* as crossing to the "further shore." The Tirthankaras were exceptional individuals who showed the way to salvation through their words and example. By their own efforts, they blazed a trail to perfect freedom and represented the highest possible attainment for the soul.

The Tirthankaras all taught the same substantial truths, but each presented his revelations in language and concepts appropriate to the people of his times. In the latest turn of the universal cycle, there have been twenty-four Tirthankaras. The twenty-fourth and most recent was Vardhamana Mahavira. Jains would not consider him the *founder* of Jainism, just its reformer or reviver. The Jains predict there will be twenty-four additional Tirthankaras in this cycle. The next one is expected in approximately 81,500 years.

---

3. Gandhi exchanged letters extensively with Srimat Rajchandra, a Jain scholar, and was influenced by him. Erik Erikson in his book *Gandhi's Truth* writes this about Srimat Rajchandra: "Young Gandhi had met a genuine seeker after truth, and we shall find essential elements of Jain thought in Gandhi's later ideology." Erik Erikson, *Gandhi's Truth: On the Origins of Militant Nonviolence* (New York: W. W. Norton, 1970), 163.

Vardhamana Mahavira

Modern scholarship must begin its study of Jainism in the Axial Age, because there is no evidence to support the historical existence of the first twenty-two Tirthankaras. The evidence for the twenty-third, an ascetic named Parshva, who was believed to have lived in the ninth century BCE, is thin. But with Mahavira, we are on more solid historical ground.

What we know about the historical Mahavira is sketchy, and there are numerous variants of his life story. Tradition says he was born in 599 BCE, although some scholars suggest a date at least fifty years later. Both Buddhist and Jain texts suggest that the Buddha and Mahavira were contemporaries living in the same region of northeastern India. The texts indicate that they knew *of* each other, although they never met. If the Buddha actually lived around 490–410, as most scholars now think, then either Mahavira's traditional dates would be inaccurate, or the stories that the sages knew of each other are fictions.

The Jain tradition says Mahavira was born in Kundagram, near Patna, a city on the Ganges in the present Indian state of Bihar. There is no reason to doubt that claim. Some of the narratives describing his birth do, however, bear the mark of myth. According to these accounts, Vardhamana was born to a King Siddhartha and Queen Trishala, rulers of the kingdom of Vaishali and followers of Parshva, the twenty-third Tirthankara. Before his birth, his mother had a series of dreams about the child she was carrying. The court sages said the dreams indicated that the child would become either a great emperor or a Tirthankara. In the legends about the Buddha, we recall, there is an almost identical prophecy. But unlike the Buddha's father, King Siddhartha did not attempt to prevent his son from becoming a spiritual master by restricting his freedom or plying him with earthly delights. Another variant of the birth story says Vardhamana was actually conceived by a Brahmin couple, and his embryo was supernaturally implanted in Queen Trishala's womb. This episode was probably added to the narrative to ease the rising tensions between the priestly and warrior castes, since many Brahmins were feeling resentment that some of the warrior caste were encroaching on their traditional territory, the realm of spirituality. Not much is said about Mahavira's youth except that, according to certain Jain traditions, he married a young woman called Yashodhara—curiously, the same name as Siddhattha Gotama's wife—and together they had a daughter. But another Jain sect denies this marriage ever took place.

At the age of thirty, Mahavira became a *shramana*, renouncing his kingdom and wealth. One account says he waited until the death of his parents to go forth as a *shramana* so as not to cause them grief. While that interpretation may be true, it is also possible that grief over his parents' death actually precipitated his decision, just as the Buddha's experience of the Four Sights catalyzed his renunciation. Often a personal tragedy or crisis sets an individual on a spiritual path.

Mahavira inaugurated his renunciation by pulling out his hair by the roots. That was a foretaste of things to come. For the next twelve years, he practiced intense asceticism, including fasting for long periods, mortification of the flesh, meditation, and silence. His goal was to discipline himself to overcome all desires and attachments. As a symbol of his objective, Mahavira discarded his clothing and spent the remainder of his days in the nude. Clothing, like anything else, could be an attachment. He scrupulously avoided harming other living beings, including animals and plants. It was his dedication to these austere practices that earned him the title Mahavira, meaning Great Hero, an epithet given to him by his admirers. At the end of this period, at the age of forty-two, he attained perfect enlightenment, a state of complete omniscience, and was recognized as a Tirthankara and a *jina*, or spiritual conqueror.

For the next thirty years, he traveled throughout the Ganges region, teaching others his principles and practices for attaining freedom from *samsara*, for which he used both the terms *moksha* and nirvana. Like the Buddha, he attracted men, women, and children from all social strata. His followers were called Jainas or Jains because they were disciples of the *jina*. Some legends say Mahavira garnered over 400,000 disciples. He organized his followers into a fourfold order: monks (*sadhu*), nuns (*sadhvi*), laymen (*shravak*), and laywomen (*shravika*). To attain liberation, one essentially had to become a monastic because of the great discipline required to achieve it. Laypersons generally expected to strive for *moksha* in a future lifetime when circumstances were more favorable to its pursuit.

Traditional reckoning says Mahavira attained his final liberation at the age of seventy-two on the last day of the year in 527 BCE, an event Jains celebrate as the festival of Diwali.[4] His chief disciple, Indrabhuti, realized enlightenment a few hours after the *jina*'s passing and later recollected his words, which subsequently became the basis for the Agam Sutras, one of the most important Jain scriptures.

---

4. Diwali is also a popular Hindu festival, celebrating the triumph of good over evil rather than Mahavira's nirvana.

The Jain Worldview

Jains, like Buddhists and Hindus, appropriated many of the basic assumptions and beliefs circulating in the Ganges basin in the early Indian Axial Age. But in almost every case, Mahavira reinterpreted these conceptions to fit his particular view of the world. We see these novel understandings in Mahavira's views on time, the world, the soul and karma, and the path to liberation.

View of Time

Mahavira believed the world was never created and will never be destroyed. Thus, cosmic time is infinite, but it follows a cyclical pattern. Each cycle is divided into two halves, a period of decline and a period of ascendancy, and each half cycle is further divided into six unequal, immensely long phases. One half cycle, called *avasarpini*, is a time of decline, and during the first part of this period, people are enormously tall and live long lives; they are extremely happy, wise, and virtuous without the need for ethics or religion. All their needs are provided for by wish-granting trees. As the cycle proceeds, conditions get progressively worse. The world and life are characterized by gradual corruption and deterioration; ethics and religion are introduced; writing is invented because people's memories begin to fail. It is during these stages that the Tirthankaras appear. At the lowest point of the cycle of decline, people will be only three feet tall and live only twenty years. They will dwell in caves, like animals, and pursue all manner of immoral activity.

When time reaches its lowest point, it begins to ascend, and the world gets increasingly better. This half cycle is called *utsarpini*. People begin to live longer, healthier lives, conduct themselves in more compassionate ways, and enjoy greater happiness. When this cycle reaches its apex, time begins its downward descent once again. This pattern repeats again and again, forever. According to Jain belief, we are presently in the fifth stage of the cycle of descent, a time when things are bad yet will get worse. The current era began a little over 2,500 years ago and will continue for a total of 21,000 years. At the end of this period, Jainism will be lost but reintroduced by the next Tirthankara after the half cycle of ascent begins.

View of the World

The physical world comprises three levels: the underworld, the earth's surface or the middle realm, and the heavens. The underworld is the location of a series of seven or eight hell realms, each colder than the next. The hells exist to punish the wicked as a way of removing negative karmas. The Jain hells are more like a purgatory than a place of ultimate condemnation. When souls have suffered enough for their sins, they may be reborn in another realm. The middle level is the home of life and is known by the lovely name Jambudvipa, or "the island of the rose-apple tree," a name also used by Buddhists and Hindus. The upper level of the world is the home of the gods. It consists of sixteen heavens and fourteen celestial regions. Souls with insight may be born in one of the higher celestial regions; those without insight may be born in one of the heavens. Above the universe's ceiling is a crescent-shaped structure where the Tirthankaras and the completely liberated souls dwell. This is the ultimate destination of those who attain *moksha*.

LIFE

Like the sages of the Upanishads, Mahavira believed the soul was real, not illusory as the Buddha thought. Mahavira conceived of the soul as unchanging in essence, although its characteristics were subject to change. He also thought there were an infinite number of souls, each an actual, separate individual, akin to what Leibniz called a monad. Thus, Mahavira would not have accepted the Vedantic idea that the soul and ultimate reality are consubstantial, since that view denies individuality. Furthermore, all souls are of equal value; one is not better than another. Souls may be embodied in gods and humans, as well as animals, plants, and even, according to some, stones, minerals, bodies of water, fire, and the winds. The souls of fire and wind are very tiny but nonetheless alive. One of the early Jain scriptures admonishes followers to avoid using fire altogether:

> The man who lights a fire kills living things,
> While he who puts it out kills the fire;
> Thus a wise one who understands the Law
> Should never light a fire.[5]

In its pure state, the soul has perfect perception, knowledge, happiness, and power. But at present, all souls except the completely liberated ones are defiled because they are embodied and stained with karma. The Jain view of karma is unlike any we have studied thus far. The Jains understand karma as a fine, material substance that clings to and stains the soul. Karmas are imperceptible particles, floating throughout the world. As a soul commits a karmic act, it attracts these fine particles, which adhere to the soul and weigh it down. These

---

5. *Sutrakrtanga* I, quoted in "The Basic Doctrines of Jainism," *Sources of Indian Tradition*, vol. 2, ed. William Theodore de Bary (New York: Columbia University Press, 1958), 61.

karmas accumulate and color the soul. If we could see souls—which we cannot because of our defiled state—we could easily detect a soul's moral and spiritual quality. The worst souls are stained black, and the purest are white. In between, from bad to good, the soul may be colored blue, gray, red, lotus pink, or yellow. As in Buddhism and Hinduism, karma determines one's future births and keeps us in bondage to the material, samsaric world.

Because they are entrapped in matter, embodied souls are not omniscient, as they are in their pure state. Karmic defilements distort our perceptions and limit our knowledge of the world. These distortions prompt the soul to seek pleasure in material possessions and temporary enjoyments, which further lead to self-centered thoughts and deeds, anger, hatred, greed, and other negative states of mind. These in turn result in the further accumulation of karmas. The cycle is vicious.

The limitations caused by karmic defilement also mean we are unable to comprehend the incredible richness and complexity of reality. The Jains say reality is *anekanta*, or many sided. What this means is that the world is composed of an infinite number of material and spiritual substances, each with an infinite number of qualities and manifestations. Because of the complexity of the universe and the limitations of our knowing, all claims to truth must be tentative. The Jains refer to this principle as nonabsolutism, which means refraining from making categorical or unconditional statements. We must be humble about our knowledge and acknowledge that we could be wrong.

The Path to Liberation

With this outline of the Jain worldview, we can now consider Mahavira's discipline for attaining liberation. The objective of the Jain path is simple and has two components. The first part is to stop the accumulations of new karmas. The second is to eliminate the old karmas that have already accumulated and weigh the soul down.

To reach the first goal, Mahavira advised his followers to fulfill five *mahavratas*, or Great Vows. The first and foremost of these is *ahimsa*, not to harm any living beings. The Jains take this precept further than the Buddhists, who drew the line at *sentient* life, not life itself. The Jains believe that even unintentionally injuring another creature generates negative karma. For Buddhists, an act must be intentional to be karmically relevant. In accord with these convictions, Jains are vegetarians and refuse to use leather or other animal products. Most avoid farming—the plow might inadvertently cut a worm in two—and other occupations that might cause harm to life forms.

Some, especially the monastics, use a cloth to cover a glass while they drink to strain out insects that may have gotten in the liquid, and they sweep the pathway before them as they walk to avoid stepping on bugs. But *ahimsa* involves more than just avoiding physical injury to life. It includes what the Jains call *ahimsa* of the mind and *ahimsa* of speech. *Ahimsa* of the mind is practicing right thought. Evil thoughts and imaginings are believed to generate negative karma. *Ahimsa* of speech is speaking in a nonhurtful way, using gentle, compassionate language. The practice of nonviolence is not entirely altruistically motivated. Abstaining from violence prevents harm to a potential victim, to be sure, but it also prevents harm to the potential perpetrator. In this sense, the practice of nonviolence is enlightened self-interest.

The other four vows all relate in some way to *ahimsa* and the cessation of karmic accumulation. They include always to speak the truth (*satya*); not to steal or take what is not given (*asteya*); chastity (*brahmacharya*), which is interpreted as celibacy for the monastics and faithfulness in marriage for the laypeople; and finally, nonattachment to people and material things (*aparigraha*).

Stopping new karmas from staining the soul is the first step to liberation; removing the stains of old karmas is the next. The elimination of accumulated karmas principally involves good deeds and asceticism. Like Mahavira, those who would attain perfect enlightenment must practice fasting, meditation, penance, yoga, and studying and reciting scripture. These observances purge the soul of its karmic residues. The ultimate ascetic practice, undertaken by many throughout Jain history, is fasting to death (*sallekhana*). The fast symbolizes and promotes absolute renunciation: prior to this point, the ascetic has given up all else but food, water, and the body. Now, in a deeply meditative state, these too are gradually given up, ending for good all attachments to *samsara*. This fast is not considered violent but an act of compassion, since there is no anger or pain associated with it.

The elimination of all karmas restores the soul to its pure, undefiled state of perfect knowledge, perception, and power. No longer weighed down by the heaviness of its karma, the soul rises to the very ceiling of the world, where it enjoys the bliss of nirvana in the company of other liberated beings.

Like the Buddha and the Upanishadic sages, Mahavira preached a path of self liberation. Because each soul is accountable for its own karmas, only the individual can reverse the karmic accumulations. The monastic community was established to provide a favorable context for the pursuit of nirvana. Because the Jain quest of nirvana involved a more austere asceticism than the Buddha's Middle Way, becoming a monk or nun was more vital to ultimate realization in

Jainism than in Buddhism. The monastics were also responsible for preserving Mahavira's teachings, first in oral tradition and then in writing.

There were, of course, numerous disagreements among the monks and nuns concerning matters of doctrine and practice, but most of these were minor. The only major division in Jainism resulted in two different orders of monastics: the sky-clad, or Digambaras, and the white-robed, or Shvetambaras. This split probably occurred between the fourth and second centuries BCE. The disagreement that led to this schism was not doctrinal but practical. The Digambaras, as their nickname implies, argued that it was essential to renounce clothing to attain liberation, as Mahavira himself had done. The Shvetambaras contended that nudity was optional for the monk and not necessary for *moksha*. But the Digambaras also maintained that women could not reach liberation as women; they would have to await rebirth as a man for that. Part of their argument was that it was inappropriate for women to renounce their clothing. Digambara nuns, therefore, wear white robes, like the Shvetambaras. The Shvetambaras, conversely, believed that women *were* capable of perfect enlightenment and that one of the twenty-four Tirthankaras was a woman, a claim the Digambaras rejected. The division led eventually to further differences, one of which is that the two groups now have substantially different sets of scriptures. As the monastic communities continued to grow, other disagreements arose, and new subsects were established. Some of the main disputes included debates about venerating images of the gods and the Tirthankaras and whether or not it was even appropriate to use temples.

Although these conflicts still exist, they should not be overemphasized. According to contemporary Jain scholar Nathmal Tatia, all Jains agree on Jainism's central message, which is nonviolence, nonabsolutism, and nonattachment. These practices are basic elements in the Jain quest for personal liberation from *samsara* and their collective goal of peace throughout the world.

PART III

East Asia

16

East Asia before the Axial Age

The final destination on our journey through the development of Asian religions in the Axial Age is the civilization of the Yellow River in the northeastern region of present-day China. The name China is actually an anachronism for this culture during the Axial Age. The people we will be discussing would not have called themselves "Chinese," because the term *China* derives from the name Qin, one of many ruling dynasties of this region, which was not established until late in the third century BCE, right at the close of the Axial Age. Therefore, to call this part of the world China or to refer to Chinese culture is to use language that would have been strange to the people of the time. Nonetheless, we will continue to use these terms because it is convenient and appropriate in view of the historical continuity with what later came to be called China.

Throughout most of its recorded history, China has been home to three major religions: Confucianism, Daoism, and Buddhism. According to conventional belief, the founders of these three traditions were contemporaries. Postaxial Chinese art often depicted Confucius, Laozi, and the Buddha taking a walk or having a pleasant conversation together. Such an event could never have happened historically, of course, but the purpose of such images is to indicate the compatibility of these three major traditions by depicting the friendship of their founders. These portrayals, though, probably exaggerate the harmony among these religions. Confucianism and Daoism had contrasting philosophical outlooks and led to fundamentally different ways of life, and Buddhism struggled with overcoming the perception that it was a foreign religion espousing values contrary to traditional Chinese virtues. Nonetheless, it would not have been unusual for an individual to participate in some manner in all three traditions. One might take part in Confucian rituals as a government official or public citizen, go to a Daoist priest for medical needs, and depart the world with a Buddhist funeral.

Our next several chapters will discuss Confucianism and Daoism, the two of the three traditions that are indigenous to China. Although Buddhism played a very significant part in Chinese religious history, it did not arrive in China until the first centuries of the current era, well after the close of the Axial Age.

Before we can begin to make sense of these two traditions, though, it is necessary to grasp what Chinese life was like before they developed. In the present chapter, we will discuss the elements of preaxial Chinese culture insofar as we are able to cobble together a picture of it. As with the preaxial cultures of Central, West, and South Asia, we are often in the position of making educated conjectures based on slim archaeological and literary evidence.

The Legendary History of China

By tradition, the Chinese trace their history as far back as some five thousand years ago. Legends speak of an era of Three Sovereigns and Five Emperors several millennia before our current era. During this ancient period, according to the traditions, the basic features of Chinese civilization were established, including such things as hunting and fishing, agriculture, boats and carts, religious rituals, silk, centralized government, and writing. Today we have no written or archaeological evidence to confirm that this period was anything more than legendary.

Whether or not there really was such a period, this epoch has held very important symbolic value for the Chinese. This mythic era helped explain why things were the way they were and provided standards for the people of later times to use in judging their own values and behavior. Almost always, when people hold up the past as a moral yardstick, contemporary life is regarded as sorely lacking. American poet Robert Penn Warren once said, "The past is always a rebuke to the present."[1] Confucius was one among many who thought the China of his day had strayed from the mores of an earlier golden age, and he believed a return to those old ways was the only option. In this sense, at least, the actual historicity of these epochs is not nearly as significant as what people believed about them.

The Religion of the Shang Dynasty

The earliest period that can be historically substantiated is the Shang dynasty, which began sometime in the fifteenth or fourteenth century BCE in the northeastern region of China. For many years, scholars believed the Shang

---

1. Gloria L. Cronin and Ben Siegel, eds., *Conversations with Robert Penn Warren* (Oxford: University Press of Mississippi, 2005), 20.

dynasty was also part of the mythic "prehistory" of China, simply because there was no tangible evidence from the Shang period.

Then, very late in the nineteenth century CE, someone noticed curious items being sold as medicine in certain Chinese pharmacies. The items, which the pharmacies called "dragon bones," were used to concoct remedies by traditional Chinese doctors. After some investigation, these dragon bones were determined to be the shoulder blades of cattle and the shells of tortoises inscribed with an early Chinese script. These animal artifacts, along with some bronze ritual implements from this same period, confirmed the historicity of the Shang dynasty and shed light on Chinese religious beliefs and practices prior to the Axial Age.

Divination Practices

Modern scholars have since determined that these bones and shells had been used by Shang rulers to communicate with the gods and ancestors. The inscriptions inquire about a wide array of concerns: the best time to plant or harvest a crop, why a particular person had fallen ill, why a military expedition had failed, the meaning of a dream, the best location to erect a building, and whether a sacrifice had been pleasing.

Apparently, the bones and shells were etched with questions of this sort and then heated or burned, causing them to crack. These cracks were then interpreted, probably by a specialist in the art. It is not known exactly *how* the cracks were evaluated—whether the diviners were interested in the shape, the direction, the sound, or the speed of the crack. But once an answer was obtained, the procedure was repeated several times to ensure accuracy. After the fissures were interpreted, the answers they rendered were also engraved on the animal part. The fact that over 100,000 such fragments of bone and shell have been recovered indicates that this procedure, known generically as divination, was an extremely important part of this early period in China and that it was used for both political and religious purposes.

Divining is a very common practice throughout the world's religions. The methods differ, but the principle behind them is basically the same. Something tangible involving an element of randomness—like crack patterns or the choice of cards in a deck—is used to allow the intangible spirits to communicate to mortal beings. Divination is one way of solving basic religious issues: how do we determine what the gods want, and what must we do to ensure that things go well with us? Divination is still popular, even in our ostensibly modern scientific world. Consider the continuing presence of tarot cards, Ouija boards, horoscopes, palm reading, and the eight ball in Western culture. There is quite a variety of divination methods in world history, including some lesser-known techniques such as observing how a rooster pecks grain (alectromancy), how a person laughs (geloscopy), and watching the movements of mice (myomancy).

> "Divining is a very common practice throughout the world's religions. The methods differ, but the principle behind them is basically the same. Something tangible involving an element of randomness—like crack patterns or the choice of cards in a deck—is used to allow the intangible spirits to communicate to mortal beings. Divination is one way of solving basic religious issues: how do we determine what the gods want, and what must we do to ensure that things go well with us?"

Still today, the use of divination is widespread throughout Asia, and many Asians would not even consider making an important decision without consulting an astrologer or some other soothsayer. In the 1980s, a minor scandal occurred when it came to light that President and Mrs. Reagan had consulted astrologers in the White House. It was never clear whether the president had ever based any decisions of state on the stars or whether the astrologers were just consulted on personal matters. Nevertheless, against the backdrop of world history, the Reagans' use of divination practices would not be considered unusual at all. In fact, for many societies, to make a political decision without conferring with the spirits would be regarded as extremely risky and perhaps downright blasphemous. In ancient China, political and religious matters were intimately connected, and no one would ever consider trying to separate them. The court astrologers and diviners were paid state officials.

HEAVEN AND EARTH

The "dragon bone" inscriptions tell us about other important aspects of Shang religion. From them, we learn of the prime importance of maintaining harmony between heaven and earth—the principal dimensions of the universe—and the role of the spirit world in keeping these realms in balance.

HARMONY

The ancient Chinese saw a very close connection between the spirit and human worlds, or as they would say, between heaven (*tian*) and earth (*di*). In Chinese thought, heaven and earth did not refer to two separate regions of the cosmos; rather, they were understood to be coterminous realms. This view of heaven meant that the gods and the spirits were immediately available to human beings.

A great part of Shang religion focused on maintaining harmony between these worlds. The well-being of everyone depended on it, and preserving this balance was one of the king's principal functions. Harmony is a common theme throughout Chinese culture and one of the primary ideals of its religions.

GODS

How did the ancient Chinese imagine the heavenly realm? Who were the beings who lived in this world, and what did they do? In Shang theology, the divine dimension was thought to be a heavenly court that paralleled the earthly royal court. Just as the king ruled on earth through a bureaucracy of nobles, advisers, and various other functionaries, the high god ruled heaven with his minions and assistants. The Chinese called the high god Shangdi, or simply Di, the Lord Supreme. Di presided over a court that included many lesser divinities who controlled, or at least influenced, the powers of the natural and human worlds. These were the gods to whom the Chinese turned for favors in matters of agriculture, hunting, military campaigns, and health and longevity. The high god would not be bothered for these trivial matters. Not all the gods were universal, either; many were decidedly local, including the municipal or village gods, whose power extended only as far as the city limits, similar to the jurisdiction of the local sheriff.

The bone inscriptions reveal that relationships between the ancient Chinese and their gods were rather businesslike. The human interest in the divine was defined by what the god could do. The bones reveal no indication that people wanted to have a friendship or some other intimate relationship with their deities. We find no expressions of love or tenderness between a god and a devotee. The kind of close relationship we see in the Bible between the god Yahweh and Moses, or between Arjuna and Krishna in the *Bhagavad Gita*, would be unimaginable in Shang religion. Furthermore, we find no evidence that the gods were concerned with the moral behavior of human beings. They did not give commandments or grant favors on the basis of how well humans treated each other. Shangdi would not bring calamity upon the country because people treated each other poorly, in the way that Yahweh killed everyone except Noah and his family because of humanity's wickedness. For the Chinese gods, the central concerns in the divine–human relationship were in receiving pleasing sacrifices and tributes; humans, in return, expected divine assistance with 'worldly' matters such as producing an abundant crop, gaining victory over enemies, healing illness, and living a long life with many descendants. Here, we might compare the religious interests in China with those of the Indo-Aryans, who at this same point in history were mainly concerned with meeting basic needs and enjoying a prosperous life. Morality and personal spirituality were not part of Chinese religious practices at this time.

THE ANCESTORS

In addition to the gods—and not sharply distinguished from them—were the ancestors. The ancestors were the deceased individuals in one's clan, who existed in the spirit world, from where they continued to exert influence on living family members. Belief in ancestors is actually a widespread phenomenon throughout the world's religions, though it is not by any means universal. It has been part of the religious beliefs of people from parts of Africa, native America, Polynesia, South and Southeast Asia, as well as China. In ancient China—and to a great extent throughout Chinese history—ancestors have been seen as having a continuing interest in the welfare of their descendants. Hence, they were to be consulted on important matters, and they were to be honored with sacrifices and gifts. They were also believed to mediate with the gods, especially if they were ancestors of a powerful earthly family, such as that of the king.

> "For the Chinese gods, the central concerns in the divine–human relationship were in receiving pleasing sacrifices and tributes; humans, in return, expected divine assistance with 'worldly' matters such as producing an abundant crop, gaining victory over enemies, healing illness, and living a long life with many descendants."

Some early theorists of religion in the nineteenth century thought belief in ancestors may have been one of the earliest forms of religion. Burial of the dead was probably the earliest religious ritual, and, if so, reverencing the dead might have been connected to it. One hypothesis suggests that the belief that one's relatives might still exist in the spirit world following death comes from the experience of dreaming. Most of us—perhaps all of us—have had dreams about someone who has died, often someone very close to us. These dreams can be very powerful. For ancient people around the globe, the dream world was just as real as—and frequently more real than—the world of waking life.

Ancestor reverence as it was practiced in China, though, involved more than just belief in the continued existence of the dead. People also felt the need to keep the ancestors happy and appeal to them for favors. We do not know much about ancestor reverence in the Shang period, because we lack historical evidence about the practice among the common people, but we do know that the king's relationship to *his* ancestors was extremely important. The bone inscriptions suggest that the king's ancestors had a great influence over his well-being and could mediate between the king and Shangdi. Each day of the week was even dedicated to one or another of the royal ancestors.

About ordinary folk and their ancestors we know very little, but judging by the importance of this practice throughout the rest of Chinese history, we can surmise that ancestor reverence was also widespread among everyday people in the Shang period. Even today, in places where traditional Chinese religions are still practiced, ancestor worship is very popular. In Taiwan, Tomb-Sweeping Day is a spring festival when extended families gather at the cemetery for a reunion to clean the graves of the departed and make offerings to them. This holiday underscores for us the great significance of the family and the sense of continuity with the past that pervades Chinese culture.

Ghosts

Ghosts, like ancestors and gods, were part of the unseen spirit world in the ancient Chinese worldview. Whereas the ancestors were generally benevolent toward the living, ghosts were not. They could cause great misfortune, sickness, and other problems. Generally, ghosts were understood to be the spirits of the dead who had not been properly buried. Like the ancient Greeks, ancient Chinese believed a ghost would haunt the living until its body received a fitting funeral.[2]

Early in the twenty-first century, ghosts became a news item in a story reporting how many East and Southeast Asians were avoiding vacationing at the beaches of Thailand and other parts of the Indian Ocean where the tsunami of 2004 killed almost a quarter million people. The great fear among these individuals was that because so many people who died in that disaster were simply washed out to sea and never received a burial, the shores would be full of ghosts wreaking havoc on human life. As this story illustrates, ghosts were to be avoided as much possible. But when they couldn't be avoided (and sometimes you just cannot avoid ghosts), the Chinese tried to appease them with offerings or, as a last resort, to banish or exorcize them.

The Concept of Virtue

Before we leave this brief sketch of preaxial China, one final concept should be noted because it plays an extremely important role in the development of Axial Age thought. That is the concept of *de*, a word found on many of the bone inscriptions used for communicating with the spirits. *De* is usually translated as

---

2. See the *Iliad* and the *Odyssey*.

"virtue," although its meaning in preaxial China is different from the way we use the word *virtue* today.

At that time in Chinese history, *de* referred to a power or force that came to exist within a person who acted generously or kindly toward another individual or to a god or spirit. *De* was generated by an act of compassion or by a sacrifice that was pleasing to a god or ancestor, but what was important was mainly the inner disposition, or the attitude, with which the act was performed. This power of virtue was believed to accumulate in an individual who performed many acts of kindness and compassion. Virtuous people were powerful people. (It would not be accurate to say, however, that powerful people were always virtuous people.) For their part, those who benefited from these compassionate acts were believed to feel indebted to the benefactor and would want to repay the benefactor with a similar act of kindness. The Chinese called this desire to respond to a kindness *bao*. Thus, virtue carries with it the power to affect the lives of others in a positive way. Your virtuous act toward me encourages my virtue, prompting me to act kindly. *De* and *bao* were regarded as being causally connected in the nature of things. These were not viewed as psychological so much as natural phenomena, operating as surely as we today think gravity works, or the way Indians view the function of karma.

This idea of virtue is important in Chinese religions in many ways. For example, let us explore how it functions in an issue we have been discussing: family obligations. Consider the importance of including ancestors as part of the ongoing life of the family. This practice is associated with what the Chinese call filial piety (*xiao*), or the reverence for parents and ancestors. According to the ancient understanding of virtue and the sense of obligation it evoked, children were greatly indebted to their parents for giving them life. The debt one owed to one's parents was immeasurable and could never, really, be repaid. The only proper response, in view of this indebtedness, was reverence.

A poem from the classic *Book of Odes* nicely captures the sense of filial indebtedness that was foundational for Chinese family life. The poem was written down in the Zhou dynasty (c. 1045–221 BCE), but it was probably composed in preaxial times. In any event, it reflects what seem to be prevalent attitudes of the Shang period. The poem is addressed to the author's parents:

> Oh father, you begat me!
> Oh mother you nourished me!
> You supported and nourished me,
> You raised me and provided for me,
> You looked after me and sheltered me,

In your comings and goings,
You [always] bore me in your arms.
The kindness [*de*] I would repay [*bao*]
Is boundless as the Heavens!³

This belief in the importance of filial responsibility has been foundational for Chinese culture up to modern times.

A similar point can be made with respect to each of the elements of Shang religion that we have examined. They all endured in some fashion into the Axial Age and have persisted through much of Chinese religious history. We have discussed the closeness of heaven and earth in the Chinese imagination and the vital importance of maintaining harmony between them. The chief method for preserving harmony was essentially ritualistic. The residents of heaven demanded less in terms of moral and ethical behavior and more in terms of sacrificial food. The responsibility for this harmony fell in great measure—if not exclusively—on the king. Thus, we see the very close association of politics and religion in Chinese culture, a closeness that may seem alien to many modern minds. We should also observe that religious practice essentially served the needs of the collective rather than the needs of individuals, including the king himself. Sacrifices and divination practices were mainly for the well-being of society. And this, we should note, is characteristic of preaxial religions. The practice of religion pertained chiefly to ritual and was performed principally for the material benefit of the community. We observed this in preaxial South Asia as well. When the Axial Age came to China, however, these central elements of religious practice began to change.

---

3. From the *Shijing* in James Legge, *The Chinese Classics 4:352*, (Hong Kong: Hong Kong University Press, 1970), quoted in Philip J. Ivanhoe, *Confucian Moral Self-Cultivation*, 2nd ed. (Indianapolis: Hackett, 2000), xii.

17

The World of Confucius

In our first glimpse of China's religious history, we discussed the prominent practices and beliefs of the preaxial period, which included divination, ancestor reverence, ritual sacrifices, and gods and ghosts. Those ancient concepts and practices endured into the Axial Age and up to modern times. In this chapter, we will examine the transition to the Axial Age and introduce the most influential individual of that era, the sage Confucius. In subsequent chapters, we will study the fundamental elements of Confucian thought, how they were interpreted by others, and some significant opposing viewpoints, including the religion of Daoism.

The Early Zhou Dynasty

Scholars are not absolutely sure when the Shang dynasty began—probably in the fifteenth or fourteenth centuries BCE—but we know when it ended. In or about the year 1045 BCE, the Shang rulers were deposed by another aristocratic family, the Zhou dynasty, who established the next period in Chinese history. The Zhou dynasty lasted, at least in name, some eight hundred years, until it was supplanted by the Qin dynasty in 221 BCE. These dates mean that the Zhou dynasty roughly spanned the entire Axial Age.

Political and Cultural Changes

To help us comprehend the religious dimensions of this period, it is essential to discuss its salient political and cultural aspects. The Zhou dynasty is traditionally traced to a King Wen, who was known as the "cultured king" and was credited with refining the book of divination called the *Yi Jing*. Despite his title, "King" Wen never actually ruled China. Wen had been a feudal lord who was imprisoned by the last Shang king. When Wen's son Wu overthrew Shang rule, he freed his father from imprisonment and bestowed on him the honorific title "king," although Wu himself was the actual ruler. When King Wu died at an early age, his younger brother Dan became regent for Wu's thirteen-year-old son. Dan was better known by his title, the Duke of Zhou. These figures in the early history of the Zhou dynasty—especially the duke—came to be regarded as the paragons of leadership and moral behavior by later Chinese, particularly Confucius, who reported that he had frequent dreams about the duke.

Despite the high regard later Chinese had for these early Zhou rulers, Zhou culture was initially not nearly as sophisticated as the Shang dynasty it replaced. Zhou culture lacked writing but quickly adopted the Shang writing system. It also appears that the Zhou rulers embraced parts of Shang religion. The Zhou kings gave a fiefdom to the Shang family members so they could continue to worship and sacrifice to their ancestors. The Zhou rulers themselves probably worshiped the Shang ancestors, even though they had ousted the descendants of these ancestors!

THE MANDATE OF HEAVEN

Like the Shang kings, the Zhou rulers worshiped a high god, in addition to the countless local spirits and divinities composing the heavenly bureaucracy. In Zhou theology, this Supreme Being was called Tian, a term that is ordinarily translated as "Heaven." In the Shang dynasty, *tian* was simply a generic term for the heavenly realm, but in the Zhou era, the idea of *tian* became more ambiguous. The Zhou people considered Tian a personal deity, a being conceptualized in anthropomorphic terms, like Shangdi; in fact, the Zhou rulers originally used the names Shangdi and Tian interchangeably to refer to the highest god. Over time, however, more impersonal associations came to dominate Zhou theology, and heaven was regarded basically as an ultimate principle, like *asha* in Zoroastrianism. So *tian* could now mean both a personal god and an impersonal principle.

But the crucial difference between the Zhou and the Shang concepts of the highest power pertains to morality. From our discussion of the Shang oracle bones, we recall that the gods, from the highest on down, simply had no interest in how humans behaved toward each other, and they did not make moral behavior a condition for granting favors. But Tian *did* care. This attribution of moral qualities represents a significant shift from preaxial understandings of the gods and is part of the general ethicization process we have seen throughout several axial centers.

Just how far Tian's moral interests extended remains uncertain. It is not clear, for instance, if Heaven was interested in how the ordinary Chinese man treated his wife or how she acted toward her next-door neighbor. But it is evident that Heaven had an interest in who the ruler was and how he treated his subjects. We know this because a new term entered the Chinese lexicon in the Zhou dynasty: *tianming*, the Mandate of Heaven. Some of the early classics of China credit the Duke of Zhou with this expression. As it came to be interpreted, the Mandate of Heaven decreed that the ruler governed with divine blessing as long as he was virtuous. Conversely, if a ruler was wicked or inept, Heaven withdrew its mandate, and the ruler's reign was no longer morally legitimate. This notion is similar to Christian Europe's belief in the divine right of kings, in the sense that a monarch reigned with the authorization of the deity. But the Chinese conception differed from those European versions that argued that the king had been chosen by god and therefore must be obeyed absolutely. Since the Chinese understanding of the Mandate of Heaven made the ruler's legitimacy contingent on his virtue and not only on birth, it could be used as moral justification for opposing and even deposing the king, which is exactly what the Zhou rulers did.

"The crucial difference between the Zhou and the Shang concepts of the highest power pertains to morality: In Shang religion, we recall that the gods simply had no interest in how humans behaved toward each other. But Tian *did* care. This attribution of moral qualities represents a significant shift from preaxial understandings of the gods and is part of the general ethicization process we have seen throughout several axial centers."

Today, most scholars think the appearance of the Mandate of Heaven shortly after the Zhou dynasty conquered the Shang is more than just an interesting coincidence. It is likely that the Zhou rulers or their supporters developed this notion precisely to justify the overthrow of their predecessors. On the basis of this idea, the Zhou people claimed that the Shang family had become corrupt—and there probably was some merit to that claim—and that consequently Heaven's mandate had passed to them.

The concept of the Mandate of Heaven came to assume a critical role throughout Chinese history, up until the twentieth century. And its significance lies in this simple proposition: that the ultimate powers that be—whether these are understood as a personal deity or an impersonal principle—have moral sensibilities and interests. To Westerners brought up with the idea of god based on the Bible or the Qur'an, this may not seem unusual. For Jews, Christians, and

Muslims, god is almost by definition moral or the source of human morality. But within the context of this period in Chinese history, to regard the divine as moral was significant.

Yet that idea was not universally or immediately accepted. Previously, we observed that the documents of the Shang religion focused almost exclusively on the king and his relationships to the gods and ancestors. But now, in the Zhou period, there is enough literary and archaeological material to allow us to glance at the religious life of common folk. From this evidence, we can discern elements of dissent from the official Zhou theology.

Some aspects of folk religion from this period are available to us in a classic work known as the *Shi-jing*, or the *Book of Odes*. In this fascinating text, certain passages are direct protests against Heaven's apparent injustice, suggesting that not everyone was convinced of Tian's moral character. The following stanza is one such instance. The author's complaint might appear as if these verses were taken directly from the book of Job:

> O vast and distant Heaven,
> Who art called our parent,
> That, without crime or offence,
> I should suffer from disorders this great!
> The terrors of great Heaven are excessive,
> But indeed I have committed no crime.
> [The terrors of] great Heaven are very excessive,
> But indeed I have committed no offence.[1]

Even at this early date, a theological conflict that has continued to plague theists to the present day looms on the horizon. This is the famous problem of evil, which has bedeviled the theistic traditions for centuries. Essentially, the difficulty arises whenever one attributes both omnipotence and morality to god. How can god be both all good and all-powerful when evil exists in the world? Either god is all-powerful but not all-good, or god is all-good but not all-powerful. That is the theistic dilemma. Countless solutions to this problem have been proposed throughout the ages, and none of them has ever gained universal approval. Evil is not really a theological problem for religions that do not believe that god is totally good and omnipotent. Some religions, such as portions of Hinduism, see god as the source of *both* good and evil. For these traditions, evil is an existential or practical problem but not a theological one. In

---

1. Ode 4, Stanza 1, *The Khiáo Yen*, c. 878–828 BCE; trans. James Legge. Available at http://www.sacred-texts.com/cfu/sbe03/sbe03116.htm.

this poem from the *Book of Odes*, the dilemma is solved by affirming Heaven's omnipotence but denying its morality, because it punishes when no sin has been committed. This was exactly Job's complaint, according to the Bible.

FOLK AND ELITE TRADITIONS

This passage from the *Book of Odes* illustrates that religious perspectives were by no means uniform at this time in Chinese history. Furthermore, this example helps show how differences in theological viewpoint might be related to one's social location. The king who lived a privileged existence and whose reign was divinely endorsed might be more inclined to regard Heaven as just and benevolent than would a peasant who struggled for daily subsistence and found him- or herself beaten down by misfortune.

Despite these differences in perspective, it would be a mistake to assume that a sharp separation existed between what have been called the folk and elite traditions in Chinese religion. For many years, scholars of Chinese religion have insisted there was a substantial divergence between the intellectual and highbrow expressions of religion and the way that religion's beliefs and practices worked in the daily lives of ordinary people. Recently, however, scholars have come to believe that folk and elite religions were not so starkly different, or at least not as much as once supposed. We might think of folk religion and elite religion as opposite ends on a continuum, on which they share a great many of the same beliefs and practices but have distinct interests and orientations.

The religious practices of ordinary people seem to have focused on exactly what one would expect ordinary people to be concerned with. Living close to the land and being very dependent on the vagaries of nature, the religious beliefs and practices of common folk concerned the matters of daily, earthly well-being. Undoubtedly, the people of the land believed in gods, ancestors, and ghosts, just as their rulers did, and surely they performed sacrifices and other rituals to gain favors from the spirit world or to remove or fend off an unwanted demon. The rituals of common people would be oriented toward securing the welfare of an individual or a family or perhaps the village, but would not extend much further. The rituals of the elite—including the king, of course—were centered on benefiting the state itself. And as we have just seen, the ruler had a keen interest in legitimating his reign by claiming the favor of Tian.

The Later Zhou Dynasty

Despite the claim to possess the Mandate of Heaven, all was not well during the Zhou period. Even though it survived 800 years and was China's longest-lasting dynasty, serious rifts began to appear just a few centuries after its establishment. In 771 BCE, the Zhou king was murdered by invading nomads, and the capital had to be moved further eastward. This move marked a division between what is known as the Western Zhou and Eastern Zhou periods. The Eastern Zhou period, which lasted about 550 years, was further divided into two periods known as the Spring and Autumn Age (722-481 BCE) and the Period of Warring States (475 or 403-221 BCE).

The Spring and Autumn Age got its designation from a book entitled *The Spring and Autumn Annals*, a chronicle traditionally attributed to Confucius. Even though the period bears such a nice name, this was not a politically or culturally agreeable time in China. The power of the Zhou rulers began to decline, creating instability and uncertainty throughout the region, and the many smaller kingdoms that had been under the control of the Zhou kings began vying with one another to gain superiority.

Outright chaos ensued when the Period of Warring States began. By now, there were advanced military technologies, and peasants were being conscripted as soldiers. This era was particularly brutal and disruptive, as the name implies, but it was also an immensely creative time philosophically and religiously. The Period of Warring States was also known as the Period of One Hundred Philosophers (or the Period of One Hundred Schools). That alternative name suggests that this age of political disorder prompted the intellectuals to address the pressing issues of the day. And obviously, the most urgent concern was the simple and practical matter of establishing and maintaining human harmony. To put the issue both concisely and precisely: What does it take for people to get along with each other? That was the question of the day, and there was no shortage of answers. Several major philosophical schools were advancing their particular solutions. In terms of subsequent influence on Chinese thought, Confucianism and Daoism were the most important.

Life of Confucius

Within this context of political upheaval and philosophical creativity arose the most important figure during the Axial Age in China and, arguably, the most influential Chinese figure of all time, Confucius.

THE HISTORICAL CONFUCIUS

What we can say about the life of Confucius is rather brief. The most historically reliable information must be gleaned from a work that most scholars believe comes from near his own time and that bears the imprint of his own thinking. This is a book called the *Analects (Lunyu)*, a collection of his sayings, conversations, and anecdotes related to his life, compiled by his disciples after his death. However, there is no consensus among historians about the extent to which the *Analects* is historically reliable. Almost everyone agrees that much of the text reflects the perspectives and words of his followers, some of whom may have been removed from him by several generations. Only the first half of the book is generally regarded as reflecting the thought and words of Confucius himself. Even within those parameters, some say only a few chapters (3–9) or just one section—a part of chapter 4—contains words that Confucius may have actually spoken. Others have gone even further to claim that Confucius was not a historical figure at all but a literary trope, an invented character that came to symbolize certain things for the Chinese elite.[2] Most sinologists (the specialists in the study of China) believe a similar thing about Laozi, the reputed founder of Daoism, so such an argument is not at all far-fetched.

These are very new and controversial claims in Confucian scholarship. By no means have these matters been sufficiently discussed among academics, much less a consensus reached. In view of this state of affairs, it best to present the majority view on the historiographical issues concerning Confucius until and if the dominant view changes. Historical questions, of course, are not the only important issues to address. Although the historical Confucius (as well as the historical Buddha, Zoroaster, and Mahavira) are of great interest, ultimately what is important are the beliefs and practices espoused in the teachings that come to us under their names. The Buddha, Confucius, and Laozi may *all* be fictions, but the words attributed to them may indeed be true.

Regardless, most scholars of Confucius do not doubt his historicity. From the *Analects* and a few other sources, historians surmise that Confucius was born around the year 551 BCE, during the Spring and Autumn Period, in the State of Lu, one of the several small principalities that began to compete with one another as the Eastern Zhou dynasty began its slow decline. The same sources suggest he died in 479. Of course, as with the other axial sages, the traditional dates for Confucius are not accepted by everyone who grants that he was a

---

2. Lionel Jensen, *Manufacturing Confucianism: Chinese Traditions and Universal Civilization* (Durham, NC: Duke University Press, 1997).

historical individual. Recently, some scholars of Confucius have made the case that he lived closer to the end of the Zhou dynasty.[3]

Although he is known in the West as Confucius, that term was neither his given name nor the name by which the Chinese have known him. Throughout the history of China, he has been called Kongzi, or Master Kong. The name Confucius is actually a Latinized name coined by Jesuit missionaries in the seventeenth century based on "K'ung-fu-tzu," an honorific title. But Confucius is the name that has endured, even for scholars in the field, so we will continue with that time-honored practice.

PERSONAL QUALITIES

In addition to the date and location of his birth, scholars believe that he was born to a family of lower nobility, and his father died when Confucius was around three. He was born relatively poor and remained so all his life. Despite his modest beginnings—or maybe because of them—he was an eager and dedicated student. "At fifteen," he says, "I set my heart on learning,"[4] and this love stayed with him for his entire life. "In a community of ten households there will certainly be someone as loyal and trustworthy as I am, but not someone so fond of learning as I am."[5] He apparently mastered the process of education as well: "When I study, I do not get bored; in teaching others I do not grow weary."[6] He expected his students to share his enthusiasm: "To those who are not eager to learn, I do not explain anything."[7]

If Confucius were merely an invention of later Confucians, then they did a superb job of portraying an individual who embodied the principles they said he taught. In the sayings of and about Confucius in the first half of the *Analects*, we encounter a man of great humility and modesty. His disciples said he was "rather unassuming and seemed as if he were an inarticulate person."[8] There seems not to have been a shred of pretense in him. His greatest concern was self-improvement, rather than passing judgment on the behavior of others. He advised his followers, "When you come across an inferior person, turn inwards and examine yourself."[9] He was passionate about the arts, particularly music and

---

3. E. Bruce Brooks and A. Taeko Brooks, *The Original Analects: Sayings of Confucius and His Successors* (New York: Columbia University Press, 1998).
4. *Analects* 2.4., trans. Raymond Dawson, (New York, NY: Oxford University Press, 1993), 6.
5. *Analects* 5.28, trans. Dawson, 19.
6. *Analects* 7.2, trans. Dawson, 24.
7. *Analects* 7.8, trans. Dawson, 24.
8. *Analects* 10.1, trans. Dawson, 35.
9. *Analects* 4.17, trans. Dawson, 14.

singing.[10] This appreciation of music extended beyond aesthetics. He believed that music had a moral dimension; listening to appropriate music, he believed, had the power to make one a better person. He was, of course, respectful of authority, and he believed that a humane society depended on respect for one's superiors. The chapter of the *Analects* that most describes Confucius's personal qualities concludes with this summary: "The Master was genial and yet strict, imposing and yet not intimidating, courteous and yet at ease."[11]

Confucius aspired to hold an office of significant political power, or at least to serve as an adviser to a king or duke, but he was never able to gain such a position. He managed to hold one or two minor posts, including the equivalent of police commissioner in his home state. In later life, he surrounded himself with about two dozen disciples, and they preserved the wisdom he imparted. He often traveled beyond the state of Lu to advise the government officials of other provinces.

Master Kong's vocation was rooted in a profound moral vision. His essential interest in politics was not for the sake of power or to advance a career but for the good of the realm and the well-being of all citizens. Confucius believed that the key to human harmony—that fundamental aspiration of the dozens of philosophers of this age—lay in good government and, even more pointedly, in the moral character of the ruler and other public servants. Moral behavior must begin at the top, and from there, virtue trickles down, as it were, to the lower rungs of society. If the leader is virtuous, the people will follow suit.

When we look more specifically at the full scope of Confucian ideas in our next chapter, we will begin to understand why personal morality was so essential to him. We will also begin to see why the thought of Confucius, out of this field of one hundred philosophers, was the one that prevailed and dominated Chinese religion, philosophy, and politics up to the twentieth century.

---

10. *Analects* 7.32, trans. Dawson, 27.
11. *Analects* 7.38, trans. Dawson, 27.

18

The Foundations of Confucianism

Although many have regarded Confucius as China's most profound and influential thinker, Confucius did not consider himself a great mind. He claimed no originality for his ideas: "I transmit but I do not create. Being fond of the truth, I am an admirer of antiquity."[1] Confucius believed that the example of the early Zhou dynasty provided his contemporaries with all the resources needed to address the moral and political concerns of the day. This was one reason why study was so important to him. Confucius's greatest desire was to understand this legacy, put it into practice in his own life, and then teach these ideas and observances to others. He was convinced that much of the trouble in his China was the direct result of neglecting the lessons of earlier eras. Like many, both Chinese and non-Chinese, Confucius believed in a golden age of the past in which life was better. In this chapter, we will begin our study of the foundations of his thinking or, as he would prefer us to say, his understanding of the lessons of antiquity.

THE THOUGHT OF CONFUCIUS

Virtually everything we know about the thought of Confucius comes from the *Analects*, the same small text we used to sketch out what few things we can say about his life. Tradition claims that Confucius had a hand in writing or editing several other Chinese classics, but most modern scholars doubt the truth of those claims. Therefore, we are dependent on the *Analects* for understanding his ideas.

With that single and rather brief book, grasping Confucian thought might seem to be relatively easy. Yet understanding his philosophy through the *Analects* is not at all a simple thing. The book is not easy to read. Unlike many other scriptures, such as the *Bhagavad Gita* or the Bible, it is not in narrative form. Nor is it systematic philosophy, like the Four Noble Truths. If there is

---

1. *Analects* 7.1, trans. Dawson, 24.

an underlying order to the *Analects*, it is difficult to recognize. Occasionally, a careful reader can glimpse a theme or concept running through one of the twenty "books" in the collection, but a general pattern remains elusive. Furthermore, the sayings often make obscure and unexplained references to persons or events, and some of these baffle even longtime Confucian scholars. No doubt this motley quality of the *Analects* is due at least in part to the many individuals involved in its compilation.

THE NATURE OF CONFUCIANISM

As we noted, Confucius lived during a particularly brutal time in Chinese history. Hostilities between kingdoms and corruption in government were on the rise. Almost by necessity, he thought about social and political matters. Many of his teachings were oriented toward the rulers and government officials, so much of his thinking falls under the category of political philosophy. He was not interested in the abstract questions of political philosophy as much as the practical ones: given the current state of Chinese civilization, how best do rulers rule? Confucius also spoke at great length about family life, and, again, his concerns are more practical than theoretical: what are our obligations to the members of our families, and how are they best carried out? Significantly, he connected family values and politics, an association that may sound familiar to current readers. Whether concerning the family or the state, Confucius's main interest was in ethics or morality. Furthermore, he restricted his moral concerns to the human domain.[2] That anthropocentrism would put Confucius at odds with the Jains' Mahavira, who insisted on the equality of all souls, regardless of their form of embodiment.

Confucius did not say much about souls, nor about gods and spirits. Ironically, the man who is generally considered China's greatest religious figure—and who himself was later worshipped as divine—had very little to say about the spirit world. In the *Analects*, a student recalled that the Master did not speak of "miracles, violence, disorder, and gods."[3] On another occasion, a student approached Confucius to ask how the gods and the ancestors should be served. The Master responded, "You are not able even to serve your fellow humans. How can you ask about the gods and spirits?" When the student asked about death, the Master said, "You do not even understand life. How can you

---

2. The *Analects* report this incident: "When the stables caught fire the Master, on returning from court, said, 'Did anyone get hurt?' He did not ask about the horses" (*Analects*, 10.11, my rendition). The anecdote suggests his relative disinterest in the welfare of animals and in money—horses were far more expensive than stable hands—and his primary concern with human beings.

3. *Analects* 7.21, my rendition.

understand death?"⁴ Elsewhere, Confucius is quoted as saying that it is wise to keep the gods and spirits at a distance, although one should be reverent toward them. Confucius never denied the existence of the gods and spirits, but neither did he make belief in them central to his perspective. He strongly urged people to be moral, to practice goodness and kindness, but never does he indicate that one will be rewarded by god or enjoy a pleasant afterlife for doing so. He says, "Those who are humane rest content with humaneness."⁵ Being good is its own reward.

Considering Master Kong's principal interest in humanity, might it be more appropriate to characterize Confucianism as a philosophy rather than a religion? There is certainly merit to that suggestion, especially if one regards religion as something having primarily to do with gods or spirits.

However, there are good reasons for including Confucianism under the rubric of religion or at least to regard it as *both* a religion and a philosophy. For one thing, Confucianism shares with the perspectives of the Buddha and Vedantic Hinduism a basic lack of interest in gods and the spirit world. Yet both Buddhism and Hinduism are ordinarily considered religions. Furthermore, Asians have never routinely made the distinction that Westerners often make between philosophy and religion. From an Asian point of view, philosophy must be pragmatic; it must be practiced, and it cannot be merely speculative or theoretical. This emphasis on practicing one's beliefs brings Asian philosophy very close to what Westerners mean when they speak of religion. Certainly, Confucius himself thought following his way required hard work and cultivation, not just holding specific philosophical convictions.

---

4. *Analects* 11.12, my rendition.
5. *Analects* 4.2, trans. Dawson, 13.

> "Confucianism may be included under the rubric of religion, regarded as both a religion and a philosophy.... Philosophy must be pragmatic; it must be practiced, and it cannot be merely speculative or theoretical. This emphasis on practicing one's beliefs brings Asian philosophy very close to what Westerners mean when they speak of religion. Certainly, Confucius himself thought following his way required hard work and cultivation, not just holding specific philosophical convictions."

There are other religious elements in Master Kong's views as well. First, although he was reticent about the gods and spirits, he did speak of Heaven, or Tian. At least once, he suggested that Heaven itself authorized him to teach, and in so doing, he applied the Mandate of Heaven to his own work.[6] By the time of Confucius, the Chinese believed the will of Heaven concerned not only the ruler but everyone. Confucius thus saw Heaven as legitimating his values. Second, even though he was not greatly concerned with divine beings as such, he was very interested in ritual, especially the sacrifices that were performed for the welfare of the state. Confucius loved rituals, not so much because they pleased the gods, but because he thought they were salutary for human life. Had he been an outright atheist, it is possible that Confucius would have nonetheless urged his contemporaries to perform their religious rituals because the act itself helped shaped moral character.

IDEAL PERSONS

The central thrust of Confucian thought is pragmatic, but these practical concerns are informed by a specific vision of the way human beings and human society ought to be. Before we turn to the practice of Confucian ethics in the next chapter, we should explore his ideals for individuals and human relationships. Beginning here will help us understand some of the subtle points of his ethics as well as connect Confucius to the other axial sages we have studied.

To Confucius, the highest type of person was the "sage." Although the sage was the complete embodiment of his values, Confucius said in his later life that he had never actually met a sage and had given up hope of ever doing so.[7] He did not regard *himself* as a sage, although his followers and many others throughout Chinese history did.

---

6. *Analects* 7.23.
7. *Analects* 7.26, trans. Lau, (London: Penguin, 1979), 89.

Confucius also mentioned the ideals of the "good man" (*shan jen*) and the "complete man," (*ch'eng jen*) which were often associated with particular stations in society. In casting these terms in the male gender, we are simply repeating the way that Confucius apparently thought about them; since he was someone who prized patriarchal values in the family and the society, it would be misleading to use more generic terms, such as the "good person" or the "complete person."

THE GENTLEMAN

Although he mentions several ideal types, Confucius stressed one above all others: the *junzi*. *Junzi* is usually translated as the "gentleman" or "superior man." We will follow the scholarly consensus and use the term *gentleman*, but it will be helpful to understand the Chinese sense of that word, since it differs somewhat from our contemporary usage. Westerners often use the word *gentlemen* as a generic term for males, as in "ladies and gentlemen," but it can be used to refer to a specific kind of man, namely, one who is courteous and observes proper etiquette, as in "A gentleman always opens a door for a lady." This latter sense is actually closer to the way Confucius used the term *junzi*, because mannerly behavior and being gentle (as the name suggests) are hallmarks of the gentleman. It is also instructive to remember that the English word *gentleman* was not always applied generically to refer to any man. In its original usage, the term was restricted to the nobility and indicated someone of high standing. In a similar way, Confucius intended the word *junzi* to designate someone who had attained a noble character and superior status. However, he understood nobility and superiority to be qualities that are earned by hard work, not bestowed as a birthright. The Buddha made the same point with his use of the word *Aryan*.

Based on his study of earlier Chinese culture, particularly the figure of the Duke of Zhou and other individuals associated with the early Zhou period, Confucius maintained that there are certain qualities or traits that define the gentleman. Because he was more interested in how and what people *are* than in what they do, Confucius characteristically discussed these ideal human beings in terms of their inner dispositions and not in terms of their deeds. Of course, there is a profound connection between being and doing, and Confucius was aware of this, but his teaching was centered on character rather than actions. He wanted people to *be* better people, not merely to behave better. Confucius thought moral improvement is part of our very humanity, the way we express and fulfill our greatest potential as persons. In other words, we become more fully human when we live the noblest and most moral life possible.

HUMANENESS

The gentleman had many qualities that distinguished him from others. The foremost among these was the quality of *ren*. *Ren* is usually translated as "humaneness" or "humanity." Some translators prefer the terms *kindness, benevolence,* or simply *goodness*. Although rarely used, "compassion" would be an excellent translation. Confucius did not invent the concept of *ren* (it was an old term meaning something like *noblesse oblige,* that is, the duty of the aristocrat to be kind to those of lower station), but he was the first to make *ren* central to his teaching.

Although it is clear that he believed humaneness was the salient trait of the gentleman, Confucius never fully defined it. In the *Analects*, he refers to it rather obliquely, preferring to discuss examples of persons possessing it. Because of that approach, it is not clear whether Confucius thought *ren* was innate to human nature or a characteristic to be acquired. In either sense, *ren* was a virtue to which one was to aspire. If it were an inborn quality, it still needed to be cultivated and nurtured to come to full expression. If it were an acquisition, then it would also need cultivation and nurturance to be instilled. However he viewed it, as a natural potential or the product of education, Confucius believed that one must commit oneself to the hard work of being good.

Fortunately, Confucius did say enough about humaneness and the gentleman for us to assemble an idea of what he meant by *ren*. He repeatedly stated that humaneness involves following a version of the Golden Rule: "Do not impose on others what you yourself do not desire."[8] For Confucius, this principle entailed another component of humaneness: reciprocity (*shu*). In response to a disciple's question about humaneness, the Master said, "Now the humane man, wishing himself to be established, sees that others are established, and wishing himself to be successful, sees that others are successful. To be able to take one's own familiar feelings as a guide may definitely be called the method of humaneness."[9] Reciprocity is the method of determining what others may want or not want. Our own feelings, something presumably familiar to us, serve as the guide for making this determination. By understanding our own wishes, we may imagine, on the basis of our common humanity, what others desire.

---

8. *Analects* 12.2; 15.24, trans. Lau, 112, 135.
9. *Analects* 6.30, trans. Dawson, 23.

The Buddha called this practice "seeing others as being like yourself."[10] We might call it empathy.

Of course, knowing what others may want or not want based on our own desires is one thing; acting on that knowledge in a compassionate way is something else. Confucius set a high standard when he explained what that means concretely. In the preceding passage, he says the humane person acts to promote the success of others. For many of us, that can be a real struggle. As Paul Tillich, the great twentieth-century Christian theologian, said, "There is something in the misfortune of our best friends that does not displease us."[11] Whether such hidden hostility is inherent to our natures, as Freud might say, or the product of our conditioning, as Buddhism would contend, Confucius believed that animosity or poor behavior toward anyone was a major obstacle to realizing our full humanity. But with great effort, the gentleman has removed such an obstacle.

In other places, Confucius speaks of humaneness in the language of love. For one student, he summarizes *ren* by saying, "It is to love others."[12] This simple directive might be misleading if it are not read in the full context of Confucian teaching. Confucius did not believe the humane person would—or even *should*—love everyone equally. In fact, it was on this very point that Confucianism was criticized by another leading school of the day, the Mohists, inspired by the philosopher Mozi. Mozi argued that the highest virtue for humans was "impartial caring" or "universal love" (*bo-ai*), unconditional love for all persons.

On the face of it, Mohist universal love sounds like a loftier ideal than the Confucian view of love. The Confucians and other philosophical schools, however, found the Mohist understanding unnatural, impractical, and actually inhumane. Impartial love, they argued, implied that one should treat one's own family and friends in the same way as anyone else, even strangers. Confucius believed we should love others in proportion to the benefit we receive from them. Since it is obvious that we have benefited most from our parents, who have given us the gift of life, and the other members of our family, we are

---

10. The *Dhammapada* offers this reflection on the practice: "All tremble before violence. All fear death. Having done the same yourself, You should neither harm nor kill. All tremble before violence. Life is held dear by all. Having done the same yourself, You should neither harm nor kill." *Dhammapada: Verses on the Way*, 10.1, trans. Glenn Wallis (New York: The Modern Library, 2007), 29.

11. Paul Tillich, *The Shaking of the Foundations*, (New York: Charles Scribner's Sons, 1976), 157. Tillich attributes this saying to Immanuel Kant, but I have not been able to verify that claim. Others attribute it to Francois De La Rochefoucauld.

12. *Analects* 12.22, trans. Dawson, 47.

obligated to love and care for them the most. The universal love of the Mohists was widely viewed as undermining the ancient and deeply ingrained practice of filial piety. Partly for that reason, Mohism died out in the Qin dynasty.

Confucius not only thought filial piety was the most natural expression of human love; he also believed it was the basis of all forms of loving. In the first book of the *Analects*, he says, "The gentleman concerns himself with the root; and if the root is firmly planted the Way grows. Filial piety and fraternal duty—surely these are the roots of humaneness."[13] Family life is the laboratory where we learn to love. Being a good son, he might say, is the key to being a good person. If I cannot learn to love my family, how can I hope to genuinely love others? By no means does Confucius believe love *stops* with the family. Love of family is the root, not the tree. From learning to fulfill our filial responsibilities, we extend our love to friends and neighbors, then to the village, the common people, and ultimately the whole of humanity. But as our love extends beyond, it rightly decreases in intensity. Confucius did not intend that we should *not* love those at a distance from ourselves, just that we love them less than those nearest to us. In promoting a love that discriminates among persons, Confucius may have chosen a more difficult path than the Mohists.

Accordingly, the disciples of Confucius found his path a hard one to walk. Discussing the Confucian way with another disciple, "Master Zeng said, 'A Gentleman must be strong and resolute, for his burden is heavy and the road is long. He takes benevolence as his burden. Is that not heavy? Only with death does the road come to an end. Is that not long?'"[14] As the final lines of this passage imply, the discipline of striving for goodness is a lifelong process, and in the end, it may be unattainable. Confucius never guaranteed a conclusion to his way, such as Buddhahood or the liberation of the soul. A gatekeeper who had heard of Confucius's reputation inquired of one his disciples, "Is that the [Kong] who keeps working towards a goal the realization of which he knows to be hopeless?"[15]

WISDOM AND EQUANIMITY

Humaneness, kindness toward others, empathy: these were the prime qualities of the *junzi*. But they were not the only ones. The gentleman was wise as well as compassionate. By wisdom, Confucius meant that one knew what was right and what was wrong, was a good judge of character, and possessed

---

13. *Analects* 1.2, trans. Dawson, 3.
14. *Analects* 8.7, trans. Lau, 93.
15. *Analects* 14.38, trans. Lau, 130.

self-knowledge. He told his followers, "When you understand something, to recognize that you understand it; but when you do not understand something, to recognize that you do not understand it—that is wisdom."[16] The quality of wisdom also meant that one thought for oneself. A gentleman did not blindly follow others, or as Confucius put it, "A gentleman does not behave as an implement."[17]

The *junzi* possessed equanimity: "In his attitude toward the world the gentleman has no antagonisms and no favouritisms. What is right he sides with."[18] Like the Buddhist *arahant* or Hindu *jivanmukta*, the gentleman did not allow external circumstances to dictate his disposition: "The Master said: A man of quality indeed was Hui! He lived in a squalid alley with a tiny bowlful of rice to eat and a ladleful of water to drink. Other[s] . . . would not have endured such hardships, but Hui did not let his happiness be affected. A man of quality indeed was Hui!"[19] The quality of equanimity pertained also to the opinions of others. In the very first passage of the *Analects*, Confucius defines this quality according to his usual high standards: "not to be resentful at others' failure to appreciate one—surely that is to be a true gentleman."[20] Later in the same section, he further emphasizes this trait, taking it almost to the level of "saintliness": "One does not worry about the fact that other people do not appreciate one. One worries about not appreciating other people."[21] With such an attitude, is there any wonder that Confucius characterized the gentleman as "calm and peaceful"?[22]

---

16. *Analects* 2.17, my rendition.
17. *Analects* 2.12, trans. Dawson, 7.
18. *Analects* 4.10, trans. Dawson, 14.
19. *Analects* 6.11, trans. Dawson, 21.
20. *Analects* 1.1, trans. Dawson, 3.
21. *Analects* 1.16, my rendition.
22. *Analects* 7.37, trans. Dawson, 27.

19

The Cultivation of Virtue

Confucius's answer to the social and political disorder of his day was to cultivate persons of virtue. He understood that the problems facing his society were too profound to be resolved by mere legislation or decree and the extensive policing of the populace. In his view, the evils confronting China were rooted in spiritual defilements: greed, hatred, the love of power, self-centeredness, and callousness toward human life. These dispositions were not aspects of life that could be controlled by the police. Speaking of racism in the United States, Martin Luther King, Jr. once said, "The ultimate solution to the race problem lies in the willingness of men to obey the unenforceable."[1] What King observed about the defilement of racism coheres exactly with Confucius's view of the deep-rooted problems of his China. The only answer to such a situation is to convince others to obey the unenforceable. Confucius sought to do this by the way of virtue.

We have already examined how the virtues that Confucius considered most important would be embodied in the ideal individual he called the gentleman. What remains to be discussed is how Confucius thought these virtues could be instilled and refined and how the virtuous individual could promote greater harmony within and among societies.

Moral Self-Cultivation

Like the Buddha, Confucius believed that kindness and compassion are qualities that require cultivation. Both sages were convinced that discipline was the key to realizing and perfecting these qualities. They each proposed different methods for doing so, although at several significant points, their recommendations are similar. Of course, they advocated these disciplines for different reasons: the Buddha to achieve liberation from *samsara*, and Confucius

---

1. Martin Luther King, Jr., *Where Do We Go from Here: Chaos or Community?*, (Boston: Beacon, 1967), 100.

to promote social harmony in this life. Yet, viewed from a different angle, they shared the belief that self-discipline is necessary to bring forth the best that is within us.

THE CONFUCIAN WAY

Master Kong never laid out anything as clear-cut as the Noble Eightfold Path for his disciples to follow, but he did set out specific landmarks for guiding them along the path of virtue, which he called the Way, or *Dao*. These markers are scattered throughout the *Analects* and, like the elements of his life and philosophy, have to be carefully culled from the text. Fortunately, a close reading highlights the basic practices that Confucius regarded as central to moral nurturance.

A few sentences out of the first book of the *Analects* capture several of these practices in a single paragraph: "A gentleman avoids seeking to satisfy his appetite to the full when he eats and avoids seeking comfort when he is at home. He is diligent in deed and cautious in word, and he associates with possessors of the Way and is put right by them. He may simply be said to be fond of learning."[2] As in the teaching of the Buddha, there is an element of moderate asceticism in the life of the gentleman and the gentleman-in-training. He avoids eating too much and becoming too comfortable. Furthermore, conscious self-restraint helps encourage what is surely a major aspect of the practice of kindness: combating the tendency toward self-absorption. Confucius called this "subduing oneself."[3]

This passage also indicates that Confucian discipline requires self-awareness in word and deed. For this, the master advocated a form of meditation, what he variously called "quiet-sitting," "abiding in reverence," and "rectifying the mind." Like the Buddha and the Upanishadic sages, Confucius recognized the value of taking time to devote attention to one's own thoughts and experiences. Such a practice sharpens the faculty of awareness and also creates space for critical self-examination. Confucius' capacity to look at himself with ruthless honesty almost certainly contributed to at least two other worthy qualities: his openness to being corrected and taught by others and his modesty, traits that are also related to one another. It takes a spirit of humbleness to be receptive to instruction. The most difficult students to teach are those who lack humility. Perhaps that is why he refused to teach someone who did not share his love of learning: "The Master said: 'To those who are not eager to learn I do

---

2. *Analects* 1.14, trans. Dawson, 4.
3. *Analects* 12.1, trans. Dawson, 44.

not explain anything, and to those who are not bursting to speak I do not reveal anything. If I raise one angle and they do not come back with the other three angles, I will not repeat myself,"[4]

Confucius seems to sum up the traits of the gentleman in the last sentence of the passage: "He may simply be said to be fond of learning." But what sorts of things did Confucius think it important to learn? For the sage, devotion to learning meant especially the study of certain Chinese classics. The Master himself spent a prodigious amount of time studying the documents and chronicles of earlier periods, books on ritual, the *Yi Jing*, and the *Book of Odes*. Eventually, the most important of these writings were designated as the Wu Jing, or the Five Classics, and they became the first canon of Confucian writings.[5] When Confucianism was later established as the basis of Chinese education, the Wu Jing formed the foundation of the curriculum. A thorough grounding in these texts was considered indispensable to a career in the government, which was regarded as the appropriate profession for a Confucian.

In his program of self-cultivation, Confucius also included an educated appreciation of the refined arts of music, dance, and poetry. Music was a particular love of Confucius's; he enjoyed singing and playing the lute. As mentioned earlier, he believed that particular kinds of music had the power to evoke and refine moral sensitivities. In this context, he was thinking mainly of music that might be performed at state occasions and in rituals such as sacrifices, weddings, and funerals. At these times, he thought the music must fit the occasion and contribute to the general purpose of the event. Apparently, Confucius was especially sensitive to the spiritual power of music. A disciple reports, "When the Master was in Qi, he heard the *shao* [a musical piece for a state ceremony], and for three months did not notice the taste of meat. He said: 'I did not imagine that music-making reached such perfection.'"[6] By the same token, certain forms of music, he thought, could be a disruptive influence and degrade our capacities for kindness and harmony.

Unlike spiritual teachers of some other traditions, Confucius encouraged his followers to devote attention to the minute details of daily life. The forest *shramanas* of the Ganges basin in India practiced a radical disregard for the things of this world; since the world was transient, the *shramanas* sought to attend only to that which is enduring: the invisible and intangible *atman*. But

---

4. *Analects* 7.8, trans. Dawson, 24.

5. The Wu Jing comprised the *Book of Odes*, the *Book of Changes*, the *Book of Rites*, the *Book of History*, and the *Spring and Autumn Annals*.

6. *Analects*, 7.14, trans. Dawson, 25.

to Confucius, such things as clothing and food and even one's posture were matters of spiritual significance. One of the books of the *Analects* contains an extensive list of rules for wearing clothes: the proper colors to wear and not wear (mauve and purple, by the way, were not acceptable for the gentleman), the appropriate types of material for particular seasons, and the correct way to fold robes. These regulations may seem rather tedious, but they served important functions in the cultivation of moral character. Some of these purposes are obscure without knowing the complete context, but others are more apparent. For example, Confucius told his students never to eat their fill in the presence of someone in mourning. Self-restriction in this case not only displayed solidarity with one in grief but also allowed one an opportunity to reflect on his or her common lot with the mourner and the deceased, bringing attention to the fact that we all mourn and we all die. That simple recognition helps deepen our sense of compassion and reverence for life. Wearing the proper clothes, folding them in the correct way, and carrying oneself with upright posture suggest a respect for oneself and for the society of which one is a part. Confucius emphasized that observing these rules should always be done with the utmost humility and never to gain advantages for oneself.

Although Confucius promoted attentiveness to these mundane aspects of experience, he also encouraged a kind of detachment from material possessions and things. He seemed to know, like the Buddha, that happiness is not found in acquisitions: "The Master said: 'Even in the midst of eating coarse rice and drinking water and using a bent arm for a pillow, happiness is surely to be found; riches and honors acquired by unrighteous means are to me like the floating clouds.'"[7] In this brief passage, Confucius expressed one of the major themes of the Axial Age religions: Happiness has nothing to do with wealth, recognition, or comfort but everything to do with righteousness.

OBSERVANCE OF *LI*

Finally, we come to what is probably the most important dimension of self-cultivation in the Confucian view, the proper observance of *li*. The term *li* has a rich history in Chinese religions. It is an ancient word that Confucius infused with new meaning. Originally, *li* meant the ritual sacrifice performed for the gods, ancestors, and other spirits, but Confucius transformed the concept of *li* in two fundamental ways. First, he extended its meaning to refer not only to public, formal occasions of ritual but to all occasions of human interaction. Just as Shakespeare compared the world to a stage and men and women to

---

7. *Analects* 7.16, trans. Dawson, 25.

actors, Confucius thought of the world as a temple and of men and women as participants in a grand ceremony. He believed that in all our dealings with others, we ought to act and comport ourselves with all the dignity appropriate to a sacred rite. He described the features of this dignified approach: "The things which the gentleman values in the Way are three: in transforming his demeanor he banishes his violence and rudeness, in composing his expression he keeps close to sincerity, and in the style of his utterances he banishes coarseness and impropriety."[8] What Confucius illustrates in this passage are examples of social etiquette. And with that observation, we return to an earlier point about the meaning of the word *gentleman*. In the Confucian sense, the gentleman is indeed a mannerly individual. Confucius was not interested in manners simply for the sake of appearing courteous or gaining personal advantages. When performed with the proper inner disposition, following the rules for correct behavior has the potential to make us more humane.

This was Confucius' second contribution to the understanding of *li:* connecting it to moral development. In the Shang and early Zhou dynasties, ritual was understood primarily as the performance of certain external acts. Simply going through the prescribed motions was sufficient to make the ritual effective. Closer to the time of Confucius, *li* came to include the inner sense of reverence and sincerity of the ritual's participants. The sacrifice had to be enacted in the proper spirit, lest it be ineffective and displeasing to those it intended to honor. Confucius took this concern with the interior dimension of ritual a step further by associating it with the quality of humaneness. Ritual thus became an act that not only pleased the divine beings but also (and perhaps more importantly for Confucius) shaped the moral character of the participant and observers.

---

8. *Analects* 8.4, trans. Dawson, 28.

Let us explore for a few moments what led Confucius to regard *li* as a discipline for refining humaneness. For clarity, we will focus on *li* as a sacred public ritual rather than the etiquette of everyday life or the private rituals of ancestor reverence. The dynamics are fundamentally the same in all cases but are more evident in public ritual.

The state rituals performed in the time of Confucius were elaborate events that required extensive study before they could be performed. These occasions often required many persons to be directly involved with the ceremony. There were ritual specialists as well as musicians, dancers, and actors who performed for the pleasure of the audience, which consisted of both human and divine beings. The gods were invited to attend with invocations and attracted to the proceedings by the smells of the food. Food offerings were made for the principal benefit of the spirits and ancestors, but humans also were allowed to partake. The offerings were usually animals sacrificed for the occasion and cooked or burnt whole. The most common victims were oxen, pigs, and sheep. A ritual that included one of each species was especially pleasing to the gods. Sometimes the spirits were offered gifts of silk and jade or rice and millet, but more important than the gifts themselves was the reverential and gracious attitude with which they were offered. According to the *Book of Odes*, the spirits rewarded with a long life those who sacrificed in the correct frame of mind.

Confucius saw many aspects of the ritual as evoking and refining the sense of humaneness. The study required to perform the ritual served as a form of discipline and self-restraint. It also provided knowledge about the meaning of the ritual itself, which Confucius believed embodied the mysteries of Heaven. Even beyond this mystical dimension, the ritual had more mundane elements that contributed to moral development. Participating in the ritual encouraged certain emotions and states of mind, such as reverence, gratitude, and humility. It promoted a spirit of cooperation among people and instilled the importance of subordinating personal needs and desires to the social endeavor. Not unlike meditation, it required concentration and attention to detail. While people were

> "Confucius transformed the concept of *li* in two fundamental ways. First, he extended its meaning to refer not only to public, formal occasions of ritual but to all occasions of human interaction.... Second, he connected it to moral development. Ritual thus became an act that not only pleased the divine beings but also (and perhaps more importantly for Confucius) shaped the moral character of the participant and observers."

conducting a ritual, it would be very difficult for them to think of things other than the events at hand. Finally, ritual could create a sense of interconnectedness between humanity and divinity, reminding the participant that he or she was part of a vast web of interdependent relationships involving the gods, the earth, and other human beings.

The relationship between humaneness and *li* was thus dialectical, each element mutually strengthening the other. The more one grows in the quality of humaneness, the easier and more authentic is the expression of that quality while interacting with others. The deeper my feelings of compassion and the greater my awareness of those feelings, the more likely I am to act on them and to do so genuinely. By the same token, the more I act kindly, compassionately, and reverentially, the more I become of aware of the roots of those qualities in my inner nature.

How Self-Cultivation Transforms Society

The purpose of moral cultivation, of course, was more than simply creating better individuals. Confucius believed the practice was essential to a better society and government. Did he think the answer to the social and political problems of the Zhou period would be solved by putting everyone on a program of moral self-cultivation? Probably. If he thought such a thing were feasible, it would undoubtedly have improved the welfare of the state, but as a realist, Confucius did not anticipate such a thing. It seems likely that he did not think the common people were equipped with the time or the intelligence to undertake this regimen. That did not mean he thought commoners were incapable of being moral; they simply required another approach.

This is where government played its greatest role in society. For Confucius, the primary function of the ruler and the ruling class was to provide for the welfare of the common people, and not for self-aggrandizement and the acquisition of power, the attitude that was becoming increasingly popular on the eve of the Warring States period. To encourage the well-being of the whole of society, Confucius thought it was vital for the ruler and the elite ruling class to practice the arts of moral self-cultivation and act as moral exemplars for all citizens. Virtue, he thought, starts at the top and spreads throughout the kingdom. The more virtuous the ruler, the more virtuous the people.

This theory of the ruler's moral influence in a country is based on the ancient Chinese understanding of virtue, which was discussed at the beginning of this section on East Asia. As we recall, virtue, or *de*, was believed to be a kind of force or power that came to reside in people of moral and compassionate character. The kinder one was, the more this virtuous power accrued to the individual. The natural and irresistible response to virtuous acts by those who benefited from them was called *bao*, the sense of gratitude and desire to reciprocate in kind by acting virtuously oneself. Through years of practicing virtue, one might accumulate enough virtuous energy to be morally charismatic. An individual with a cache of moral charisma could inspire others to become more virtuous themselves. Confucius believed this transaction occurred almost by magic. Without legislation or proclamations, the virtuous ruler could affect the well-being of his state effortlessly simply by being a moral example: "The Master said, 'Guide them by edicts, keep them in line with punishments, and the common people will stay out of trouble but will have no sense of shame. Guide them by virtue, keep them in line with the rites, and they will, besides having a sense of shame, reform themselves.'"[9] In this way, Confucius assumed that humans would "obey the unenforceable." Confucius advised rulers to refrain from the use of force: "In administering your government, what need is there for you to kill? Just desire the good yourself and the common people will be good."[10] He even predicted that one hundred years of moral rule could completely eliminate killing within the realm.

The direction of moral charisma does not move only from the top down. Confucius taught that social superiors could be influenced by their subordinates. This is one reason why he encouraged his followers to take government positions, where they would be situated to influence both the lower classes and the ruler and his court. Even the commoners could contribute to the welfare of society by cultivating virtue. Once someone approached Confucius and asked why he did not participate in government, and he answered this way: "The *Book of History* says, 'Simply by being a good son and friendly to his brothers a man can exert an influence upon government. In so doing a man is, in fact, taking part in government.'"[11] For Confucius, the personal moral character of each citizen has an impact throughout a society. The goodness of the individual does make a difference in the world.

---

9. *Analects* 2.3, trans. Lau, 63.
10. *Analects* 12.19, trans. Lau, 115.
11. *Analects* 2.21, trans. Lau, 66.

20

Early Confucianism and the Rise of Daoism

Mention the name Confucius, and many Americans will conjure the image of an old Chinese man sporting a Fu Manchu beard and moustache spouting wise sayings that are just pithy enough to fit on those little slips of paper in fortune cookies. This impression of Confucius is due mainly to the immense popularity of the forty-four *Charlie Chan* movies made in 1930s and '40s. These films reflected stereotypes of East Asians in the early twentieth century, and many Chinese and Chinese Americans today consider the films offensive. Charlie Chan, who was played by European American actors and not an actor of Chinese heritage, was a bright and often funny detective who supposedly had an encyclopedic knowledge of Confucius and quoted him at critical junctures in the movie. He would often preface a statement with "Confucius say . . ." and repeat a proverb in Pidgin English. Some of the proverbs were fairly funny: "Optimist only sees doughnut, pessimist sees hole."[1] Some were gems of wisdom: "Death one appointment we must all keep, and for which no time set."[2] There is actually a website listing nearly five hundred of these witticisms, but as far as I can tell, not one of them actually came from Confucius.[3]

Be that as it may, I mention Charlie Chan simply to note that many of us think of Confucius as a wise old man with an aphorism for every occasion. That image, actually, is not far off the mark. To the degree that the *Analects* portray Confucius accurately, he seems to have preferred to make brief statements to provoke further thought or to make forthright assertions, rather than to construct logical arguments to persuade people to accept his viewpoint. Rarely

---

1. *Charlie Chan in Paris,* directed by Lewis Seiler (Los Angeles: Fox Film, 1935).
2. *Docks of New Orleans,* directed by Derwin Adams (Los Angeles: Monogram Pictures, 1948).
3. "Charlie Chan's Aphorisms: The Complete Sayings of Charlie Chan," *The Charlie Chan Family Home,* n.d. http://charliechanfamily.tripod.com/id6.html. Accessed 27 April 2013.

did he feel the need to justify his position rationally. He was more of an Aesop than an Aristotle.

Just How Good Are We, Really? The Mengzi–Xunzi Debate

Because of his style of teaching, Confucius's disciples, following his death, found themselves in the position of not only interpreting his words for themselves but also of defending his views against criticism from other schools of philosophy. This was the Period of One Hundred Philosophers, after all. Increasingly, members of the Confucian school, which was known as the School of Scholars (*rujia*), were challenged to discuss issues with rival philosophers and to provide rational arguments for their perspective.

Mengzi

The first noteworthy thinker to attempt a comprehensive argument for Confucius's philosophy was Mencius (385–312 BCE), a fourth-century disciple of Confucius's grandson. Mencius is the Latinized form of Mengzi, or Master Meng. Because he was the first major Confucian interpreter, Mengzi's explanation of the sage's thought was very influential. Mengzi's version was officially accepted as Confucian orthodoxy, although not until the Song dynasty, over one thousand years later. But even before that, many Confucians understood Confucius through the mind of Mengzi. Mengzi was to Confucius as Paul was to Jesus.

A few aspects of Mengzi's personal life are worth noting. One is that he took a three-year leave of absence from his job to mourn for his mother following her death. Even Confucius would have been impressed with such filial piety! He spent much of his life as an itinerant political consultant, like Confucius, traveling from state to state offering advice to rulers. Apparently, not even one monarch accepted his guidance. He ultimately settled and gathered a small school of disciples around him. These disciples compiled his teachings into a collection known as the *Mengzi*, or the *Mencius*. At the time, it was common simply to use the author's name for a book's title. The *Mencius* consists primarily of his conversations with his students, who reputedly recorded their teacher's words verbatim.

Two matters in particular seem to have been of special concern to Mengzi: the role of government in promoting the human good and the fundamental quality of human nature. The first item he shared with Confucius, who also had much to say about the function of government. Like Confucius, Mengzi encouraged rulers to foster moral development in their subjects, as parents would in their children. He also maintained that virtue was a much more effective means of governance than was the use of force or punishment.

He based his confidence in virtue on the second item: his understanding of human nature. This is where Mengzi parted company with Confucius. Confucius said a great deal about government but virtually nothing about human nature. Either he thought the matter irrelevant to his practical concerns, or the concept of human nature was not a notion current in his day. It was probably more the latter. The term *ren xing*, human nature, was not discussed much by any Chinese philosopher until about the Period of the Warring States, at which time it became a central issue of debate.

Mengzi contended that human nature was inherently good. In one of the most famous passages in the *Mencius*, Mengzi defended the idea of human goodness with a thought experiment:

> The reason why I say that all human beings have hearts that are not unfeeling toward others is this. Suppose someone suddenly saw a child about to fall into a well: anyone in such a situation would have a feeling of alarm and compassion—not because one sought to get in good with the child's parents, not because one wanted fame among one's neighbors and friends, and not because one would dislike the sound of the child's cries. . . . From this we can see that if one is without the feeling of compassion, one is not human. If one is without the feeling of disdain, one is not human. If one is without the feeling of deference, one is not human. If one is without the feeling of approval and disapproval, one is not human. The feeling of compassion is the sprout of benevolence.[4]

Mengzi used this argument to demonstrate that something deep within the human heart responds naturally out of compassion, without any ulterior motivation. This is a strong argument for Mengzi's view, but not an incontrovertible one. The bystander's response might be motivated by something other than compassion or humaneness. Today, sociobiologists, for example, might argue that the motivation is the genetically determined instinct to act in ways that preserve the species.[5] If true, humans are no different from other species in this respect, and humaneness could not be the trait that distinguishes humans from other animals, as the Confucians believed. Still, for many, Mengzi's case was compelling.

---

4. *Mengzi* 2A6.4-6.5, trans. Brian W. Van Norden (Indianapolis/Cambridge: Hackett, 2008), 46.
5. Edward O. Wilson, *On Human Nature* (Cambridge: Harvard University Press, 1979).

Yet if all humans are born with intrinsic benevolence, Mengzi must explain why humaneness does not seem to be the prevailing condition of daily life. Based on empirical evidence, one might easily draw the opposite conclusion: people are just no damn good. In the Period of Warring States that would have been an easily substantiated claim, but Mengzi had a response to that criticism: The reason we fail to be good in our daily lives is that we have neglected to cultivate our innate virtue or have had most of that goodness stripped away from us by environmental factors, such as growing up under abusive conditions. As goodness diminishes, evil tendencies begin to manifest themselves. In the Parable of Ox Mountain, Mengzi explained how a fundamentally compassionate nature can be distorted into an inhuman one simply by disregarding the need to nourish it:

> The trees of Ox Mountain were once beautiful. But because it bordered on a large state, hatchets and axes besieged it. Could it remain verdant? Due to the respite it got during the day or night, and the moisture of rain and dew, there were sprouts and shoots growing there. But oxen and sheep came and grazed on them. Hence, it was as if it were barren. Seeing it barren, people believed that there had never been any timber there. But could this be the nature of the mountain? . . . Kongzi said: "Grasped then preserved; abandoned then lost. Its goings and comings have no fixed time. No one knows its home." Was it not the heart of which he spoke?[6]

With this little story, Mengzi effectively countered the argument that empirical evidence refutes the claim of humanity's innate goodness. The denuding of the mountain forest is similar to the way our environmental conditioning can strip away our natural goodness. Constant exposure to wickedness gradually degrades us. The parable also helps us understand what Mengzi may have meant when he asserted that humans are innately humane. The quality of goodness is like a plant shoot that requires careful tending in order to thrive. Compassion is native to the human heart but needs encouragement to mature and come to full expression. Even when it appears that people are evil to the core, shoots of humaneness still lurk just beneath surface, simply awaiting appropriate conditions to come forth. Mengzi thought the home was especially important in providing those conditions for nurturing goodness. The practice of filial piety and the parental love for the child were essential to actualize the potential for kindness.

---

6. *Mengzi* 6A8.1, 6A8.4, trans. Brian W. Van Norden (Indianapolis/Cambridge: Hackett, 2008), 152.

Because humans have this innate quality, they are naturally more responsive to a ruler who governs by virtue than one who rules by force. There is something within us that is naturally attracted to goodness. Seeing others acting morally and compassionately evokes within us the desire to do the same. Kindness begets kindness.

Mengzi was also responsible for drawing out some of the religious dimensions of Confucian thought. Confucius stated that Heaven had endowed him with virtue. It is not clear whether Confucius was referring to himself alone or simply including himself in an endowment given to all people. For Mengzi, it is unambiguous: all humans are furnished by Heaven with goodness. Our proper response to this gift is to foster those good qualities within, and by so doing, we serve Heaven itself. Serving Heaven is now less a matter of feeding choice cuts of sacrificial meat to the gods and more a matter of following the Way of Heaven in our daily lives. Heaven prefers the sacrifice of self to the sacrifice of sheep.

XUNZI

The chief opposition to Mengzi's views came from a Confucian who was born about the time Mengzi died. Xunzi lived most of his life in the third century (310–219 BCE), near the end of the Zhou dynasty and the East Asian Axial Age. Although he and Mengzi were probably more alike than different, Xunzi took exception to Mengzi's belief that human nature is basically inclined toward the good. This difference in views was really the first major disagreement within Confucian ranks.

Most interpreters of Xunzi understood him to be saying that human nature is fundamentally wicked, which was just the opposite of Mengzi's view. Because humans are basically evil, they naturally tend toward selfishness and a state of anarchy. Some interpreters tried to explain Xunzi's harsh position in a way that mitigated its negativity. They contended that Xunzi was too influenced by his political context—the Warring States Period—which they said made him overemphasize human depravity. Others suggested he was merely trying to balance Mengzi's overly sanguine estimation of humanity. Mengzi saw the doughnut, but Xunzi reminded everyone that there was also a hole.

Recent scholarship on Xunzi suggests he was not so much saying that humans are naturally immoral but that their natures are *amoral*, without moral inclinations one way or the other.[7] What we require, he thought, was a reformation of this amoral nature into one that has a refined moral sensitivity.

---

7. Ivanhoe, *Confucian Moral Self-Cultivation*, 32.

For this reason, humanity needs moral cultivation. Because the work of instilling morality was essentially a matter of creating a "second nature" for humans, moral cultivation would be a long, hard process, involving the family, educational institutions, and the state. Like Confucius, Xunzi thought the practice of rituals and social etiquette was central to this procedure. However, he did not see *li*—these rituals and manners—as a natural expression of human nature. In fact, he believed them to be artificial human constructs designed for the benefit of people living in society. This was a rather novel point of view. Xunzi was in effect saying the Way was rooted not in Heaven, but in human societies that deemed morality essential to their existence and welfare.

Xunzi advocated moral education, particularly an education that featured the study of tradition and ritual, just as Confucius and Mengzi did. And like the other two, Xunzi believed that human beings were morally perfectible. The difference seems to be in the way Mengzi and Xunzi conceptualized the process. For Mengzi, perfection came by nurturing a natural development. For Xunzi, it involved using humanly devised strategies for shaping amorphous raw material. At the end of the day, I think they both saw the doughnut.

> "For Mengzi, perfection came by nurturing a natural development. For Xunzi, it involved using humanly devised strategies for shaping amorphous raw material."

Confucianism after the Axial Age

Xunzi died near the end of the Zhou dynasty and the beginning of the Qin dynasty. After his death, Confucianism was temporarily suppressed by China's new rulers but ultimately emerged as the dominant cultural force that shaped the Chinese ethos for two thousand years.

Qin Dynasty

The Qin dynasty ruled briefly in the last quarter of the third century BCE (221–206 BCE). This dynasty marked the unification of China, but it was not a happy time for Confucians or Confucianism. The ruling philosophy of the Qin was Legalism, one of the many competing schools of thought in that age. Legalism was essentially a Machiavellian approach to governance. It embraced the use of military and police force as a way to keep order and relied on the centralization of authority. Because the Qin rulers perceived Confucianism as a threat to their sovereignty, Confucian texts were burned, and many Confucians themselves were tortured and killed. Although their regime was often cruel and lasted only fifteen years, the Qin rulers were impressive enough that the country of China is now known by their name.

HAN DYNASTY

The Qin rulers were succeeded by the Han dynasty, which lasted from 206 BCE to 220 CE. These were prosperous times for China and widely considered one of the greatest periods in Chinese history. Many in China today still refer to themselves as the "People of Han." The Han rulers not only reinstituted Confucianism; they made it the official state religion. It was during this dynasty that government officials were required to study the Confucian texts and pass civil service exams based on them. By the first century CE, sacrifices were offered to Confucius, and temples constructed in his honor.

Around this same time, Mahayana Buddhism was introduced to China, and Daoism began to establish institutional structures. From this point onward, Confucian history is intertwined with that of these other two religions. During the Song dynasty (960–1279 CE), for example, a new philosophical movement called Neo-Confucianism developed that attempted to synthesize Buddhism and Confucianism.

CURRENT ERA

Confucius's prestige has waxed and waned at various points in the last two thousand years, but overall, he has enjoyed overwhelming admiration from the Chinese. His philosophy was also influential in some of the countries with which the Chinese had significant contact, especially Korea, Japan, and Vietnam. In 1906, he was formally declared by imperial decree to be "Co-Assessor with the deities of Heaven and Earth."[8] That proclamation was made a few decades before the Communist takeover of China, led by Mao Zedong. Under Mao's rule, Confucius and Confucianism were portrayed as quaint, backward, and antirevolutionary. Mao did much to eradicate Confucianism in China, but now in the post-Mao era, Confucianism seems to be enjoying renewed interest among Chinese and others around the world.[9]

---

8. Hick, *An Interpretation of Religion*, 257.

9. See Annping Chin, *The Authentic Confucius: A Life of Thought and Politics* (New York: Scribner, 2007).

The Rise of Daoism

From Confucianism, we turn now to the last tradition we will consider, Daoism. In a way, our study of Confucianism has been a necessary prerequisite to the exploration of Daoism, because much of early Daoist philosophy was a response to the same social and political conditions addressed by Confucianism. The Daoists, however, took a very different approach to these circumstances. While Confucianism and Daoism shared much in common—such as the conviction that the problems of the Zhou dynasty were rooted in greed and an obsession with power—they proposed almost diametrically opposite solutions. In this way, Daoism emerged as a counterbalance to particular elements of Confucianism.

Philosophical and Religious Daoism

As we examine Daoism, the first item we must address is *which* Daoism we are talking about. Sinologists have often distinguished between what they called "philosophical Daoism," known by the Chinese word *daojia*, which means the school of the Way, and "religious Daoism," known as *daojiao*, the teaching of the Way. This distinction was part of the broader division that analysts made between the elite and folk dimensions of the Chinese traditions. Philosophical Daoism was part of the elite form of the tradition, oriented toward the literate and intellectual class, whereas religious Daoism was the folk expression, developed principally for the common people, whose needs and interests differed somewhat from those of a higher social station.

Philosophical Daoism is primarily associated with two classic texts, the *Daodejing* and the *Zhuangzi*, which came into being during the later Axial Age. Religious Daoism, which is also called the Daoist "church," was a later development, beginning around the second century ce, during the Han dynasty, when the tradition began to establish ecclesiastical structures, including priests, temples, rituals, hierarchies, and so on. On the surface, the two forms of Daoism appear quite different from one another, but the extent to which they really are different is an intriguing question in current

> "While Confucianism and Daoism shared much in common—such as the conviction that the problems of the Zhou dynasty were rooted in greed and an obsession with power—they proposed almost diametrically opposite solutions. In this way, Daoism emerged as a counterbalance to particular elements of Confucianism."

Daoist studies. The conviction seems to be growing among scholars that the distinction between the two forms of Daoism is not as sharp as once believed. Some have even suggested that the original distinction was a misguided fabrication of Western sinologists who were fascinated by the intellectual dimensions of the tradition but put off by its popular religious manifestations. This is an important issue, but it cannot detain us at this point, since the origins of religious Daoism fall outside the purview of the Axial Age.

Our attention, therefore, will focus on what has been called philosophical Daoism. Despite the terminology, philosophical Daoism had many religious components. What it lacked, as far as we can tell, were rituals, communities, clergy, gods, and similar features that are often associated with religion in the West. But like any religion, it provided a comprehensive view of the world that involved the sacred and a concept of the ultimate.

> "Despite the terminology, philosophical Daoism had many religious components. What it lacked, as far as we can tell, were rituals, communities, clergy, gods, and similar features that are often associated with religion in the West. But like any religion, it provided a comprehensive view of the world that involved the sacred and a concept of the ultimate."

LAOZI AND THE DAODEJING

Some have claimed that the origins of philosophical Daoism lie in the Shang dynasty or even before. Most scholars, however, date its beginnings to around the third or fourth century BCE, the time when its principal text, the *Daodejing*, was composed. This would be within or near the Warring States Period. It is evident that the text as we have it today appeared after the rise of Confucianism, because much of it was clearly intended as a refutation of central Confucian ideas.

According to Chinese tradition, the *Daodejing* was written by a man named Laozi, who lived in the sixth century and was several years older than Confucius. Some traditions suggest that Confucius was at one time a student of Laozi's, but that seems doubtful. A "biography" of Laozi written in the Han dynasty says he worked in the archives of the Zhou rulers. In his later years, he became increasingly frustrated with society and government and decided to leave the capital city to spend the remainder of his life in solitude and quiet contemplation. As he departed the city on a buffalo, the keeper of the Jade Gate asked him to leave a remembrance of his wisdom before he departed forever. Laozi dismounted, grabbed a brush, and quickly wrote out a text of five thousand characters. Then he got back on his buffalo and rode off. The text he left with the gatekeeper became the *Daodejing* or, as it is also known, the

Laozi. According to one account, Laozi continued his journey to India, where he appeared as the Buddha, and then on to West Asia, where he was known as Mani, the founder of Manichaeism.

Although the figure of the old man sadly departing society is a fitting image for philosophical Daoism, it has no historical basis. Today, virtually every scholar of Daoism believes Laozi to be a fiction, a creation of the early Daoists, intended probably to provide a counterpart to the figure of Confucius and an author for the *Daodejing*. The evidence for this conclusion is compelling. The stylistic and linguistic differences throughout the text make it quite evident that the *Daodejing* was the work of many minds, not of a single individual. These differences also suggest that the book was composed and edited over a long period of time, perhaps as long as a century. Furthermore, Laozi is not really a name in Chinese; it means "old master" or "old baby."

Whether or not Laozi was a historical person hardly matters. Of far greater interest are the ideas contained within the work that bears his name and the role they played in China's Axial Age. In the next chapter, we will begin our exploration of these novel ideas.

21

The *Daodejing*

The *Daodejing* is a book of mystery. We are not certain of its origins or authorship, nor is there much certainty about its meaning. The book's style is poetic, impressionistic, and evocative. And it is very brief, comprising eighty-one chapters, each no longer than a page. It was written, of course, in Chinese, which is notoriously ambiguous and difficult to translate. The combination of these factors resulted in a text that has been interpreted and translated in many, many ways. There are several hundred commentaries on the *Daodejing* written in Chinese, Korean, and Japanese, and it has been translated into English more times than any other book except the Bible.

THE *DAO*

Fortunately, the book's title is straightforward. *Daodejing* is translated as the *Classic (Jing) of the Way (Dao) and the Virtue (De)*. The difficulties begin when we start to parse the words *dao* and *de*.

DAO IN CHINESE PHILOSOPHY

Dao was a concept used by all forms of Chinese philosophy, not just the school that incorporated its name. It was often the topic of debate among and within the various schools. *Dao* is ordinarily translated as the "way" or the "path." In a formal, philosophical sense, *Dao* meant the ideal way of things or the manner in which something goes well, but different philosophers employed the word in different ways. When used by Confucius, the term meant the discipline of becoming a sage and the path to social harmony.

The *Daodejing* also employs the term in this manner but gives it another, more primary significance as well. For Daoists, the *Dao* meant "the way of nature," in a sense similar to the concept of ultimate reality. The *Daodejing* calls the *Dao* the "universe's mother," suggesting it is the source of all things and that which nurtures and sustains them. Of course, the metaphor of "mother" should not be taken too literally. The *Dao* is not a personal entity; it is not a god or goddess. Yet its jurisdiction is universal. It is the way of all things in the universe.

THE NAMED AND THE NAMELESS DAO

The *Daodejing* cautions us from the very beginning not to try to understand the *Dao* too clearly or concretely. It is not amenable to precise definition or complete understanding. According to the opening lines of the *Daodejing*, one of the most quoted passages in Chinese literature:

> The way that can be spoken of
> Is not the constant way;
> The name that can be named
> Is not the constant name.
> The nameless was the beginning of heaven and earth;
> The named was the mother of the myriad creatures.
> Hence always rid yourself of desires in order to observe its secrets;
> But always allow yourself to have desires
> in order to observe its manifestations.
> These two are the same
> But diverge in name as they issue forth.[1]

This rather cryptic passage suggests there are two aspects to the *Dao*: that which can be talked about and discussed and that which cannot. Both are part of the same reality. The deeper, eternal dimension is the latter, the ineffable and inscrutable Way. Like the Hindu concept of *nirguna* Brahman, this aspect of the *Dao* sets limits to human understanding and analysis, but it does not mean that the *Dao* is absolutely unattainable or unreachable. It simply indicates that observing the *Dao* goes beyond understanding and speaking of it. As with the idea of *saguna* Brahman, there is also an aspect of the *Dao* that *can* be discussed; the dimension of the *Dao* that is available to name and concept is its embodied form, its manifestation in the "myriad things," the many individual entities that make up the world. Despite the liberty to speak of the *Dao* in this respect, its ultimately inexpressible quality sets restrictions on what and how we may

---

1. *Tao Te Ching*, ch. 1, trans. D.C. Lau, (Harmondsworth, Middlesex, UK: Penguin Classics, 1963), 57.

speak of it. The Daoist conception of the *Dao* well fits the dictum of Irish poet William Butler Yeats: "Man can embody the truth, but he cannot know it."²

This tension between the named and the nameless *Dao* accounts for the form of the *Daodejing* itself. The medium is an almost perfect reflection of its message. As if heeding the admonition of chapter 1, the entire text is brief and terse, avoiding overanalysis and rational justification. Its poetic style appeals more to intuition and the imagination than to the discursive mind. Its paradoxes and rich imagery often confuse and confound.

"There are two aspects to the *Dao*: (1) the deeper, eternal dimension is the ineffable and inscrutable Way, and (2) the dimension of the *Dao* that is available to name and concept is its embodied form, its manifestation in the "myriad things," the many individual entities that make up the world."

In fact, the *Daodejing* rarely discusses the *Dao*. To quote chapter 56, "Those who know do not talk [about it]; those who talk [about it] do not know."³ Nowhere is it defined. Rather than describe the *Dao*, the book characterizes the persons or things that follow or possess it. We learn about the *Dao* mainly by reading about those who live in accord with it. When the text does refer to the *Dao*, it does so obliquely, through rich, multivalent images or through paradoxes, statements that frequently baffle more than they illuminate. Both strategies serve to stress the *Dao*'s indistinct and mysterious nature. "As for the Way," says chapter 21, "it is vague and elusive."⁴ Such a statement both reveals and conceals.

The twofold nature of the *Dao* helps to explain a paradox that runs throughout the *Daodejing*. Some passages depict the *Dao* as stable, eternal, and constant. Others describe it as the source of change, or perhaps even change itself. We could easily attribute this discrepancy to a difference of opinion among the various contributors to the text, but what if the difference is deliberate? It is more in keeping with the paradoxical nature of the *Dao* to affirm both its constant qualities and its changing qualities. The eternal, stable dimension can be identified as the primordial, ineffable *Dao*, as suggested by chapter 1. The changing *Dao* can then be understood as that which manifests

---

2. William Butler Yeats, in a letter to Lady Elizabeth Pelham (4 January 1939) quoted in David A. Ross, *A Critical Companion to William Butler Yeats: A Literary Reference to His Life and Work* (New York: Facts on File, 2009), 29.

3. *The Daodejing of Laozi*, ch. 56, trans. Philip J. Ivanhoe (New York: Seven Bridges, 2002), 59.

4. *The Daodejing of Laozi*, ch. 21, trans. Ivanhoe, 21.

through the myriad things, the items of the world that come into existence and pass out of it.

A particular Chinese icon may illuminate this paradox, although it will not explain or resolve it. Most Westerners are familiar with the *Taijitu*, although they may not know it by name. It is the symbol of two curved shapes, one black and one white, swirling around each other, together composing a circle. Inside the white swirl is a black circle; inside the black is a white one. The symbol represents the Chinese ideal of harmony and wholeness by suggesting that all things require an equal and opposite thing to maintain balance. One swirl can represent day, the other night. One can be life, the other death. One is female, the other male. One is hot, the other cold. And so on and on. The Chinese term for the black swirl is *yin*, and it represents everything that is dark, hidden, passive, receptive, yielding, cool, soft, and feminine. The white swirl is called *yang*, and it represents everything that is light, open, active, aggressive, controlling, hot, hard, and masculine. Sometimes the emblem is called the *yinyang* symbol. Like the *Dao*, the concept of *yinyang* was shared by Confucianism and Daoism and other Chinese schools of thought, and it probably antedated all of them. The *Dao* is the power underlying yin and yang.

Yin and yang are indeed opposites, but they are also complementary and interdependent. One cannot exist without the other, and each supports the other. Like all opposites, they have things in common (such as size and shape). And neither is completely what it appears to be. Yin is not wholly yin, and yang is not wholly yang. Each contains the seed of the other, as represented by the circle within each swirl. Life contains the seed of death; death contains the seed of life. Essentially, the relationship between yin and yang accounts for the phenomenon of change. Yin gives rise to yang; yang gives rise to yin. This is an eternal, harmonious pattern.

> "The Chinese term for the black swirl is *yin*, and it represents everything that is dark, hidden, passive, receptive, yielding, cool, soft, and feminine. The white swirl is called *yang*, and it represents everything that is light, open, active, aggressive, controlling, hot, hard, and masculine.... Yin and yang are indeed opposites, but they are also complementary and interdependent. One cannot exist without the other, and each supports the other."

The *Taijitu* icon represents the coexistence of change and constancy within the *Dao*. The *Dao* causes—or is—the change in the world, as represented in the swirling movement of yin and yang. Simultaneously, it is the source of balance, harmony, and wholeness, suggested by the circle, the symbol of eternity and completeness. The pattern of constant change is its unvarying quality. Understanding the importance of keeping yin and yang in balance is helpful in understanding the relationship of Daoism to Confucianism. Perhaps one reason for the rise of Daoism was to offset the very strong yang elements in Confucianism. For this reason, the *Daodejing* valorized many things associated with the yin side of life: depth, mystery, intuition, the feminine, receptivity, darkness, enigma, passivity. Throughout the text, yin items such as these are affirmed, as if to balance the yang emphasis in Confucianism.

Imagining the *Dao*

A few examples of the images associated with the *Dao* will illustrate how the *Daodejing* performs its work as a text. The principal function of the *Daodejing* is to bring the reader into accord with the *Dao*, and to do this, the work appeals to imagination rather than reason. Being in accord with the *Dao* means being both clear and confused.

Water

One of the frequent images for the *Dao* is water. In chapter 78, we read:

> In all the world, nothing is more supple or weak than water;
> Yet nothing can surpass it for attacking what is stiff and strong
> And nothing can take its place.
> That the weak overcomes the strong
> and the supple overcomes the hard,
> These are things everyone in the world knows

but none can practice.⁵

This passage suggests that the *Dao*, or the sage who abides in it, is yielding, flexible, and compliant, the qualities of yin. She, he, or it avoids strife and conflict and thus appears weak to others; yet what is apparently weak is in reality a powerful force, able to overcome resistance with patience. Imagine a stone in a mountain streambed. The water in the stream does not contend with the stone; water yields to its presence and flows around it. Over time, the water erodes the stone particle by particle, until it has dissolved into nothing. Thus, the weak and flexible conquers the stiff and strong.

EMPTINESS

Another common metaphor for the *Dao* is emptiness. Representing emptiness is a tricky thing, yet that is part of the point. Chapter 11 develops this image in several ways:

> Thirty spokes are joined in the hub of a wheel.
> But only by relying on what is not there,
> do we have use of the carriage.
> By adding and removing clay we form a vessel.
> But only by relying on what is not there,
> do we have use of the vessel.
> By carving out doors and windows we make a room.
> But only by relying on what is not there,
> do we have use of the room.
> And so what is there is the basis for profit;
> What is not there is the basis for use.⁶

Three ordinary items: the hub of a wheel, a clay vessel, and a room. All three would be considered yin things because of their receptivity and emptiness. Usually, we define and think about such things in terms of what they are made of. A room is four walls, a ceiling, and a floor. This chapter invites us to think about such things in a different way, not in terms of what is there, but what is not there. Four walls, a ceiling, and a floor form the *boundaries* of the room. The room is actually the empty space within the boundaries. The true usefulness of the room is its emptiness. The same is true for the clay vessel. It is made out of something, but what is of use is what is not there: the space inside the clay.

---

5. *The Daodejing of Laozi*, ch. 78, trans. Ivanhoe, 81.
6. *The Daodejing of Laozi*, ch. 11, trans. Ivanhoe, 11.

Likewise with the hub of a wheel. The spokes meet at the place of emptiness. Without the empty place, the wheel is useless; it cannot be connected to the carriage, and the wheel cannot turn.

These images encourage us to reorient our perceptions and to recognize the value of what appears to be valueless. This is one sense in which it is meaningful to say the *Daodejing* "performs." It does not just express an idea to be absorbed by the mind; it prompts us to think in an altogether different way and encourages us to be like water, to be empty.

Following the *Dao*

The *Daodejing* is clearly more than a book of insightful poems or evocative descriptions of nature and simple objects. Its images and tropes are metaphors for living life with the very grain of the universe. As a didactic text, it provides both implicit criticisms of other philosophies and ideals for living in accord with life's ultimate reality.

Contra Confucianism

Like the Confucians, the Daoists who composed the *Daodejing* understood the *Dao* as the appropriate way for humans to order and live their lives. The Daoists, however, thought of following the way as participating in the *Dao* of nature, the changes and rhythms of the universe and the natural world. The *Dao* of humanity *was* the *Dao* of nature; humans are part of the natural world. The Confucians, in contrast, connected the Way not with nature but with culture: the proper observances of tradition, ritual, and rites. For the Daoists, the very neglect of the Way of nature was at the root of society's misery. Early Daoism saw Confucianism not as the solution to the problem but as its very manifestation. Confucianism served to further alienate human beings from the *Dao* of nature by its anthropocentrism and close regulation of human relationships. To Daoists, Confucianism ruined the very spontaneity of life with its carefully thought-out rules and well-rehearsed rituals. Spontaneity, not calculation, was nature's way.

The Daoists used a Confucian strategy to criticize their opponents. They accused Confucianism of advocating the very things that led to the corruption of an earlier golden age. In the following passage from chapter 38, the Confucians are not mentioned by name, but the four major Confucian ideals are singled out, so there is no mistaking the reference:

When the Way was lost there was Virtue [*de*];

> When Virtue was lost there was benevolence [*ren*];
> When benevolence was lost there was righteousness [*yi*];
> When righteousness was lost there were the rites [*li*].
> The rites are the wearing thin of loyalty and trust,
> and the beginning of chaos.[7]

In better times there were no virtues, no talk of benevolence or compassion, no need to discriminate right from wrong, and no ritual to cultivate moral goodness. People naturally followed the Way and lived happily; they had no need for ethics or religion. The appearance of rites and moral discourse, the Daoists claimed, had only revealed the extent to which people had departed from the Way.

The solution to human suffering, the Daoists believed, was a return to the Way of the universe, to the Way of an older age. Initially, this advice was intended for the rulers and the ruling class, for like the Confucians, the Daoists believed that the welfare of society depended greatly on the character of its rulers. Consequently, much of the *Daodejing* expounds a social and political philosophy, particularly in the second half of the book. Many interpreters of the *Daodejing* have given scant attention to the political dimension of the text and instead emphasize its mystical component. As a result, the book is often read primarily as a manual for individual spiritual development. To understand the *Daodejing* thoroughly, however, we must attend to both its political and spiritual elements. We will start by outlining the Daoist ideal of the sage, the material that most explicitly pertains to personal spirituality. Then, in our next chapter, we will turn to the key aspects of its social and political philosophy.

THE DAOIST SAGE

It is easy to understand why many read the *Daodejing* primarily as text on spiritual development. The master who embodied the *Dao* was a mystic, one who sought to lose the perception of being an isolated, individual self by participation in a much greater reality, especially the natural world. This kind of mystical experience was encouraged by the *Daodejing* through specific practices and ways of being in the world.

---

7. *The Daodejing of Laozi*, ch. 38, trans. Ivanhoe, 41. Chinese transliterations of Confucian terms have been added.

BLENDING INTO THE WORLD

The first and perhaps most important of these practices involves diminishing the ego, relinquishing that part of who we are that craves attention, recognition, and control. In a statement reminiscent of Confucius, the *Daodejing* says, "sages know themselves but do not make a display of themselves; they care for themselves but do not revere themselves."[8] True sages, and hence truly good rulers, were not self-promoters. They were not interested in career advancement or receiving credit for their accomplishments. Their principal concern was the welfare of others. The Daoists believed that such self-effacement accorded with the Way of nature, and they pointed to Heaven and Earth as examples:

> Heaven is long lasting:
> Earth endures.
> Heaven is able to be long lasting
> and Earth is able to endure,
> because they do not live for themselves.
> . . . .
> This is why sages put themselves last and yet come first;
> Treat themselves as unimportant and yet are preserved.
> Is it not because they have no thought of themselves,
> that they are able to perfect themselves?[9]

Chinese philosophers often spoke of the triad of Heaven, Earth, and Humanity and of the ideal of maintaining balance among the three domains. In the Daoist view, human beings had caused a great imbalance in the triad by becoming too consumed with themselves as individuals and neglecting their place in the great nexus of the universe. "Sages" in contrast, "blend into the world," says the *Daodejing*.[10]

Blending into the world included living a simple existence, close to nature. Chinese literature contains countless stories about individuals who forsook the life of the city to wander the mountains and valleys of China or to settle in ramshackle huts on the side of a mountain, doing little else but enjoying the delights of nature. These individuals were the counterparts to India's *shramanas*, who also wandered or lived simply with little or no possessions. The Indian *shramanas* were more ascetic and inwardly focused than the Daoist sage, who

---

8. *The Daodejing of Laozi*, ch. 72, trans. Ivanhoe, 75.
9. *The Daodejing of Laozi*, ch. 7, trans. Ivanhoe, 7.
10. *The Daodejing of Laozi*, ch. 49, trans. Ivanhoe, 52.

was more likely to contemplate the moon and the stars on a warm summer night while sipping a cup of wine. The Daoists were not seeking to escape the vicious cycle of rebirth, nor did they consider the world covered by a veil of illusion. The world was real and, for those on the Way, was a source of genuine pleasure and insight.

Nevertheless, the *shramanas* of India and the sages of Daoism shared certain ideals. Both groups sought to minimize and eventually give up all self-centered desires and attachments. The *shramanas* did this to eliminate the karmas that kept them in bondage to *samsara*; the Daoists wanted to restore harmony between themselves and the world. The *Daodejing* characterizes the sages' decentering of self in language similar to the *Bhagavad Gita*: "They produce without possessing. They act with no expectation of reward."[11] To be without goal or objectives characterized the best sort of life. Toward the end of his life, Charles M. Schulz, the creator of "Peanuts," reflected, "My life has no purpose, no direction, no aim, no meaning, and yet I'm happy. I can't figure it out. What am I doing right?"[12] The Daoists would have understood.

EQUANIMITY

The Daoist sage also practiced a Buddhist-like equanimity based on the way of nature. Just as the *Dao* embraces and supports all things, so does the sage. He or she seeks to avoid the dualisms of good and bad, right and wrong, beautiful and ugly, praise and blame by welcoming everything, even those aspects of life that are conventionally shunned, ostracized, and rejected. The sage affirms, "I am good to those who are good; I am also good to those who are not good."[13]

The ideal of overcoming the dualisms created by human judgments had far-reaching consequences for Daoist thought and practice. In later Daoist art, for example, new aesthetic ideals revered the warped, twisted, imperfect, indistinct, impermanent, and asymmetrical. Such artistic values helped provide a balance to conventional forms of beauty. Like the metaphor of emptiness, the Daoist aesthetic was intended to challenge ordinary perceptions and modes of thinking. The strategy was subtly subversive because it served to draw attention to the fact that values were human constructions and not necessarily absolute, and perhaps not necessarily the best we are capable of.

---

11. *The Daodejing of Laozi*, ch. 2, trans. Ivanhoe, 2.

12. Charles M. Schulz quoted in *The Wordsworth Dictionary of Quotations*, 3rd ed. (Ware, Hertfordshire, UK: Wordsworth Editions, 1998), 371.

13. *The Daodejing of Laozi*, ch. 49, trans. Ivanhoe, 52.

22

Daoist Politics and Mysticism

The *Daodejing* was initially intended to provide advice on how to manage government rather than one's personal life. In this case, however, the paths for governing a state well and living one's life well coincide. The qualities that make one a sage are the exact qualities that characterize a good ruler. In short, the *Daodejing* advocates letting the wise rule.

Daoist Political Philosophy

Because the well-lived life according to the *Daodejing* is marked by a preference for yin qualities, the sagely ruler takes a minimalist approach to politics. In governance as well as the rest of life, the less one interferes the better.

Wu Wei

Nowhere is this convergence of political and spiritual excellence seen more clearly than in the Daoist practice of *wu wei*. *Wu wei* is often translated as "nonaction"; it might better be rendered as "actionless action" or "acting by not acting." *Wu wei* does not mean doing nothing; rather it suggests acting in the easiest, simplest way possible to accomplish what needs to be done. *Wu wei* has the appearance and feel of not acting at all.

The greatest obstacle to living in accord with the *Dao* is our compulsive desire to control. We want to regulate the course of our lives, coerce others to do what we want them to do, and rid ourselves of unpleasant situations. The practice of *wu wei* is the relinquishing of this tendency to control. It recognizes that the world—Heaven, Earth, and Humanity—follows its own path, its own rhythms. Letting the world follow its *Dao*—which it will do in any event—is the only way we will find harmony and happiness within ourselves and with others.

Why Government Is Bad

The recommendation of *wu wei* as a political strategy is connected with the Daoist analysis of suffering in ancient China. The *Daodejing* regards widespread misery as the result of governments that act contrary to the *Dao* of nature. Two characteristics of those governments seem to be especially at fault: first, the self-centeredness of the ruling class and its disregard for the well-being of the common people, and second, governments' tendency to interfere in the lives of individuals. These two traits are connected to one another. Chapter 75 explains the situation in very plain terms:

> "The greatest obstacle to living in accord with the *Dao* is our compulsive desire to control. We want to regulate the course of our lives, coerce others to do what we want them to do, and rid ourselves of unpleasant situations. The practice of *wu wei* is the relinquishing of this tendency to control."

The people are hungry because
those above eat up too much in taxes;
This is why the people are hungry.
The people are difficult to govern
because those above engage in action;
This is why the people are difficult to govern.
People look upon death lightly
because those above are obsessed with their own lives.
This is why people look upon death lightly.[1]

There is no doubt that the *Daodejing* regarded the extravagant self-indulgence of China's rulers as contributing to the problem:

The court is resplendent;
Yet the fields are overgrown.
The granaries are empty;
Yet some wear elegant clothes;
Fine swords dangle at their sides;
They are stuffed with food and drink;
And possess wealth in gross abundance.
This is known as taking pride in robbery.

---

1. *The Daodejing of Laozi*, ch. 75, trans. Ivanhoe, 78.

Far is this from the Way!²

Understanding the contemporary political situation in these terms, the *Daodejing* recommends that rulers themselves practice the natural way by reducing their desires and living simply. "In bringing order to the people or in serving Heaven," says chapter 59, "nothing is as good as frugality."³ The rulers' cultivation of the virtues of simplicity and nonaccumulation should become the basis for the policy of the government.

NONINTERFERENCE

This policy and the whole Daoist political philosophy can probably be summed up in this statement: "Ruling a great state is like cooking a small fish."⁴ Unless you have experience cooking small fish, you might find this simile a bit mystifying. The statement assumes that you know how delicate fish flesh becomes when it is cooked; it flakes off the bone very easily and, without proper attention, disintegrates. The implication for both cook and ruler is to refrain from interfering with the process. If you keep poking and turning the fish with chopsticks, it will break up and lose its savor. Intervene as little possible. Cook one side, turn over, and cook the other. That's it. That is *wu wei*.

As a political philosophy, this means that government should stay out of people's lives as much as possible. An English translation of the *Daodejing* was probably not available when Henry David Thoreau penned his essay on "Civil Disobedience," but the first paragraph of that famous essay precisely expresses the early Daoist view of governance: "I heartily accept the motto,—'That government is best which governs least'; and I should like to see it acted up to more rapidly and systematically." The *Daodejing* clearly advocates a minimalist government as envisioned by Thoreau. But Thoreau takes this idea even further: "Carried out, it finally amounts to this, which I also believe,—'That government is best which governs not at all'; and when men are prepared for it, that will be the kind of government which they will have. Government is at best but an expedient; but most governments are usually, and all governments are sometimes, inexpedient."⁵ When he takes this position, Thoreau unwittingly aligns himself with Zhuangzi, whose interpretation of Daoism we will take up shortly. Both Thoreau and Zhuangzi would have

---

2. *The Daodejing of Laozi*, ch. 53, trans. Ivanhoe, 56.
3. *The Daodejing of Laozi*, ch. 59, trans. Ivanhoe, 62.
4. *The Daodejing of Laozi*, ch. 60, trans. Ivanhoe, 63.
5. Henry David Thoreau, "Civil Disobedience," in *Walden and Civil Disobedience*, ed. Owen Thomas (New York: W. W. Norton, 1966), 224.

thought that until governments are eliminated altogether, the best we can hope is for them to leave us alone.

THE RULER AS SAGE

As a result of noninterference, leaving things alone, everyone benefits. The sage-ruler affirms to himself:

> "I do nothing and the people transform themselves;
> I prefer stillness and the people correct and regulate themselves;
> I engage in no activity and the people prosper on their own;
> I am without desires and the people simplify their own lives."[6]

It is not exactly clear from the text how *wu wei* was able to effect these profound social changes. Was it because the ruler made spiritual cultivation his chief priority and so modeled the same for the people? Was it because the Daoists believed in the near-magical power of accumulated virtue, as did Confucius and other Chinese of the past? Was it because the ruler's trust in the people inspired them to be worthy of the confidence he placed in them? Or did the early Daoists have a kind of sentimental and romantic view of the common people, like that of Leo Tolstoy and Mao Zedong, leading them to believe the ordinary folk were naturally more virtuous than the scholars and aristocrats? Any of these are plausible.

In the end, the *way* it works is not nearly as important as *that* it works. Unfortunately, the Daoists had no contemporary examples of virtuous leaders to support that claim and could only appeal to the legendary rulers of bygone eras. But Daoism and Confucianism were agreed on the point: for the ruler to diminish his selfish desires and the pursuit of power—whether by *wu wei* or *li*—was essential to the country's well-being.

ZHUANGZI

In the figure of Zhuangzi, however, Daoism—or at least Zhuangzi's interpretation of it—seems to have shifted its interests from the political arena to an exclusive focus on individual spirituality. Zhuangzi does not specifically address the ruling class but the individual seeking to live in accord with the *Dao*.

Most scholars think Zhuangzi was an actual person—and a quirky one at that. He was said to be totally unconcerned with status, physical appearance, and comfort. Zhuangzi's traditional dates are 369–286 BCE, which make him

---

6. *The Daodejing of Laozi*, ch. 57, trans. Ivanhoe, 60.

a contemporary of Mengzi and situates him in the Period of Warring States. Unlike virtually every other philosopher of this period, Zhuangzi had little to say about the political and social realms, as if he considered them not in the least important. According to legend, Zhuangzi was offered a high-ranking position in the court of a King Wei. Zhuangzi laughed in the face of the messenger who brought the invitation and compared the job to an ox that was well cared for, dressed in embroidered cloth, and led to the temple to be slaughtered. He said he would rather enjoy life as a pig in the mud.[7]

Perhaps Zhuangzi had become jaded by the political situation of his day and had lost hope that things would ever change, even under the rule of a Daoist sage. Or maybe he simply believed that society did not matter; to follow the *Dao* was an individual and not a communal concern. Nonetheless, it is clear that Zhuangzi was inspired by the old masters who had written and compiled the *Daodejing*, although he did not seem to accept their political philosophy. Perhaps he thought of himself as taking their insights to their logical conclusions. In any event, Zhuangzi is the principal person responsible for drawing out and emphasizing the mystical components of Daoism.

Zhuangzi is credited with writing what are called the "Inner Chapters" of the book that bears his name; others, it seems, wrote the so-called "Outer" and "Miscellaneous" chapters of the book. The *Zhuangzi* is a masterpiece of literature, and it is unfortunate that it is not better known in the West. There are far fewer translations of the *Zhuangzi* than the *Daodejing*, but many consider the *Zhuangzi* to be the superior work. It is provocative, entertaining, and often humorous. Much of the humor derives from the way Zhuangzi and the later writers enjoy poking fun at Confucius and other leading philosophers of the day. Unlike the dense and terse *Daodejing*, the *Zhuangzi* has a free-flowing, easy style that is consistent with its message. Though written in prose, it has a rhythmic, poetic quality.

Let us briefly examine several of the Zhuangzi's salient themes and illustrate them with passages from the text. Most of Zhuangzi's ideas were anticipated in the *Daodejing*, but the *Zhuangzi* highlights these concepts and expresses them with a vividness and concreteness that the earlier text lacked.

A fundamental part of Daoist practice was, of course, the acceptance of change, one of the basic features of the *Dao*. Like the Buddha, the early Daoists believed resistance to change was a primary cause of suffering. The *Zhuangzi* not only cautions against such resistance, it actually encourages a

---

7. Victor H. Mair, trans. *Wandering on the Way: Early Taoist Tales and Parables of Chuang Tzu* (New York: Bantam, 1994), xxxii.

hearty welcoming of the impermanence of life: "Before long, Sir Come fell ill. Gasping and on the verge of death, he was surrounded by his wife and children who were weeping. Sir Plow, who went to call on him, said to his family, 'Shush! Go away! Do not disturb transformation!' Then, leaning against the door, he spoke to Sir Come: 'Great is the Transforming Creator! What next will he make of you? Where will he send you? Will he turn you into a rat's liver? Will he turn you into a bug's leg?'"[8] Zhuangzi conveyed exhilaration at the prospect of change, even the change that occurs with death. Apparently, Zhuangzi did not see the change brought by death as a form of reincarnation or as transport to a heavenly realm. He regarded it in material terms, as the physical elements of the body now take shape in another form. There seems to be some question about the extent to which Zhuangzi embraced a materialist view of the world; at one point he even suggested that the mind dies with the body. In any event, whatever is left of us becomes something else, and he found that concept thrilling.[9] He obviously enjoyed the spontaneity and surprise associated with the movements of the *Dao*.

As the story indicates, Zhuangzi especially encouraged the acceptance of death and saw this as vital to happiness in life. A story from the Outer Chapters reports Zhuangzi's response to the death of his own wife. Shortly after she died, Zhuangzi was visited by a friend who intended to console him. The friend was astounded to see that Zhuangzi was not only *not* in mourning but was sitting on the floor, beating on a basin and singing a song. The scene scandalized the friend, and he asked Zhuangzi the meaning of it all. Zhuangzi said:

> "When she first died, how could I of all people not be melancholy? But I reflected on her beginning and realized that originally she was unborn. Not only was she unborn, originally she had no form. Not only did she have no form, originally she had no vital breath. Intermingling with nebulousness and blurriness, a transformation occurred and there was vital breath; the vital breath was transformed and there was form; the form was transformed and there was birth; now there has been another transformation and she is dead. This is like the progression of the four seasons—from spring to autumn, from winter to summer. There she sleeps blissfully in another chamber. If I were to have followed her weeping and wailing, I think it would have been out of keeping with destiny, so I stopped."[10]

8. *Wandering On the Way* (6.5), 58–59.
9. *Wandering on the Way* (2.3), 13–14.
10. *Wandering on the Way*, (18.2), 168–69.

For Zhuangzi, the acceptance of impermanence entailed seeing all points of view as relative and tentative. Like the Jains, he cautioned against making absolute judgments, not because of the defilements of the soul but for the simple reason that things change. What appears today as the worst of news may turn out tomorrow to be a blessing in disguise. As the *Daodejing* says:

> Good fortune rests upon disaster;
> Disaster lies hidden within good fortune.
> Who knows the highest standards?[11]

The following story is a Daoist tale, although not attributed to Zhuangzi. Yet it dramatically illustrates his point:

> There is a story of a farmer whose horse ran away. That evening the neighbors gathered to commiserate with him since this was such bad luck. He said, "Maybe so, maybe not." The next day the horse returned, but brought with it six wild horses, and the neighbors came exclaiming at his good fortune. He said, "Maybe so, maybe not." And then, the following day, his son tried to saddle and ride one of the wild horses, was thrown, and broke his leg. Again the neighbors came to offer their sympathy for the misfortune. He said, "Maybe so, maybe not." The day after that, conscription officers came to the village to seize young men for the army, but because of the broken leg the farmer's son was rejected. When the neighbors came to say how fortunately everything had turned out, he said, "Maybe so, maybe not."

The practice for overcoming the tendency to rush to judgment is what Zhuangzi called emptying the mind, or "sitting and forgetting." The idea is based largely on the metaphor of emptiness that was used in the *Daodejing*. Zhuangzi thought that much of our misery is caused by our preconceptions, which predispose us to see the world in particular ways, ways that disrupt our capacities to respond out of spontaneity to whatever life throws our way. These prejudices are what compel us to evaluate things before it is time. The discipline he encouraged was quite similar to meditation practices of the Buddha and to the form of Buddhism that would develop later in dialogue with Daoism, Zen. The consistent practice of sitting and forgetting allows the practitioner to relinquish habitual beliefs and patterns of thinking. It enables him or her to

---

11. *The Daodejing of Laozi*, ch. 58, trans. Ivanhoe, 61.

perceive the world afresh with openness to the present moment and freedom from precalculated responses.

We cannot leave our discussion of the *Zhuangzi* without mentioning the most famous story within it, the butterfly dream. Many people who know nothing else about *Zhuangzi* have heard this brief anecdote: "Once upon a time Zhuang Zhou dreamed he was a butterfly, a butterfly flitting about happily enjoying himself. He didn't know that he was Zhou. Suddenly he awoke and was palpably Zhou. He didn't know whether he was Zhou who had dreamed of being a butterfly or a butterfly dreaming that he was Zhou. Now, there must be a difference between Zhou and the butterfly. This is called the transformation of things."[12] This little story has been interpreted in many ways. A popular contemporary Western interpretation sees the parable as an argument for the relativity of views, and hence the relativity of all claims to truth. Since we are all in a state of not knowing for certain whether we are dreaming or awake, how can we be sure of anything? Who is to say the reality of a dreaming butterfly is less real than the waking reality of a man, or the dreaming reality of a man is less real than the waking reality of a butterfly?

Early Chinese commentaries on the story see it in a different way altogether. In English, the story is usually presented from the perspective of Zhou, who is reflecting after waking from the dream, but in the original Chinese, Zhou is not reflecting on the dream; he has forgotten it. The story is told from the perspective of an omniscient narrator and not by Zhou. The narrator knows that Zhou was dreaming, but Zhou does not. In the commentator's view, the story is an allegory about life and death, which are compared to waking and dreaming. The commentator thinks being awake and dreaming are both real phases of existence, as are life and death. It is presumptuous to assume that death is a wholly negative experience. Who knows? In death we may be as happy as a butterfly flitting about without a care, unaware of a previous existence or identity. This may be why the story ends with the line "This is called the transformation of things."[13]

Daoism after the Axial Age

These few remarks on the *Zhuangzi* bring to a close our examination of early philosophical Daoism. Before we leave the tradition altogether, though, let us consider so-called religious Daoism that developed after the Axial Age. The

---

12. *Wandering on the Way* (2.14), 24.
13. This interpretation is based on Hans-Georg Moeller, *Daoism Explained* (Chicago: Open Court, 2004), 44–55.

Daoist church comes into being in the second century CE, during the Han dynasty. Confucianism had just been established as the official religion of the state, and Mahayana Buddhism had finally arrived in China. It was partly in response to Buddhism that Daoism began to develop ecclesiastical structures and assume new beliefs and interests. Prompting these developments were several popular movements that predicted a Second Coming of Laozi and his establishment of a *taiping*, a great peace, similar to the Christian expectation of the Second Coming of Jesus. By this time Laozi had been deified and considered the incarnation of the *Dao*. Temples were built, and sacrifices made in his honor, just as had been done for Confucius. Soon, several Daoist devotees began to receive revelations from Laozi. One man, Zhang Daoling, received instructions on ritual, meditation, healing, and moral observances. These teachings became the basis for a new, popular Daoist movement called the Celestial Masters.

As Daoism spread through China, it came into contact with the indigenous folk religions and tended to blend with them. In some areas, the Daoists encountered Chinese alchemists who were experimenting with the magical potential of various substances. By this time, Daoists had already developed a keen interest in prolonging life and believed that certain substances might actually confer immortality. Many Daoists believed they had found this substance in cinnabar, which they used to mix elixirs of immortality.

With these new developments in religious Daoism, the tradition became firmly embedded in the popular religious practices of ordinary Chinese. Philosophical Daoism continued its existence in various forms, experiencing moments of prominence and patronage, such as the Tang dynasty, and moments of ridicule and obscurity, usually when Confucianism was in the ascendancy. Good times and hard times: such is the way of the *Dao*.

Conclusion: Reflections on the Axial Age

More than two thousand years now separate us from the Age of Sages. As we pause to reflect on our study of this era, we might well ask what significance this period has for us today as persons of the twenty-first century. Answers to this question will fall into two categories: historical and theological. In the first category, this study of the Axial Age has revealed certain dynamics involved in the phenomenon of human religiousness. I will summarize these general principles governing religion in history. Under the category of theology, our study has disclosed the particular ways in which the axial sages understood human existence and prescribed ideals for living life. The broad shape of their visions for authentic human life will be reviewed, drawing special attention to those features of their perspectives that seem most relevant for us today.

The Axial Age and Our Understanding of Religion

We begin by asking what the study of the Axial Age teaches us about religion as a phenomenon in human life. First and perhaps most obviously, our examination has made it abundantly evident that religions change and develop over time. Even Jainism, which purports to be an eternal religion, propagating the same substantial message age after age, still acknowledges that the form of that message has to change to fit the needs of the persons to whom it is addressed and that human beings interpret aspects of that message in different ways. Although the message of religious traditions is often grounded in the eternal, religions are human creations, products of finite and transitory minds that are subject to the vagaries of time.

Frequently, the changes we witnessed in our study were quite dramatic and could be interpreted as even contrary to the intention of those who first laid the tradition's foundations. The Buddha, for example, constantly emphasized that he was not a god but a human being who had perfected himself through his own efforts and who encouraged his disciples to do the same, yet later he was conceived to be a divine being who assisted individuals to escape *samsara*. The founder's or founders' message and the way that message is received and practiced can be very different things. But it would be a mistake to think such developments are inauthentic or illegitimate. There is no world religion in which the founder's or founders' original vision did not undergo some refinement or even complete reinterpretation. This fact is simply inherent in the nature of religions and, indeed, of all human institutions.

Religions develop and change because they are not self-contained entities unrelated to other domains of human experience. They are profoundly shaped by—and they profoundly shape—human culture on many levels. The Confucian traditions arose in response to difficult political and economic times in ancient China and then in turn became the philosophical and religious basis for training government officials. Zoroastrianism was a reform movement responding to widespread lawlessness and later evolved into the Iranian state religion that lasted for centuries. Buddhism and Jainism began as ways to cope with *samsara*, an idea wrought within ancient Hinduism, and then influenced the Hindu traditions by insisting on the centrality of nonviolence.

These examples remind us that distinctions between religions and other aspects of culture cannot always be sharply drawn. The Chinese and Indian kings employed astrologers and sages as state officials. Daoist thought was the basis for Chinese medicine. Greek aesthetic ideals shaped the first anthropomorphic representations of the Buddha. It is not really until modernity that religion and the rest of culture came to be thought of as sharply separated. That dichotomy, our study proves, is clearly misguided.

Nor should we think of religions as isolated from one another. They constantly interact in positive and negative ways. The negative ways that religions interact—crusades, pogroms, jihads—are quite familiar, but the constructive dimensions of those interactions are less well known. Our study of the Axial Age has brought to light some of the creative aspects of interreligious encounter. Daoism developed in dialogue with Confucianism, and Buddhism in dialogue with what came to be called Hinduism. Both Daoism and Buddhism adopted many of the ideas and practices of their counterparts and reinterpreted and rejected others. Then, centuries later, the encounter of Buddhism and Daoism helped produce another form of spirituality, Ch'an (or Zen, to use its better-known Japanese name).

It is also evident that different religions functioned differently in different cultures. Not only was there a general shift in religious function from cosmic maintenance to personal transformation in the Axial Age; we have also seen how different axial religions functioned differently within their societies. Throughout much of South Asia, Buddhists have relied on the teachings of the Buddha to guide them toward the ultimate goal of release from *samsara*, but these same Buddhists prayed to the gods of Hinduism for everyday favors such as healing and protection from evil. A Chinese bureaucrat might have practiced Confucianism during his work hours and come home to enjoy life as a Daoist. Recognizing the ways that different religions affect an individual's life differently challenges our modern Western ways of thinking about religions as being mutually exclusive of one another. A principal identification with one religious perspective is no reason a person cannot participate in some fashion in other religions.

This fact, which we observed in the Axial Age, still has contemporary resonance. In India today, some Hindus worship at the tombs of Muslim saints, and some Muslims celebrate the Hindu and Jain festival of Diwali. One Hindu acquaintance of mine, an immigrant to the United States, began to attend a local Roman Catholic church to worship her goddess through the church's image of the Virgin Mary when there was no Hindu temple in her area. In the West, we are now seeing an increasing incorporation of features from other religions into some forms of Christianity and Judaism. A growing number of churches and synagogues in Europe and North America have begun to offer courses in yoga, tai chi, and meditation, although they tend to downplay the religious connections of these disciplines by calling them "exercise," "relaxation," and "stress reduction" classes. It is inevitable that we will continue to see more of this kind of borrowing between religions in the future. Whether such appropriation will have an effect on the substantive aspects of Christianity and other religions that have traditionally tried to remain exclusive is yet to be seen. But sharing ideas and practices among religions is a fact of history.

THE THEOLOGY OF THE AXIAL AGE

To begin our examination of the theological importance of the Axial Age, let us review the dynamics of this era in broad strokes. As these driving impulses come into greater relief, we begin to see the lessons of the Axial Age that we are still learning to learn, as well as the ways this epoch fails to speak to us.

As we have seen, the Axial Age was the historical moment in which the "self" makes its appearance. Prior to the axial period, human beings did not experience themselves as autonomous individuals with agency and moral responsibility in the way most of us now do. The Axial Age did indeed mark a turn in the way human beings thought about being human. Of course, this change in thinking did not occur all at once. There were intimations of individual selfhood in very rare instances in the preaxial period, but in the Axial Age, the experience of the self became increasingly common in the axial centers. That the sense of selfhood was becoming more extensive is reflected in the way certain sages democratized spiritual attainment. The Buddha and Mahavira, in particular, contended that perfection and liberation were possible for anyone, not simply the men of upper castes, as had traditionally been assumed. And although Confucius oriented his teachings toward the ruling elites and thought the abilities of common people were rather limited, he nonetheless believed that ordinary folk had an important role in fostering the harmony of family and society. He even welcomed into his school men of all social and economic classes, provided they were passionate about learning. The movement toward spiritual equality was reflected in the debate surrounding the true meaning of nobility. Against the tide of their culture's history, the Indian *shramanas*, the Buddha, Mahavira, and Confucius all argued that nobility was not a matter of birth but of spiritual quality.

Yet as the sense of self became more widespread, it also became more problematic. Human self-consciousness brought with it a feeling of greater freedom as well as greater responsibility. Both aspects of selfhood were reflected in new conceptual developments of the axial sages. Zoroaster's call for people to choose between the principle of good and the powers of evil assumed that humans had the freedom to make this choice and that they were accountable for the choice they made. The doctrine of karma, espoused by all the Indian sages presented here, was based on this same principle of freedom and accountability. Karma implied that everything the individual did, thought, or said could be significant. That fact could promote a sense of liberating power through knowing that one's destiny is in one's own hands, or it could generate a tremendous feeling of burden through knowing that one's destiny is in one's own hands! The Confucian discipline of moral self-cultivation also assumed this fundamental dynamic of freedom and responsibility. As individual persons, the axial sages tell us, we can and should behave morally because our welfare as individuals and the welfare of society depend on it.

To say that the self becomes a problem, however, means more than simply a greater sense of responsibility and the burden that entails. The problem of the self is also its imperialism, the tendency to imagine that one's self is at the center of the world and has the right to arrogate unto itself whatever it pleases. This egocentrism was a vital concern of every axial sage we have encountered, and each one of them proposed a solution. This fundamental concern accounts for why the basic function of religion during this era (as well as in the postaxial age) is characterized as personal transformation. The self-centered individual poses a problem that requires some manner of change. Zoroaster saw the problem of the self in the lawlessness of the *drujvants*, the ones whose arrogance led them to follow the god of the Lie and slay other human beings to gain wealth and power. His solution was for people to orient their lives to the power of good, which involved subordinating oneself to will of Ahura Mazda.

In the Upanishads, acting out of selfish desires with attachment to the results of one's actions created the negative karma that kept one bound to incessant reincarnation. One of the solutions offered for this problem of selfhood was identifying with a "higher" sense of self, that is, with Brahman or the *atman*. In so doing, one could overcome the fears and attachments that resulted from regarding the self as a transient body, an unstable mind, or a separate and lonely individual by recasting the self as eternal and consubstantial with ultimate reality. While the Buddha saw virtually the same problems in selfhood that the Upanishadic sages did, his solution was not to create a larger, more permanent sense of self but to eliminate the concept of selfhood altogether. "Self," he said, is an illusion and an unwholesome way of thinking about human life. He promoted a comprehensive slate of practices for eradicating the misapprehension of separate selfhood that was at the root of all suffering.

The Chinese thinkers also had concerns with the self. Confucius advocated "subduing the self," that is, not destroying the sense of self altogether but subordinating its wishes to the welfare of the greater human community. His practices of *li* were specifically tailored to instill the virtues of reverence, humility, and gratitude. Daoism fostered an even greater form of self-effacement. "Blending into the world" was the Daoist ideal. Although philosophical Daoism was essentially an individualist religion, especially as it was interpreted by Zhuangzi, its ideal was a greatly diminished sense of self. The Daoist sage was one who gave up all attempts to control the world and society and tried to let go and let be, trusting in the way of nature.

If there is anything on which one could say the Axial Age religions seemed to agree, it may be this point: that an unbridled sense of self leads to devastating consequences for the individual, society, and the world. And although they proposed many different ways of understanding and addressing this concern, the response of the axial sages seems equally unanimous: practice self-awareness and compassion.

Ironically perhaps, the axial teachers contended that a central component of relinquishing self-centeredness was attaining greater self-consciousness. One of the hallmarks of the Axial Age, especially in South and East Asia, was the development and refinement of practices intended to enhance awareness of interior experience. The meditative techniques of the Indian *shramanas*, the Buddha, and Mahavira, as well as the contemplative exercises of Confucianists and Daoists, are perhaps the clearest instances of this inward turn. Yet the same focus on interiority is witnessed in the traditions that emphasized ritual. Whereas the early Indo-Aryans concentrated on the outward dimensions of their rites, in the later Vedas, we find a growing concern with the sacrificer's mental state and self-consciousness. Throughout their teachings, the axial sages urged methodical and disciplined activity oriented toward discovering the truth about the self.

The quest for self-understanding was always coupled in the minds of the axial sages with the practice of compassionate behavior. Buddhism identified wisdom (the virtue of seeing things as they are) and compassion (willing the happiness of all beings) as the two wings of the tradition. The great Sage of China put it this way: "The humane person, wanting to establish himself, helps others establish themselves, and wanting to be successful, helps others to be successful. Taking one's own feelings as a guide may be called the method of humaneness."[1] Knowing oneself is the essential guide to the exercise of compassion. And compassion, we learn from the sages, is the way we keep our overweening self in check. Not only does compassion rein in our selfish desires through thoughts and acts of generosity, but when compassion is self-directed—as the axial teachers said it must be—we cultivate the quality of humility, because we understand that the self-centered life is an unhappy one.

INSIGHTS OF THE AXIAL AGE FOR TODAY

The sages of the Axial Age forged and taught their wisdom in a time of great cultural and social turmoil, not unlike our own turbulent era. In the face of change and uncertainty, conflict and dissension, they professed a vision of mindfulness and humaneness. For us today, this message is more relevant than ever.

Although their message of compassionate and mindful virtue was revolutionary for its time, few today would take issue with it. Since our lives have been decisively shaped by the insights of axial thinkers, it is not surprising that we take much of their teachings as normative. Yet though we profess admiration for the qualities of self-awareness and humaneness, what our times lack is a broad and deeply rooted commitment to their cultivation. "Know thyself." "Love thy neighbor." We believe in these precepts, but we find it difficult to practice them. What the ancient teachers tell us is that accepting the truth of the message is merely the first step on the long path of implementation and perfection. We have taken the first step, no doubt. Yet after more than two thousand years, we still falter as we try to tread the way of virtue. Perhaps

---

1. *Analects* 6.30. My rendition.

because religion in the modern age has too often become a matter of intellectual assent to beliefs about god, we find it too difficult to practice virtue in the dedicated and risky fashion taught by the sages millennia ago. Perhaps we have been so schooled in the theology of salvation by faith that we have wrongly concluded that deeds have little place in our spirituality.

Against the cheap grace propounded by many modern religious institutions, the teachers of the Axial Age extolled the necessity of hard work and self-discipline in matters of virtue. Simply expecting humaneness to appear because it may be innate to our nature or because we think we ought to be nicer to others is insufficient. Whether compassion and mindfulness are intrinsic to what we are, as the Buddha and Mencius thought, or are qualities that must be formed out of an inchoate nature, as Xunzi believed, the Axial Age thinkers all considered specific practices to be essential to becoming good and happy people. Yet more than simply urging us to nurture virtue, they showed us how. Our study has revealed a wellspring of techniques that can be appropriated in modern life. What our world still has not learned is that the disciplined cultivation of compassion and wisdom must become the central pursuit of our lives.

Yet while the axial sages were on the mark with this insight, their teachings were not complete, and we would be wrong to think that the lessons of this era contain everything needed to bring happiness to the modern world. For in the transition to the Axial Age, something profoundly important was lost, and something else had yet to be fully grasped.

The shift in religious function from cosmic maintenance to personal transformation was a positive change in the sense that human beings no longer needed to shoulder the burden of supplying the gods with food or performing ceremonies in order to keep the sun coming up or the cattle fertile. The downside of relieving this burden, however, was the fact that humans began to lose the sense of needing to collaborate in the maintenance of the world. The turn toward self-transformation ultimately resulted in a loss of concern with keeping the world in good working order. Postaxial humans have generally adopted the attitude that the world can take care of itself, allowing us to do whatever we wish to it and with it. At least now, over the last half century, we have become increasingly aware of the problems caused by such violence to the earth. One lesson to be gained from our study, then, is the need to reincorporate cosmic maintenance into postaxial religion in ways that go beyond preaxial theology and yet strengthen the human sense of connectedness with the natural world.

Another deficiency of the axial transformation has not become evident until modernity. In the modern era, especially within the last 150 years, human beings have become more sensitive to the corporate dimension of our existence. Due largely in part to the insights of Western social sciences, we have started to appreciate more fully the role of society in shaping human experience. Today, we readily speak of the "social construction of reality" and are more aware than ever of the manner in which structural injustices—racism, sexism, genocide, slavery, economic disparity, global hunger, and the like—perpetuate the unhappiness that the axial sages sought to address. But during their era, these sorts of structural injustices were poorly understood, if at all. The thinker whose ideas seem most attuned to the social dimension of human experience was Confucius. Yet there is nothing in the *Analects*, for example, to suggest that Confucius had any awareness of the destructive nature of sexism (although he seems fully aware of the problems of economic inequality). We cannot fault the axial sages for not being far enough ahead of their times. But we can recognize that appropriating the message of awareness and compassion must not be limited to the goal of personal transformation alone. Personal discipline is essential, even fundamental, to the insights of the axial sages, yet it must be complemented with the unique discernments of the modern period. It would, in fact, violate the critical spirit of the Axial Age to believe we should adopt the teachings of that era wholesale. The Buddha reminds us never to accept anything as true simply because it is traditional or is professed by well-respected teachers.

Taking seriously the social dimension of human experience would mean seeking ways to apply the practices of mindfulness and humaneness in institutional, commercial, and political settings. Perhaps it is time for us to begin to ask ourselves what it would mean to practice compassion at the level of international and national governance. Perhaps it would mean discovering ways to use our educational institutions to teach ways of being more kindhearted and more self-aware. Perhaps businesses and corporations might learn to measure their successes not in terms of profit but in terms of how well they promote universal well-being. The possibilities for imagining humaneness at the corporate and institutional levels are prodigious. But at this moment in history, we have barely begun to explore these opportunities. What is required is an extensive recognition that the virtues of mindfulness and compassion should inform not only personal transformation but social reform as well.

If axial thinkers seem most closely to converge on the matter of practice, then belief is the area where they seem most sharply to diverge. The Axial Age offered a wide array of ways to conceptualize ultimate reality. Zoroaster taught a theology centered upon one supreme divine being. The Indian *shramanas* imagined a reality beyond the gods that they called Brahman. The Buddha termed the absolute reality *nibbana*, and the Chinese called it the *Dao* or sometimes Heaven. The development of these conceptions was a product of what Eisenstadt calls transcendental consciousness, the effort to grasp the world in a comprehensive sense by reflecting on the powers that might ground and explain it.[2] These transcendental concepts, however, did not necessarily supplant preaxial images of and ideas about the divine. Usually, concepts like Brahman and the *Dao* simply took their place alongside the more ancient ways of thinking of the divine anthropomorphically or in other forms. Hence, Confucius acknowledged the importance of sacrificing to the gods and ancestors, but he was reticent about them, to the chagrin of some of his protégés. Likewise, the Buddha did not dispute the existence of the *devas*; he merely thought they were of no benefit for realizing ultimate bliss.

Despite divergent ways of thinking about absolute reality, our examination of these many traditions suggests a point upon which some strands of axial thought seem to agree: the conviction that the highest reality is beyond our grasp. We find traces of this idea in the Confucian reluctance to speculate about Heaven or speak of "gods and prodigies." This same reluctance is evident in the Buddha's refusal to answer certain metaphysical questions about the origin and extent of the universe and the realization of *nibbana*. We see it in the concept of *nirguna* Brahman, the ultimate reality that so exceeds the mind that the Upanishadic sages only hint at it by saying what it is not. The first chapter of the *Daodejing* indicates that the *Dao* has both nameable and unnameable aspects.

Drawing together these strands of thought, we see within the Axial Age a trajectory toward recognizing and preserving a sense of ultimate mystery against the countervailing tendency within all religious traditions to conceal what they do not know. That may sound paradoxical, since "mystery" seems to be religion's stock-in-trade. But from the perspective of the axial sages, who knew when to keep silent, it appears that most religions attempt to banish or cover up mystery. Rather than allow us to feel the sometimes exciting and sometimes terrifying state of *not* knowing, most purveyors of religion have rushed in with explanations and answers. How did the world come to be? God created it. What happens after death? Rebirth in heaven, a Day of Judgment, or dissolution into the elements. Why must we die? Our ancestors ate forbidden

---

2. S. N. Eisenstadt, *The Origins and Diversity of Axial Age Civilizations* (Albany: State University of New York Press, 1986).

fruit in paradise. Why are things going badly for us? We disobeyed the divine commandments. A problem with many religions today is that they tell us too much and with too much conviction. There is no place for mystery in their temples. We find in the notions of *nirguna* Brahman, the nameless *Dao*, and *nibbana* an essential corrective to this propensity to conceal what we really do not know by saying too much. In the face of genuine mystery, the most appropriate response may be simple silence.

Glossary

Agam Sutras (Āgam Sutras): the central Jain scriptures, believed by Jains to be the words of Vardhamana Mahavira as recalled by his chief disciple Indrabhuti.

ahimsa (ahimsā): the practice of doing no harm to living beings according to Hinduism, Buddhism, and Jainism.

Ahriman: the evil god in Zoroastrian theology; also known as Aeshma and Angra Mainyu.

ahuras: the Avestan word for the gods or spirits aligned with the principle of good.

airyana vaejah (airyana waējah): "the land of the noble" in the ancient Iranian language; the name from which "Iran" is derived.

Analects: the collection of sayings and dialogues of Confucius, compiled (and at least partially composed) by his students after his death; known in Chinese as the *Lunyu* (Conversations).

Ananda: the Buddha's personal attendant who memorized the Buddha's discourses and recited them at the First Buddhist Council; his recollections became the Suttas of the Pali Canon.

anatta: the Pali term for Buddha's denial of a permanent, substantial self or soul. Translated as no-self or not-self; known in Sanskrit as *anatman*, or no-*atman*.

ancestor reverence: treating one's forebears as living spirits whom one should honor, worship, and consult on important family decisions; an especially important practice throughout Chinese religious history.

anekanta (anekānta): "many-sided"; the Jain idea that the world is composed of an infinite number of material and spiritual substances, each with an infinite number of qualities and manifestations. Because of this complexity of the universe, all claims to truth must be tentative.

anicca: Pali word for impermanence.

arahant: a living individual who has attained awakening.

Ardhanarishvara (Ardhanārīsvara): iconic representation of the god as half Shiva, half Parvati; intended to symbolize the male/female, form/power aspects of the divine.

ariya: noble.

Arjuna: the warrior whose ethical dilemma forms the basis of a wide-ranging dialogue with Lord Krishna in the *Bhagavad Gita*.

Aryans (Āryans): the central Asian pastoral nomads who migrated into Iran and India prior to the Axial Age.

Aryavarta (Āryavarta): "the land of the noble"; the Indo-Aryans' name for their homeland in northern India.

ascetic: one who practices forms of self-denial (e.g., fasting, celibacy, abstaining from luxury and comforts) in order to attain higher spiritual goals.

asha: the Iranian principle of right and order; opposed to *druj*, the principle disorder and chaos.

ashavans: those who follow and revere *asha*.

Ashoka (Aśoka): ruler of the Mauryan Empire in India (reigned 273–232 BCE); a Buddhist convert who was responsible for the spread of Buddhism throughout India and other parts of Asia.

asuras: Sanskrit term for a class of divinities opposed to the *devas*; usually demonic in character.

atman (*ātman*): the essential self. Initially understood as the breath in the early Vedic era, the *atman* is later regarded by Hindus as immortal and transmigratory.

Avesta: the central scripture of Zoroastrianism. The most sacred sections of the Avesta are the Gathas, or Verses of Zoroaster.

Avestan: the Indo-European language in which the Zoroastrian Avesta was originally written.

avijja (*avijjā*): Pali word for ignorance or misknowing.

awakening: traditional metaphor for the experience of realizing the highest spiritual wisdom. When Siddhattha Gotama completely understood the causal factors of *dukkha* and the way to *nibbana* while sitting under the bodhi tree, he claimed to have had this experience; sometimes called enlightenment.

Axial Age: term coined by philosopher Karl Jaspers to denote the era of exceptional religious and philosophical creativity between 800 and 200 BCE that gave rise to the major world religions.

Babylonian Captivity: the deportation and exile of a large segment of the population of Judah to Babylon by King Nebuchadrezzar (586–536 BCE); this event marks the start of the Jewish Diaspora; also known as the Exile.

Banaras (Banāras): the holiest city in India; situated on the Ganges River in the present state of Uttar Pradesh. The Buddha gave his first discourse at the Deer Park near Banaras; also known as Varanasi and Kashi.

bao: Chinese word for the desire to repay kindness with a similar act of kindness.

Bhagavad Gita (Bhagavad Gītā): much-beloved Hindu text recounting the dialogue of Lord Krishna and Arjuna prior to the war between the Kurus and the Pandavas.

bhikkhu/bhikkhuni: Buddhist monk/nun.

bodhi tree: Buddhist term for the tree (*Ficus religiosa*) under which Siddhattha Gotama realized awakening and became the Buddha.

brahman: the absolute, ultimate reality. Originally, *brahman* was the Vedic word for the power inherent in ritual; later, the term came to designate the highest reality beyond all conceptualization.

Brahmin (Brāhmana): the South Asian caste of priests and intellectuals.

Buddha: one who grasps the causes of suffering and puts an end to it. In the Theravada Buddhist tradition, "the Buddha" is a title reserved for one who realizes awakening on his or her own; those who see *nibbana* through the teaching of a Buddha are called *arahants*. Buddha literally means "the Awakened One."

Buddhism: religious tradition whose origins date to the ferment that initiated Jainism and classical Hinduism. Following the conversion of Emperor Ashoka, Buddhism became a dominant religion of India and remained so until the medieval period.

caste: term to describe the stratification of Hindu society based on occupation and purity. Caste usually refers to the *varna* system, the fourfold classification of priests, warriors, producers, and servants (Brahmins, Kshatriyas, Vaishyas, and Shudras). Derived from the Portuguese *casta*, meaning pure.

Celestial Masters: early movement of the Daoist "church," whose followers sought to attain immortality through elixirs.

Charlie Chan: character in American movies in the 1930s and 1940s who shaped popular Western impressions of Confucius.

Confucius (Kongzi, Master Kong), c. 551-479 BCE: perhaps the most influential Chinese philosopher, Confucius maintained that human harmony lies in moral action and good government, which support the well being of the state and the people. In the Han dynasty, Confucianism was adopted as the state ideology, and Confucius himself was later deified and worshiped.

cosmic maintenance: the preaxial function of religion in which the processes of the world are supported or controlled by human activity.

cosmogony: creation story.

daeva (daēva): Avestan cognate of *deva*, a "shiny one"; considered by Zoroaster to be a class of malevolent divinities; the word from which "devil" derives.

Dao: Chinese for "the way."

Daodejing: the Chinese classic (*jing*) of the Way (*dao*) and the virtue (*de*); the basis of philosophical Daoism.

daojia: philosophical Daoism; literally, the school of the Way.

daojiao: the Daoist "church"; literally, the teaching of the Way.

darshan (darśan): to "take *darshan*" means to see and to be seen by the deity in Hinduism. *Darshan* is also the word for a philosophical system, such as Yoga or Vedanta.

Day of Judgment: the end of the world as we know it. According to Zoroaster, the Day of Judgment will entail the final triumph of good over evil; this concept also appears in Judaism, Christianity, and Islam.

de: Chinese for virtue or power.

Deer Park: the site of the Buddha's first discourse; located in present-day Sarnath, near Banaras, India.

deva: Sanskrit term for god; literally, "shiny one."

devi (devī): Sanskrit term for goddess.

Dhamma: Pali term for the teaching of the Buddha. Sanskrit: Dharma.

Dharma: in Hinduism, dharma is one's sacred duty according to caste; the principle of cosmic order. Dharma is the principle that succeeded the Vedic concept of *rita*.

di: Chinese term for earth.

Di: shortened form of Shangdi, the early Chinese high god.

Digambaras: one of the two orders of monastics in Jainism; members of this order renounce even their clothes, inspiring its name, the "sky-clad."

divination: the practice of communicating with the spirits through the interpretation of tangible elements.

Diwali: popular South and Southeast Asian holiday celebrated by Hindus and Jains in the autumn. Known as the Festival of Lights.

dragon bones: nickname for the inscribed cattle bones and turtle shells used for divination in the Shang Dynasty; so-called by modern Chinese pharmacies when they were sold as ingredients in medicines.

druj: Avestan term for the principle of disorder, evil, chaos; Sanskrit: *druh*.

drujvants: "Followers of the Lie"; those who, according to Zoroaster, aligned themselves with the principle of *druj*.

dukkha: Pali term usually translated as suffering, disappointment, and unsatisfactoriness.

Durga (Durgā): one of the manifestations of the goddess in Hinduism.

Dyaoš, Dyaus-Pitr: ancient names for the high god in the Avesta and Veda, respectively; cognates of Zeus and Jupiter.

Eastern Zhou: see Zhou Dynasty.

epistemology: the philosophical study of knowledge.

equanimity: the attitude of calmness and serenity.

eschaton: the end of time.

ethicization: the interpretation of events or practices in ethical terms; one of the characteristic processes of Axial Age religions.

evil, problem of: the dilemma posed by the belief in a god who is considered both all-good and all-powerful in a world in which evil exists; logically, according the traditional formulation of the problem, if evil exists, then god must be either not all-good or not all-powerful.

Ezekiel: prophet of ancient Judah.

Ficus religiosa: scientific name for the bodhi tree.

filial piety: the practice of reverencing and honoring one's parents; Chinese: *xiao*.

Five Aggregates of Being: according the Buddha's teaching, the ever-changing forces composing what is conventionally called the "self": matter, sensation, perception, mental formations, and consciousness.

Five Precepts: the vows taken by Buddhists to guide wholesome action. They include the promise to abstain from harming sentient beings, to abstain from false speech, to abstain from misusing sexuality, to abstain from taking what is not offered, and to abstain from taking intoxicating substances.

Four Noble Truths: the essence of the Buddha's teaching as expressed in his first discourse following awakening. They are *dukkha* (suffering and disappointment), the cause of *dukkha*, the cessation of *dukkha*, and the eightfold path to *nibbana*.

Four Sights: the experience that prompted Siddhattha Gotama to renounce home life to seek an end to suffering. According to tradition, Gotama saw a sick person, an old person, a corpse, and a *shramana* in an excursion outside the palace precincts.

Frashokereti: the "making glorious"; Zoroaster's term for the eschatological battle in which the forces of good defeat the forces of evil once and for all, ushering in an everlasting reign of peace and harmony.

Gandhara (Gandhāra): the region in present Afghanistan and Pakistan where the first anthropomorphic Buddha images were produced nearly five hundred years after the life of the Buddha.

Gathas (Gāthās): the "Verses"; part of the oldest Avesta, the foundational scripture of Zoroaster's religion. These verses are believed to have been actually composed by Zoroaster himself under moments of religious inspiration.

Gaya (Bodh Gaya): northeastern India town, location of the Buddha's awakening.

ghosts: in Chinese religion, the spirits of the unburied dead.

Gotama, Siddhattha (Sanskrit: Gautama, Siddhārtha) ca. 490–410 BCE: the given name of the Sakyan noble who became the Buddha.

guru: teacher.

Han dynasty: the family who ruled China in 206 BCE–220 CE, one of most prosperous and stable periods in Chinese history.

Haoma: see **Soma**.

Heptad: "the seven"; the spirits or gods including Ahura Mazda seen by Zoroaster in his call to be a prophet.

High Hara: the holiest mountain on earth, where souls will be judged on the fourth day following death, according to Zoroastrian theology.

Hinduism: the Western term for the Indian religions that regard the Vedas as the highest authority.

householder: the second stage of life for both men and women of caste. At the householder stage, Hindus marry, raise children, work, and contribute to the good of family and society.

idolatry: confusing the ultimate reality with what is less than ultimate.

Indo-Aryans (Indo-Āryans): modern designation for the Central Asian people who eventually settled in India in the second millennium BCE.

Indo-European: modern term for the Central Asian ancestors of many of the inhabitants of India and Europe.

Indo-Iranians: modern term for the Central Asian people who migrated southward from the steppes and eventually split, with some settling in Iran (the Iranians or Irano-Aryans) and some in India (the Indo-Aryans).

Indra: the war god of the Indo-Iranians; the ascendant deity of the Rig Veda; the *deva* who also controlled the waters.

Indus Valley Civilization: one of the great cultures of the ancient world; flourished in 3300–1900 BCE in northwestern India along the Indus River system; also known as the Harappan (Harappān) civilization.

"Inner Chapters": part of the *Zhuangzi*, a text of early philosophical Daoism; probably written by Zhuangzi himself.

ishta-devata (*ishta-devatā*): one's personal deity of choice in Hinduism.

Jainism: religious tradition whose origins date to the ferment that initiated Buddhism and classical Hinduism. Jainism and Buddhism are regarded by Hindus as heterodox philosophies because they deny Vedic authority.

Jambudvipa (Jambudvīpa): "the island of the rose-apple tree"; a term used by Jains, Buddhists, and Hindus to refer to the earthly realm.

Jaspers, Karl, 1883–1969: German philosopher; often associated with Existentialism; coined the term *die Achsenzeit*, or Axial Age, to designate the period 800–200 BCE.

jina: a spiritual victor in Jainism.

jivanmukta: in Hinduism, a living, liberated soul.

jñana (*jñāna*): Sanskrit word for knowledge; related to the Greek gnōsis.

jñana-marga: the path of liberation from *samsara* based on the quest for wisdom and the dissolution of illusion. The *jñana-marga* usually requires ascetic practice and great discipline.

junzi: the gentleman or noble man in Confucianism; the most important ideal type for Confucius.

karma: action and its consequences; a principle of justice, ensuring that the effects of one's actions return to the agent. Karma is what binds the self to the cycle of endless existence and determines the self's station in future existences.

Kisagotami: a young woman who begs the Buddha to bring her dead son back to life; the Buddha instructs her to find a mustard seed from a home that has never been touched by death.

Krishna: one of the principal avatars or manifestations of the Hindu god Vishnu; Krishna instructs Arjuna on devotion to god in the *Bhagavad Gita*.

Kshatriyas (Kśatriyas): the caste of warriors and administrators.

Kushinagara: northeastern Indian village near the site of the Buddha's *parinibbana*, or final liberation.

Laozi: the legendary founder of Daoism and the traditional author of the *Daodejing*, which is sometimes known as the *Laozi*.

Legalism: the Chinese philosophical school opposed to Confucianism; embraced by the Qin Dynasty, Legalism advocated a strict law-and-order approach to maintaining social stability.

li: originally, the Chinese term for religious rituals and ceremonies. Confucius broadened the term to include everyday behavior and manners.

lingam: aniconic symbol of the god Shiva.

Magi: term for the "wise men from the East" who visited Jesus as an infant; derived from *magus*, a priest.

Mahavira (Mahāvīra) c. 599–527 or 540–468 BCE: the "Great Hero"; a traditional title for Vardhamana (Vardhamāna), the twenty-fourth Tirthankara of Jainism.

Mahayana (Mahāyāna): Sanskrit for the "Great Vehicle"; a branch of Buddhism that developed in the early centuries CE and brought a new understanding of the Buddha and the nature of liberation.

manas: Vedic word for that which animates the body; translates as mind, heart, or life-force.

Mandate of Heaven: the moral authority by which the ruler rules. The concept—believed to have been first articulated by the Dan, the Duke of Zhou—was used to justify the Zhou overthrow of the Shang Dynasty; Chinese: *tianming*.

mantra: Sanskrit word for a sound or phrase embodying sacred power.

Mara: the tempter in Buddhism; as Siddhattha Gotama approached awakening while sitting under the bodhi tree, Mara attempted to thwart attainment of his goal.

maya (māyā): illusion; the veil over reality that prevents the unenlightened from seeing the world as it truly is. *Maya* causes us to see multiplicity where there is in reality only unity.

Maya, Queen: wife of King Suddhodana and mother of Siddhattha Gotama. Queen Maya died seven days after the birth of Siddhattha, who was then raised by Queen Prajapati, Maya's sister.

Mazda: an *ahura* of early Iranian religion; according to Zoroaster, Mazda was the principal (and perhaps sole) benevolent deity, locked in combat with the Evil One until the end of time.

Mencius (Mengzi, Master Meng), c. 385–312 BCE: Chinese philosopher who was one of first and most influential interpreters of Confucius. He was especially interested in the question of human nature and argued that human beings were fundamentally good.

Middle Way: the course of life promoted by the Buddha in which one avoids the extremes of indulgence and deprivation.

Mitra: one of the major gods of Indo-Iranian religion initially associated with promise keeping.

Mohism: school of Chinese philosophy developed by Mozi. In contrast to Confucianism, Mohism advocated universal love of humanity.

moksha (mokṣa): release or liberation from the wheel of *samsara*. Pursued and conceptualized in a variety of ways, *moksha* is the ultimate goal of dharmic religions.

Mozi, c. 470-390 BCE: Chinese philosopher who advocated "impartial caring" or "universal love" and criticized Confucius's belief that one should love others in proportion to the benefit one receives from them.

Nachiketas: young Brahmin in the Upanishads who engaged Yama, the King of Underworld, in a dialogue about death.

Nanak, Guru, 1469–1539: the founder of Sikhism.

nibbana (nibbāna): Pali term for the end of suffering and rebirth; Sanskrit: *nirvāṇa*.

Nietzsche, Friedrich, 1844-1900: German philosopher; author of *Thus Spoke Zarathustra*.

nirguna **Brahman:** Sanskrit term for ultimate reality without qualities. This term is used to describe the aspect of Brahman that is ineffable.

Noble Eightfold Path: the Buddha's prescription for realizing *nibbana*; includes right understanding, right intentions; right speech; right action; right livelihood; right effort; right concentration; and right mindfulness.

no-self, not-self: the Buddha's denial of a permanent, substantial self or soul; Pali: *anatta*; Sanskrit: *anatman*.

Nowruz: Persian for "New Day"; the celebration of the new year in Iranian religion.

Odes, Book of: a collection of over three hundred poems from the early Zhou to the Spring and Autumn Periods; perhaps the earliest such collection in Chinese literature; considered part of the Wu Jing, the Five Classics of Confucianism; Chinese: *Shijing*.

One Hundred Philosophers, Period of: the Chinese era of the late Spring and Autumn and Warring States periods, during which many schools of philosophy were established, including Confucianism and Daoism.

oracle: a communication from the spirit world or the medium of that communication.

pairi-daeza: ancient Iranian term meaning "enclosed garden"; the basis for the word "paradise."

Pali (Pāli): a simplified vernacular form of Sanskrit in which the discourses of the Buddha were first written.

Pali Canon: the earliest collection of Buddhist scriptures, comprising the Suttas (discourses) the Vinaya (monastic rules), and Abhidhamma (the codification of the Dhamma).

parinibbana (parinibbāna): the final liberation of a fully realized person.

Parsis: the Zoroastrians (and their descendants) who fled to India to escape the Islamic conquest of Iran.

Prajapati, Queen: aunt and foster mother to Siddhattha Gotama; sister of Queen Maya; the first Buddhist nun.

prophet: one who speaks for the god, often urging people back to an authentic form of religious practice at a time when religion has become corrupt.

puja (pūjā): Sanskrit word for the ritual worship of a god, goddess, or object representing sacred reality.

Purusha: the primordial human who was sacrificed and dismembered to create the parts of the cosmos, society, and the ritual according to the Veda.

Qin dynasty: the period of Chinese history between the Zhou and Han Dynasties; from to 221 to 206 BCE; during the Qin, China was unified and Legalism was the dominant philosophy.

Rahula (Rāhula): son of Siddhattha Gotama and his wife Yashodhara; in later life, Rahula became a Buddhist monk.

Ramanuja (Rāmānuja), c. 1077–1157 CE: Indian philosopher; founded the school of the Vishishtadvaita Vedanta, or qualified non-dualism.

redeath: the Vedic belief that the soul may ascend to heaven at death, live there for a while until it exhausts its karma, and die again to be reborn on earth.

ren: Chinese word for humaneness.

renunciation: in the South Asian context, giving up home, possessions, social standing, and family ties to "go forth" into the world to seek liberation from *samsara*.

Rig Veda: the oldest and most important of the Vedas, compiled between 2300 and 1200 BCE. The Rig Veda comprises over 1,000 hymns to various Vedic deities; *rig* means "praise."

rishis: Sanskrit term for "seers," individuals with extraordinary insight into the nature of reality.

rita: the Vedic principle of order and harmony.

ritual purity: the state of cleanliness that is necessary for being in the presence of the sacred.

rose-apple tree: a South and Southeast Asian tree with small, edible fruits. It was under this variety of tree that Siddhattha Gotama had his first meditation experience as a boy.

saguna Brahman: that aspect of ultimate reality that can be conceptualized and discussed.

Sakya: the clan of Siddhattha Gotama.

samsara (samsāra): the phenomenal world of change and transience. *Samsara* denotes the situation in which the self, according to Hinduism, sequentially incarnates in different bodies at different levels of existence.

Sangha: the order of monks and nuns in Buddhism.

Sanskrit: Indo-European language in which the Vedas were composed.

Saoshyant: a savior or judge who appears at the end of time, according to Zoroaster; literally, "one who brings benefit."

satya: Sanskrit word for truth and, specifically, the *higher* truth.

satyagraha (satyāgraha): literally, "grasping for the truth"; Gandhi's term for his philosophy and practice of nonviolent resistance to injustice.

Shang dynasty: c. 1500–1045 BCE; the earliest Chinese dynasty for which there is historical evidence.

Shangdi: term for the high god of early Chinese religion; also known as Di.

Shankara (Śankara), c. 788–820 CE: Indian philosopher; founder of the school of Advaita Vedanta, or nondualism, based on the Upanishads.

shaykh: Sufi master.

Shiva (Śiva): one the great cosmic gods of Hinduism and the center of one of Hinduism's largest and most important religions.

shramana: Sanskrit term for a wandering ascetic. Pali: *samana*.

shrauta (śrauta) **ritual:** ordinarily complex Vedic ceremonies using the verses of the Vedas for the purpose of maintaining divine-human relations.

***shruti* (*śruti*):** sacred literature of the highest authority in Hinduism; believed to have been revealed to the ancient *rishis*, or seers. *Shruti* includes the Vedas and the Upanishads.

Shudras (Śudras): the lowest of the four *varnas* in India; the caste of peasants and servants.

Shvetambaras (Śvetāmbaras): one of the two orders of monastics in Jainism; the "white-robed."

Siddhartha (Siddhārtha), King: the father of Vardhamana Mahavira, the twenty-fourth Tirthankara of Jainism.

Siddhattha: the given name of the one who became the Buddha; *Siddhattha* means "he who attains the goal."

Sikhism: an indigenous Indian religion inspired by Kabir, a mystic-poet from Banaras, and founded by Guru Nanak, a Hindu from Punjab. Both men condemned Hindu and Muslim sectarianism and sought to establish authentic worship of the one true god.

Soma: the Sanskrit name for the god whose manifestation as a particular plant produced visions and a sense of well-being in those who ingested it. Avestan: Haoma.

Son of Man: Jewish concept of the individual who appears at the apocalypse as a divine judge; the title Jesus most often applies to himself in the Gospel of Mark.

Soul of the Bull: the divine being in ancient Iranian religion who sustained and nurtured animal life.

Spring and Autumn Period c. 722–481 BCE: the first of two eras of the Eastern Zhou Dynasty in China.

***stupa* (*stūpa*):** a Buddhist reliquary; also known as *dagoba* and pagoda.

Suddhodana, King: ruler of the Shakya Kingdom; husband of Queen Maya and Queen Prajapati; father of Siddhattha Gotama.

Suttas: the discourses of Buddha.

swastika: ancient Indo-Aryan symbol for the sun.

sympathetic magic: the practice of attempting to affect realities by manipulation of objects or words representing those realities.

taijitu: the Chinese diagram representing the relationship of the yin and yang principles.

tanha: Pali term for craving; literally, "thirst."

Theravada (Theravāda): the "way of the elders"; the oldest extant variety of Buddhism; also called "Southern Buddhism" because of its prominence in South and Southeast Asia.

Three Sovereigns and Five Emperors, Era of the: mythic period of early Chinese history preceding the Xia Dynasty.

tian: Chinese word for heaven.

tianming: see **Mandate of Heaven.**

Tirthankara: according to Jainism, one who teaches the truth and the way to liberation; literally, a bridge builder or ford maker.

transcendental consciousness: term used by S. N. Eisenstadt to refer to the Axial Age's thrust to gain a larger and deeper understanding of the nature of reality.

transmigration of the self: reincarnation.

Triple Practice: the traditional division of the Noble Eightfold Path into Moral Behavior, Concentration, and Wisdom.

Triple Refuge: a statement of Buddhist identity: "I take refuge in the Buddha; I take refuge in the Dhamma; and I take refuge in the Sangha."

Trishala (Triśala), Queen: wife of King Siddhartha and mother of Vardhamana Mahavira, the twenty-fourth Tirthankara of Jainism.

Upanishads (Upaniṣads): collection of early Hindu writings in which the ideas of transmigration of the soul and the identity of Brahman and *atman* are first proposed; considered *shruti*, the highest form of authority in Hinduism.

Vaishyas (Vaiśyas): the caste of farmers, cattle herders, artisans, and businesspeople.

Vajrayana (Vajrayāna): the third major form of Buddhism, practiced mainly in Tibet and Mongolia; literally, the "diamond" or "thunderbolt" vehicle.

Varuna: Indo-Iranian god associated with promise keeping.

Vedanta (Vedānta): the "end of the Veda." Vedanta is one of the most important and influential of the Hindu philosophies. Deriving inspiration particularly from the Upanishads, the last part of the Vedas, Vedanta emphasizes unity of the self and the Absolute.

Vedas: sacred wisdom believed to have been revealed to ancient *rishis*, or seers. The Vedas are now the most sacred of Hindu scriptures.

Vesak: festival that celebrates the birth, awakening, and *parinibbana* of the Buddha.

via negativa: the way of negation; a theological technique of referring to ultimate reality by saying what it is not.

Vishnu: a minor Vedic god who ultimately became one of Hinduism's most important gods and the object of a large Hindu religion; according to tradition, Vishnu has assumed ten principal manifestations, including Krishna, Rama, and the Buddha.

Warring States, Period of: the second of the two eras of the Eastern Zhou Dynasty in China; 475 or 403 until 221 BCE; a time in which the warlords of small feudal kingdoms sought to annex other states to extend and consolidate their power.

Wen, King: the symbolic first ruler of the Zhou Dynasty.

Western Zhou: see **Zhou Dynasty**.

Wu: the man who led the overthrow of Shang rulers and established the Zhou Dynasty of China; son of King Wen.

Wu Jing: the "Five Classics"; used by Confucianism as a basis for study; includes the *Book of Odes (Shī Jīng)*, the *Book of Changes (Yī Jīng)*, the *Book of Rites (Lǐ Jīng)*, the *Book of History (Shū Jīng)*, and the *Spring and Autumn Annals (Lín Jīng)*.

wu wei: actionless action; one of the fundamental virtues of Daoism.

Xunzi, c. 310–219 BCE: early Confucian thinker who opposed Mengzi's position on human nature. A native of the state of Zhao in north-central China, Xunzi provided a rigorous explanation and defense of Confucian thought in the work that bears his name, the *Xunzi*.

yajña: sacrifice. Avestan: *yasna*.

Yama: the Vedic/Hindu god of death and ruler of the underworld. Avestan: Yima.

Yashodhara (Yaśodhara): wife of Siddhattha Gotama; mother of Rahula; later a Buddhist nun.

yazatas: class of divinities in Zoroastrianism associated with the principle of good; perhaps the prototype for angels in the Abrahamic religions.

yin and yang: the Chinese principles accounting for change; yin is associated with the feminine, and yang with the masculine; the Chinese ideal is to maintain a balance between yin and yang.

yoga: a discipline for the purposes of enlightenment and liberation. Yoga literally means "yoke." In a narrower sense, Yoga refers to a specific school of orthodox philosophy.

zaotar: an Iranian priest. Literally, the "libation pourer."

Zhou, Duke of (Dan): the brother of King Wu, founder of the Zhou Dynasty, who ruled as regent for his nephew following Wu's death; the Duke of Zhou embodied many of the highest virtues according to Confucius.

Zhou dynasty: the period of Chinese history between the Shang and the Qin Dynasties; 1045–221 BCE; divided into the Western and Eastern Zhou when invaders forced the move of the capital eastward.

Zhuangzi, c. 369–286 BCE: The Daoist thinker most responsible for drawing out the mystical implications of the foundational Daoist principles. Unlike other philosophers of the Warring States period, Zhuangzi was decidedly disinterested in the political and social affairs.

Zoroaster: Iranian prophet and founder of the religion of Zoroastrianism, or Mazdaism. Some scholarly estimates suggest he lived as early as the fifteenth century BCE and as late as the sixth century BCE. Zoroaster is the Greek transliteration of Zarathustra.

Zoroastrianism: the religion based on Zoroaster's reforms of ancient Iranian religion.

Bibliography

Works Cited

Aristotle. "On the Soul." In *The Basic Works of Aristotle*, ed. Richard McKeon. New York: Random House, 1941.

Augustine. *Concerning the City of God against the Pagans*. Translated by John O'Meara. London: Penguin, 1984.

———. *Confessions*. Translated by R. S. Pine-Coffin. London: Penguin, 1961.

Becker, Ernest. *The Denial of Death*. New York: Free Press, 1973.

Bodhi, Bhikkhu. *The Connected Discourses of the Buddha: A Translation of the Samyutta Nikāya*. Boston: Wisdom, 2000.

———, and Nyanaponika Thera. *Numerical Discourses of the Buddha: An Anthology of Suttas from the Anguttara Nikaya*. Walnut Creek, CA: AltaMira, 1999.

Boyce, Mary. *Zoroastrians: Their Religious Beliefs and Practices*. London: Routledge, 2001.

Brooks, E. Bruce, and A. Taeko Brooks. *The Original Analects: Sayings of Confucius and His Successors*. New York: Columbia University Press, 1998.

Bryant, Edwin. *The Quest for the Origins of Vedic Culture: The Indo-Aryan Migration Debate*. Oxford: Oxford University Press, 2001.

Chin, Annping. *The Authentic Confucius: A Life of Thought and Politics*. New York: Scribner, 2007.

Cronin, Gloria L., and Ben Siegel, eds. *Conversations with Robert Penn Warren*. Oxford: University Press of Mississippi, 2005.

Dawson, Raymond, trans. *The Analects*. Oxford: Oxford University Press, 1993.

De Bary, Wm Theodore. *Sources of Indian Tradition: Vol 1*. New York: Columbia University Press, 1958.

Dhammika, Ven., trans. "Gemstones of the Good Dhamma." http://www.accesstoinsight.org/lib/authors/dhammika/wheel342.html.

Doniger, Wendy, trans. *The Rig Veda*. New York: Penguin, 2005.

Dundas, Paul. *The Jains*. 2nd ed. London: Routledge, 2002.

Eisenstadt, S. N., ed. *The Origins and Diversity of Axial Age Civilizations*. Albany: State University of New York Press, 1986.

Eliade, Mircea. *The Sacred and the Profane: the Nature of Religion*. Orlando, FL: Harcourt, Inc., 1987.

Eliot, T. S. *Four Quartets*. New York: Harcourt Brace Jovanovich, 1971.

Erikson, Erik. *Gandhi's Truth: On the Origins of Militant Nonviolence.* New York: W.W. Nortony, 1970.

Foster, Elon. *Cyclopaedia of Poetry*, 1st series. New York: Funk and Wagnalls, 1872.

Frazer, James George. *The Golden Bough.* Sioux Falls, SD: NuVision, 2006.

Harvey, Peter. *Introduction to Buddhism*, 2nd. Edition, Cambridge: Cambridge University Press, 2013.

Hick, John. *An Interpretation of Religion: Human Responses to the Transcendent.* 2nd ed. New Haven: Yale University Press, 2004.

Ivanhoe, Philip J. *Confucian Moral Self Cultivation.* 2nd ed. Indianapolis: Hackett, 2000.

———, trans. *The Daodejing of Laozi.* New York: Seven Bridges, 2002.

Jaspers, Karl. *The Origin and Goal of History.* Trans. Michael Bullock. New Haven: Yale University Press, 1953.

Jensen, Lionel. *Manufacturing Confucianism: Chinese Traditions and Universal Civilization.* Durham, NC: Duke University Press, 1997.

King, Martin Luther. *Where Do We Go from Here: Chaos or Community?* Boston: Beacon Press, 1967.

Kulke, Hermann, and Dietmar Rothermund, *A History of India.* 3rd ed. New York: Routledge, 2004.

Lau, D.C., trans. *The Analects.* London: Penguin, 1979.

———, trans. *Mencius.* London: Penguin, 1970.

———, trans. *Tao Te Ching.* Harmondsworth, UK: Penguin Classics, 1963.

Lax, Eric. *Woody Allen: A Biography.* Boston: Da Capo, 2000.

Legge, James. *The Chinese Classics*, Vol. 4. Hong Kong: Hong Kong University Press, 1970.

Mair, Victor H., trans. *Wandering on the Way*: *Early Taoist Tales and Parables of Chuang Tzu.* New York: Bantam, 1994.

Malandra, William W., trans. and ed. *An Introduction to Ancient Iranian Religion: Readings from the Avesta and Achaemenid Inscriptions.* Minneapolis: University of Minnesota Press, 1983.

Mascaró, Juan, trans. *The Upanishads.* New York: Penguin, 1965.

Moeller, Hans-Georg. *Daoism Explained.* Chicago: Open Court, 2004.

Ñanamoli, Bhikkhu, and Bhikkhu Bodhi. *The Middle Length Discourses of the Buddha: A Translation of the* Majjhima Nikaya. Rev. ed. Boston: Wisdom, 1995.

Niebuhr, Reinhold. *Moral Man and Immoral Society: A Study in Ethics.* 2nd ed. 1932. Reprint, Louisville: Westminster John Knox, 2013.

Nietzsche, Friedrich. *Thus Spoke Zarathustra.* In *The Portable Nietzsche*, trans. Walter Kaufmann. New York: Penguin, 1982.

Obeyesekere, Gananath. *Imagining Karma: Ethical Transformations in Amerindian, Buddhist, and Greek Rebirth.* Berkeley: University of California Press, 2002.

Olivelle, Patrick, trans. *Upaniṣads.* Oxford: Oxford University Press, 1996.

Poo Mu-Chou. *In Search of Personal Welfare: A View of Ancient Chinese Religion.* Albany: State University of New York Press, 1998.

Robertson, Connie. *The Wordsworth Dictionary of Quotations*, 3rd ed. Ware, UK: Wordsworth, 1998.

Ross, David A. *A Critical Companion to William Butler Yeats: A Literary Reference to His Life and Work.* New York: Facts on File, 2009.

Tolstoy, Leo. *The Death of Ivan Ilyich.* New York: Bantam, 1981.

Thoreau, Henry David, Owen Paul Thomas, and Henry David Thoreau. *Walden and Civil Disobedience: Authoritative Texts, Background, Reviews, and Essays in Criticism.* New York: W. W. Norton, 1966.

Tillich, Paul. *The Shaking of the Foundations.* New York: Charles Scribner's Sons, 1976.

Van Norden, Brian W., trans. *Mengzi.* Indianapolis/Cambridge: Hackett, 2008.

Wallis, Glenn, trans. *Dhammapada: Verses on the Way.* New York: The Modern Library, 2007.

Walshe, Maurice, trans. *The Long Discourses of the Buddha: A Translation of the Dīgha Nikāya.* Boston: Wisdom, 1995.

Whitehead, Alfred N. *Process and Reality.* New York: Free Press, 1979.

Wilson, Edward O. *On Human Nature.* Cambridge: Harvard University Press, 1979.

For Further Study

The Axial Age

Armstrong, Karen. *The Great Transformation: The Beginning of Our Religious Traditions.* New York: Anchor, 2007.

Bellah, Robert N. *Religion in Human Evolution: From the Paleolithic to the Axial Age.* Cambridge: Harvard University Press, 2011.

———, and Hans Joas. *The Axial Age and Its Consequences*. Cambridge: Harvard University Press, 2013.

EAST ASIA

GENERAL WORKS

Adler, Joseph A. *Chinese Religious Traditions*. Upper Saddle River, NJ: Prentice Hall, 2002.

Fung Yu-Lan. *A History of Chinese Philosophy*. Vol. 1 of *The Period of the Philosophers*. Princeton: Princeton University Press, 1952.

Graham, A. C. *Disputers of the Dao: Philosophical Argument in Ancient China*. Chicago: Open Court, 1989.

Ivanhoe, Philip J., and Bryan W. Van Norden. *Readings in Classical Chinese Philosophy*. New York: Seven Bridges, 2001.

Waley, Arthur. *Three Ways of Thought in Ancient China*. Palo Alto: Stanford University Press, 1982.

CONFUCIUS AND CONFUCIANISM

Berthrong, John H., and Evelyn Nagai Berthrong. *Confucianism: A Short Introduction*. Oxford: Oneworld, 2000.

Fingarette, Herbert. *Confucius: The Secular as Sacred*. New York: Harper Torchbooks, 1972.

Tu Weiming, and Mary Evelyn Tucker, eds. *Confucian Spirituality*. Vol. 1. New York: Crossroad, 2003.

Van Norden, Bryan W., ed. *Confucius and the* Analects: *New Essays*. Oxford: Oxford University Press, 2002.

Watson, Burton, trans. *Xunzi: Basic Writings*. New York: Columbia University Press, 2003.

———, trans. *Zhuangzi: Basic Writings*. New York: Columbia University Press, 2003.

DAOISM

Kohn, Livia, and Michael LaFargue, eds. *Lao Tzu and the Tao-te-ching*. Albany: State University of New York Press, 1998.

Miller, James. *Daoism: A Short Introduction*. Oxford: Oneworld, 2003.

Oldstone-Moore, Jennifer. *Taoism*. Oxford: Oxford University Press, 2003.

SOUTH ASIA

GENERAL WORKS

Fairservis, Walter A., Jr. *The Roots of Ancient India.* 2nd ed. Chicago: University of Chicago Press, 1975.

Feuerstein, Georg, Subhash Kak, and David Frawley. *In Search of the Cradle of Civilization: New Light on Ancient India.* Wheaton, IL: Quest, 2001.

"Harrapa." http://www.harappa.com/.

Kenoyer, Jonathan Mark. "Mohenjo-daro!" http://www.mohenjodaro.net/.

Radhakrishnan, Sarvepalli, and Charles A. Moore, eds. *A Sourcebook in Indian Philosophy.* Princeton: Princeton University Press, 1967.

HINDUISM

Basham, A. L. *The Origin and Development of Classical Hinduism.* New York: Oxford University Press, 1995.

———. *The Wonder That Was India.* New York: Grove, 1959.

Brereton, Joel. "The Upanishads." In *Approaches to the Asian Classics*, ed. William Theodore de Bary and Irene Bloom. New York: Columbia University Press, 1990.

Eck, Diana L. *Darśan: Seeing the Divine Image in India.* 2nd ed. Chambersburg, PA: Anima, 1985.

Edgerton, Franklin. *The Beginnings of Indian Philosophy.* Cambridge: Harvard University Press, 1965.

Hopkins, Thomas J. *The Hindu Religious Tradition.* Belmont, CA: Wadsworth, 1971.

Hume, Robert Ernest, trans. *The Thirteen Principal Upanishads.* 2nd ed. New York: Oxford University Press, 1971.

Huyler, Stephen P. *Meeting God: Elements of Hindu Devotion.* New Haven: Yale University Press, 1999.

Klostermaier, Klaus. *A Survey of Hinduism.* Albany: State University Press of New York, 1991.

Mahony, William K. *The Artful Universe: An Introduction to the Vedic Religious Imagination.* Albany: State University of New York Press, 1998.

Miller, Barbara Stoler, trans. *The Bhagavad-Gita: Krishna's Counsel in Time of War.* New York: Bantam, 1986.

Muesse, Mark W. *The Hindu Traditions: A Concise Introduction.* Minneapolis: Fortress Press, 2011.

Sharma, Arvind. *Classical Hindu Thought: An Introduction.* New Delhi: Oxford University Press, 2000.

THE BUDDHA AND BUDDHISM

"Access to Insight: Readings in Theravāda Buddhism." http://www.accesstoinsight.org/.

Bodhi, Bhikkhu. *The Noble Eightfold Path: Way to the End of Suffering.* Seattle: BPS Pariyatti, 1994. Available free online at http://www.vipassana.com/resources/8fp0.php.

———, trans. *In the Buddha's Words: An Anthology of Discourses from the Pali Canon (Teachings of the Buddha).* Boston: Wisdom, 2005.

Buddha Dharma Education Association. BuddhaNet. http://www.buddhanet.net/.

Carrithers, Michael. *Buddha: A Very Short Introduction.* Oxford: Oxford University Press, 1996.

Collins, Stevens. *Selfless Persons: Imagery and Thought in Theravada Buddhism.* Cambridge: Cambridge University Press, 1982.

Dhamma, Rewata. *The First Discourse of the Buddha.* Boston: Wisdom, 1997.

Gunaratana, Henepola. *Mindfulness in Plain English.* Rev. ed. Boston: Wisdom, 2002.

Harvey, Peter. *An Introduction to Buddhism: Teachings, History, and Practices.* 2nd ed., Cambridge: Cambridge University Press, 2013.

Mitchell, Robert Allen. *The Buddha: His Life Retold.* New York: Paragon, 1989.

Ñanamoli, Bhikkhu. *The Life of the Buddha: According to the Pali Canon.* Rev. ed. Seattle: Pariyatti, 2001.

Rahula, Walpola. *What the Buddha Taught.* New York: Grove, 1959.

THE JAINS

Jaini, Padmanabh S. *The Jaina Path of Purification.* Delhi: Motilal Banarsidass, 1998.

Tatia, Nathmal, trans. *That Which Is: Tattvārtha Sūtra.* San Francisco: HarperCollins, 1994.

WEST ASIA

ZOROASTER AND ZOROASTRIANISM

Avesta—Zoroastrian Archives. Published by Joseph H. Peterson. http://www.avesta.org/.

Foltz, Richard C. *Spirituality in the Land of the Noble: How Iran Shaped the World's Religions.* Oxford: Oneworld, 2004.

Hultgård, Anders. "Persian Apocalypticism." In *The Continuum History of Apocalypticism*, ed. Bernard J. McGinn, John J. Collins, and Stephen J. Stein, 30–63. New York: Continuum, 2003.

World of Traditional Zoroastrianism. http://www.zoroastrianism.com/.

Index

Achaemenid (Persian) Empire, 30
Afghanistan, 138
afterlife, 4; Buddhism and *parinibbana*, 125; classical Hinduism, 55–57, 60–61; Indus Valley Civilization, 42; Judaism, 34; Rig Veda, 45–47; Vedic Period, 45–47, 55–57, 60–61; Zoroastrian paradise, 30, 34; Zoroastrianism and bodily resurrection of the dead, 29; Zoroastrianism and individual destiny after death, 27–28. *See also* heaven; rebirth
Agam Sutras, 146
Agni, 45
ahimsa: the Buddha's Five Precepts, 128–29, 143; Jainism, 143, 149–50; of the mind/of speech, 150
Ahriman, 24–25, 34
Ahura Mazda, 12, 13; and Zoroaster, 22, 23, 25, 31, 227
ahuras, 12, 24–25, 45
Alara Kalama, 104
Alexander the Great, 138
Analects (*Lunyu*) of Confucius, 171, 172–73, 175–77, 180, 182, 183, 186, 187–88, 193
Ananda, 136, 138
anatta (*anatman*), 119–22
ancestor reverence: contemporary Taiwan, 161; Shang dynasty, 160–61, 162, 168. *See also* family/filial piety
anekanta, 149
arahants, 125, 133; female, 135–36
Ardhanarishvara, 91
Aristotle, 89
Arjuna, 94–95

Aryans: the "Aryan question," 43; the Buddha's subversion of the word, 134; Hitler and symbols of, 43; "Noble Ones," 10, 43–44. *See also* Indo-Aryans; Indo-Iranians
asceticism: and Confucian self-cultivation, 186; fasting to death (*sallekhana*), 150; of Gotama, 104–5, 107; Jain practices, 150; of Mahavira, 146; self-mortification, 86, 105, 107, 146; techniques for disciplining the lower self, 86. *See also shramanas*
asha, 12–13, 14, 17, 21, 27, 166
ashavans, 17
Ashoka, King, 139-140
asuras, 24, 45
atman: Brahman-*atman*, 80–82, 87–88; Indo-Aryan, 46, 76; as mind, 76–77; Upanishadic human essence/higher self, 76–77, 227
Augustine of Hippo, 34, 82
Avesta, 10; the Gathas of Zoroaster, 21–22, 24–25, 30
Avestan cosmogony, 13–14, 50
avijja, 118
Axial Age, 1–6, 223–32; attitudes about death, 3–4; compassion and mindful virtue, 228–29; defining, 1–6; human freedom and accountability, 226; individual selfhood, 3–4, 6, 225–28; insights for today, 225, 228–32; moral obligation, 25–26; and phenomenon of human religiousness, 223–25; political/social disorder and instability, 3; shift from cosmic maintenance to personal transformation, 5–6, 229–30; theology, 225–28; transcendental

261

consciousness, 4–5, 231; urbanization and mobility, 2–3. *See also* preaxial period

bao, 162, 192
Becker, Ernest, 60
Bhagavad Gita, 89, 94–95, 212
bhikkhus/bhikkhunis, 111, 135–36
al-Bistami, Bayazid, 87
bodhi tree, 108, 137, 138
Bodhisattva, 141
Book of Odes (*Shi-jing*), 162–63, 168–69, 187, 190
Boyce, Mary, 21
Brahman: Brahman-*atman*, 80–82, 87–88; *nirguna* Brahman, 79–80, 90, 93; *saguna* Brahman, 90; Vedantic school, 78–80, 89, 90, 93; Vedic word for power in ritual, 53–54, 78
Brahmin priests, 52–54, 78; mantras, 53; and the power *brahman*, 53–54, 78; Vedic *shrauta* rites, 52–53
Bryant, Edwin, 43n
Buddhism, 97–141; Ashoka and development in India, 140; concept of the self, 119–22, 227; contemporary practitioners, 143; death/individual destiny after death, 125; Dhamma, 109–11, 127, 133–35, 138–39, 140; and divine worship, 139; early divisions and separate schools, 141; early doctrinal disputes and Sangha councils, 138–39; Four Noble Truths, 109–32; images of the Buddha, 138, 224; institutionalization, 138–39, 141, 199, 221; and Jainism, 143; karma, 125, 128; Mahayana (Eastern Buddhism), 141, 199, 221; meditation practice, 108, 131, 135; ritual practice, 139; the Sangha (monastic community), 133–36; *stupas*, 137–38, 139, 140; Theravada, 141; Triple Refuge (creed), 139; Vajrayana, 141; the West's early negative evaluation, 123; women/nuns, 135–36; Zen, 125–26, 224. *See also* Four Noble Truths; Gotama, Siddhattha

caste: Brahmin priests, 52–54, 78; and the Buddha's message, 134; Indo-Iranian warrior caste, 17–18, 52; and myth of Purusha, 67; and rebirth, 67; *shramanas*, 69–70, 71
Celestial Masters, 221
change (impermanence): Four Noble Truths, 112, 118–19, 121; the *Zhuangzi* and Daoist acceptance of, 217–19
Charlie Chan movies, 193
China: Communist rule and Confucianism, 199; contemporary divination practices, 157–58; mythic prehistory and golden age, 156, 175; Period of Warring States, 3, 170, 191, 194, 196, 197, 201, 217; preaxial, 155–63; Shang dynasty religion, 156–63, 168; Spring and Autumn Age, 170, 171; transition to the Axial Age, 165–73; Zhou dynasty, 165–69, 170. *See also* Buddhism; Confucianism; Daoism; East Asia, preaxial (ancient China); East Asian transition to the Axial Age
Christianity: contemporary, 225; human conception and the soul's creation, 77; Zoroastrian influences, 32–36. *See also* Jesus
clothing: and Confucian discipline, 187–88; Mahavira's renunciation, 146, 151
compassion: Axial Age, 228–29; *bao*, 162, 192; and concept of virtue in ancient Chinese religion, 161–62,

191–92; *de*, 161–62, 191–92; Mengzi and innate human goodness (*ren xing*), 194–97
Confucianism, 170–99; anthropocentrism, 176, 209; as both religion and philosophy, 177–78, 197; and China's earlier golden age, 156, 175; and the *Dao*, 186–88, 203, 209–10; and Daoism, 200–202, 209–10; evil, 196, 197; family life and filial piety, 176, 182, 196; the gentleman (*junzi*), 179–83, 185–86, 189; government and society, 191–92, 194–95; heaven (Tian), 178; humaneness (*ren*), 180–82, 194–97; ideals for individuals and human relationships, 178–83; innate human goodness (*ren xing*), 194–97; *li*, 188–91, 198; Mengzi (Mencius), 194–97; moral self-cultivation, 173, 176–77, 185–92, 197–98; political philosophy, 173, 176; ritual, 178, 188–91; School of Scholars (*rujia*) and the Mengzi-Xunzi debate, 194–98; self and community, 227, 230; Wu Jing (the Five Classics), 187; Xunzi, 197–98. *See also* Confucianism after the Axial Age; Confucius; Daoism
Confucianism after the Axial Age, 198–99; Communist China, 199; current era, 199; Han dynasty, 199, 221; Qin dynasty, 165, 182, 198–99; Song dynasty and Neo-Confucianism, 199; suppression/persecution, 198–99
Confucius: *Analects* (*Lunyu*), 171, 172–73, 175–77, 180, 182, 183, 186, 187–88, 193; early life, 172; historical, 171–72; ideals for individuals and human relationships, 178–83; life of, 170–73; and Mandate of Heaven, 178; name, 172;

personal qualities, 172–73; thought of, 175–83, 193–94; on worship, 176–77, 231. *See also* Confucianism
cosmic maintenance, 5–6, 14–16, 50–52, 229–30; Indo-Aryans, 50–52; Indo-Iranians, 14–16; story of the Purusha, 50–52
cosmogonies, 13; seven-stage Avestan cosmogony, 13–14, 50; Vedic story of the Purusha, 50–52

daevas, 12, 24–25, 34
Dalai Lama, 141
Daniel, book of, 33, 35
Dao, 203–7, 209–12; Chinese philosophy, 203–4; Confucian Way, 186–88, 203, 209–10; *Daodejing* and paradoxical nature of, 205–7; Daoist "way of nature" and the "universe's mother," 203–4; emptiness, 208–9, 219–20; images and metaphors, 207–9; limits to understanding and analysis, 204–5; *taijitu* symbol (*yinyang*), 206–7; twofold nature (named and nameless), 204–7; water, 207–8
Daodejing, 200–202, 203–12; Laozi and, 201–2; and paradoxical nature of *Dao*, 205–7; social and political philosophy, 210
Daoism, 200–221; aesthetics, 212; after the Axial Age, 220–21; and change/impermanence, 217–19; and Confucianism, 200–202, 209–10; the *Dao*, 203–7, 209–12; the *Daodejing*, 200–202, 203–12; the Daoist church, 221; the Daoist sage, 210–12, 216; and death, 218–19; following the *Dao*, 209–12; Laozi, 155, 201–2, 221; philosophical Daoism (*daojia*), 200–202, 213–21, 227; political philosophy, 210, 213–16; popular movements, 221;

practice of *wu wei*, 213; religious
Daoism (*daojiao*) (folk expression),
200–201, 220–21; rise of, 200–202;
self-effacement, 211–12, 227; the
Zhuangzi, 200, 215–16, 217–20;
Zhuangzi and individual spiritual/
mystical Daoism, 216–20
darshan, 92
Day of Judgment, 33
de, 161–62, 191–92
death: Axial Age attitudes, 3–4;
Buddhist question of the individual
after, 125; classical Hinduism and
anxiety about, 55–57, 59–65; Indus
Valley Civilization, 42; Nachiketas's
dialogue with Yama, 55–57, 60, 69;
Rig Veda hymns, 45–47; Vedic
Period, 45–47, 55–57, 60–61;
Zhuangzi and Daoist acceptance of,
218–19; Zoroastrianism and bodily
resurrection of the dead, 29;
Zoroastrianism and individual
destiny after death, 27–28. *See also*
afterlife; rebirth
desire: attachment (clinging), 116–19,
124; frustration/fulfillment and
unhappiness, 113–14; Second Noble
Truth, 115–19; *tanha*, 116, 123–24;
Third Noble Truth, 123–26
devas, 12, 44–45, 139
devil: Ahriman, 24–25, 34; *daevas*,
24–25, 34; Hebrew Bible, 34; Mara,
108; Satan, 34, 108; temptation by,
34, 108; Zoroastrianism, 24–25, 29,
34. *See also* evil
Dhamma, 109–11, 127, 133, 140;
Ashoka's embrace of, 140; the
Buddha's first discourse ("Turning
the Wheel of Dhamma"), 109;
Buddhist methodology and the
principle of criticism, 111; early
Sangha councils, 138–39; Four
Noble Truths, 109–32; pragmatic
criterion of truth, 111; the Sangha
and dissemination of, 133–34, 135;
stupas as physical representations,
137, 139
Dhammapada, 181n
di (earth), 158
Di (Shangdi), 159, 166
Digambaras (the sky-clad), 151
divination practices: contemporary Asia
and the West, 157–58; oracle bones
("dragon bones"), 157, 158; Shang
dynasty, 157–58; the *Yi Jing*, 165,
187
Diwali, festival of, 146, 225
dragon bones, 157, 158
druj, 13
drujvants, 17
Duke of Zhou (Dan), 166, 179
dukkha: and attachment (clinging),
116–19, 124; cause of (desire or
craving), 115–19; of change
(impermanence), 112; First Noble
Truth, 111–14, 115; *nibbana* and the
end of, 124; of physical pain and
distress, 112; Second Noble Truth,
115–19; Third Noble Truth and
cessation of, 123–26. *See also* Four
Noble Truths
Durga, 91
Dyaoš (Dyaus-Pitr), 11–12

East Asia: Confucianism, 170–99;
Daoism, 200–221; preaxial, 155–63;
transition to the Axial Age, 165–73
East Asia, preaxial (ancient China),
155–63; ancestor reverence, 160–61,
162, 168; concept of virtue, 161–63,
191–92; divination practices,
157–58; divine-human relationships,
159–60; filial piety/indebtedness,
162–63; ghosts, 161; gods, 159–60;
harmony between heaven and earth,
158–59, 163; mythic prehistory and

golden age, 156, 175; politics and religion, 163; Shang dynasty religion, 156–63, 166, 168; Shang dynasty's end, 165, 167. *See also* East Asian transition to the Axial Age

East Asian transition to the Axial Age, 165–73; Eastern Zhou period, 170; folk religion, 168–69; and life of Confucius, 171–72; Mandate of Heaven, 167–68, 178; political and cultural changes, 165–66; political/social disorder and Period of Warring States, 3, 170, 191, 194, 196, 197, 201, 217; Shang dynasty's end, 165, 167; Spring and Autumn Age, 170, 171; Western Zhou period, 170; Zhou dynasty, 162, 165–69, 170; Zhou theology, 166–69. *See also* Confucius; Zhou dynasty

Ecclesiastes, book of, 33

Eisenstadt, S. N., 5, 231

Eliade, Mircea, 13n

Eliot, T. S., 104

Emerson, Ralph Waldo, 130

equanimity: the Confucian gentleman, 182–83; the Daoist sage, 212

Erikson, Erik, 144n

"ethicization," 28

evil: *Book of Odes* and theistic problem of, 168–69; Confucianism, 196, 197; *daevas*, 24–25, 34; Frashokereti (eschatological battle), 29; Indo-Aryan *asuras*, 24, 45; and Mandate of Heaven, 168–69; Mengzi on human nature and, 196; Xunzi on human nature and, 197; Zoroastrianism, 24–25, 28–29, 34

Ezekiel, 22

family/filial piety: ancient Chinese religion, 162–63; Confucianism, 176, 182, 196. *See also* ancestor reverence

fire: Agni, 45; Indo-Iranian deity, 11, 14; Indo-Iranian rituals, 14, 15; Jainism and soul of, 148; and seven-stage Avestan cosmogony, 13–14; Vedic *shrauta* rites, 52–53; Zoroastrianism, 31

First Noble Truth, 111–14, 115

Five Aggregates of Being, 121–22

Five Precepts, 128–29; *ahimsa*, 128–29, 143; concerning use of intoxicants, 129; concerning misuse of language/speech, 129; concerning sexual misconduct, 128–29; concerning stealing/coveting, 128–29

Four Noble Truths, 109–32; attachment (clinging) and *dukkha*, 116–19, 124; First Noble Truth (*dukkha*), 111–14, 115; the idea of change/impermanence, 112, 118–19, 121; and *nibbana*, 124–25, 126–32; not-self (*anatta*), 119–22; Second Noble Truth (causes of *dukkha*), 115–19; and *tanha*, 116, 123–24; Third Noble Truth (cessation of *dukkha*), 123–26; Fourth Noble Truth (Noble Eightfold Path), 126–32. *See also* Buddhism; Gotama, Siddhattha; Noble Eightfold Path

The Four Sights, 101–4

Fourth Noble Truth, 126–32. *See also* Noble Eightfold Path

Frashokereti, 29

Frazer, Sir James, 51

Gandharan Buddha images, 138

Gandhi, Mohandas, 143, 144n

Ganesha, 91

Ganges River basin (Gangetic Plains), 3, 55, 70, 104, 133, 145–47, 187

Gathas (Verses of Zoroaster), 21–22, 24–25, 30

Genesis, book of, 33–34, 75
gentleman (*junzi*), 179–83, 185–86, 189; humaneness (*ren*), 180–82; wisdom and equanimity, 182–83
Geush Urvan ("Soul of the Bull"), 12, 15
ghosts, 161
goddess worship, 40–41
gods/goddesses: *ahuras*, 12, 24–25; ancient Greek, 11–12, 138; anthropomorphic images, 91, 138, 224; *asuras*, 24, 45; the Buddha and the Hindu pantheon, 139; Confucius on, 176–77, 231; *daevas*, 12, 24–25, 34; *devas*, 12, 44–45, 139; Hindu iconography, 90–93; Hindu personal deities, 88–95; Indo-Iranian, 11–12, 14, 15–16; Indo-Iranian nature deities, 11, 14; *ishta-devata*, 92; Shang local gods, 159; Shang theology, 159–60; and Soma, 12, 15–16, 18, 53; and *yazatas*, 24; Zoroastrian theistic dualism, 24–25. *See also* worship; *names of individual divine beings*
Gotama, Siddhattha, 97–105, 107–14; awakening under the bodhi tree, 108; death and *parinibbana*, 136–37; early meditation teachers, 104; epiphanies near age of thirty, 99, 101–2, 103; first discourse ("Turning the Wheel of Dhamma"), 109; The Four Sights, 101–4; the historical Buddha and story embellishments, 98–104, 145; images/likenesses of, 138, 224; and Mahavira, 145; mindfulness meditation, 108; Pali Canon and Suttas, 98, 99, 101, 105, 109, 138, 141; renunciation/becoming novice *shramana*, 104–5, 107; royal family and early years, 99–101, 145; self-mortification, 105, 107; setting in motion the wheel of Dhamma, 109–11, 133; title of the Buddha, "the Awakened One," 108. *See also* Buddhism; Four Noble Truths
government. *See* politics and government
Greece, ancient: aesthetics and first anthropomorphic representations of the Buddha, 138, 224; ghosts, 161; gods, 11–12, 138; notion of rebirth, 61–62

Han dynasty, 199, 221
harmony: and *druj* (disharmony and chaos), 13; heaven-earth and ancient Chinese maintenance of, 158–59, 163; *taijitu* symbol and Chinese ideal, 206–7
heaven: ancient Chinese maintenance of heaven-earth harmony, 158–59, 163; Jain home of the gods, 147–48; Mandate of Heaven (*tianming*), 167–68, 178; Mengzi on human goodness and, 197; paradise, 30, 34; Shang dynasty, 158–61; Tian, 166–67, 178; Zhou dynasty, 167–68; Zoroastrian, 33–34. *See also* afterlife
Hebrew Bible, 33–34, 75, 168
hell: Hebrew Bible (Sheol), 34; Jain underworld, 147; Satan, 34, 108; Zoroastrian, 28–29, 33–34
Heptad (the Seven), 22
Hick, John, 5
High Hara, 28
Hindu iconography, 90–93; anthropomorphic/nonanthropomorphic images, 91; and idolatry, 92–93; incarnations of divine reality, 91–92
Hinduism, classical, 54–95; *atman*, 76–77, 227; Brahman, 78–80, 89, 90, 93; Brahman-*atman*, 80–82, 87–88; concept of the self, 75–77, 227; death, 55–57, 59–65; end of Vedic

Period/advent of the Axial Age, 54–57, 60–61; karma and the ethicization of rebirth, 64–65, 67–68, 71; knowledge, 71–73; paths to accommodate individual beliefs and tastes, 85–95; quest for liberation, 67–73, 94–95; rebirth/reincarnation, 61–65, 67–68; *samsara* and the problem of rebirth, 62, 68–73, 87–88; *shramanas*, 69–73, 85–87; Vedantic school, 75–83, 85–88, 89; worship of personal deities, 88–95. *See also* karma; Upanishads; Vedantic school

Hinduism, contemporary: bathing rituals, 42; the Buddha and, 139; goddess worship, 41; and Indus Valley Civilization, 39, 41, 42; and the Vedas (as *shruti*), 44

Hitler, Adolf, 43

householders, 70–71, 134

human nature: *atman*, 76–77; classical Hindu concept of human essence, 75–77; Confucian debate, 194–98; Confucian ideal of *ren*, 180–82, 194–97; Mengzi on innate human goodness (*ren xing*), 194–97; preaxial Aryans' view of, 45–47; Xunzi on, 197–98. *See also* humaneness; self, concept of

humaneness: Confucian ideal of *ren*, 180–82, 194–97; at corporate and institutional levels, 230; *li* and Confucian program of self-cultivation, 188–91; and love, 181–82; Mengzi on innate human goodness (*ren xing*), 194–97; and reciprocity, 180–81

India: Ashoka and development of Buddhism in, 140; Jainism's influence on, 143; preaxial South Asia, 10, 39–57. *See also* Buddhism; Hinduism, classical; Hinduism, contemporary; Indo-Aryans; Jainism

Indian Ocean tsunami (2004), 161

Indo-Aryans, 10, 43–57: *asuras* (evil beings), 24, 45; *atman*, 46, 76; *brahman*, 53–54, 78; Brahmin priests, 52–54, 78; caste, 52; cosmic maintenance and regeneration, 50–52; death and afterlife, 45–47, 55–57, 60–61; *devas*, 44–45; end of Vedic period/advent of Axial Age, 54–57, 60–61; expansion and urbanization, 55; human nature and destiny, 45–47; "Noble Ones," 43–44; origins and the "Aryan question," 43; Purusha and story of the world's creation, 50–52, 78; *shrauta* rites, 52–53; and the Vedas, 44, 45–47; Vedic ritual and religion, 44, 47, 49–54, 55–57, 72. *See also* Hinduism, classical; Indus Valley Civilization; Vedic Period

Indo-Europeans, 9–19; cosmic maintenance, 14–16; cosmogonies, 13–14, 50; gods, 11–12, 15–16; Indo-Aryans, 10, 43–57; Indo-Iranians, 10–19; Irano-Aryans, 10, 12; languages, 9–10; morality and order, 12–13; the Rig Veda, 10, 43; ritual, 14–16; Soma, 12, 15–16, 18; split/divergence of branches, 10; worship of Indra, 18–19, 44–45. *See also* Indo-Aryans; Indo-Iranians; Zoroaster

Indo-Iranians, 10–19; *ahuras*, 12, 24; the Avesta, 10; cosmic maintenance, 14–16; *daevas* (*devas*), 12, 24; gods, 11–12, 15–16; Indra worship, 18–19, 44–45; laity, 11; language dialects, 10; migration and split, 10, 19, 43; morality and order, 12–13; nature deities, 11, 14; prayer, 31; priests, 11, 21–22; principle of order (*rita/asha*),

12–13; as raiders, 16–19, 22; religion, 11–16, 17–19; the Rig Veda, 10, 43; ritual, 14–16; sacred spaces, 14; sacrifices, 14, 15; seven-stage Avestan cosmogony, 13–14, 50; society and economy, 10–11; Soma, 15–16, 18, 53; warrior caste, 17–18, 52. *See also* Indo-Aryans
Indra, 18–19, 44–45, 76
Indrabhuti, 146
Indus Valley Civilization, 39–42, 43, 52, 61n; absence of afterlife/death concerns, 42; artifacts depicting sexuality and procreation, 40–41; bathing and ritual purity, 41–42; decline, 43; goddess religion, 40–41; meditation practices, 85; urban centers, 40. *See also* Indo-Aryans
"Inner Chapters," 217
Irano-Aryans, 10, 12
ishta-devata, 92
Islam: human conception and the soul's creation, 77; Zoroastrian influences, 32–36

Jainism, 143–51; and the Agam Sutras, 146; *ahimsa*, 143, 149–50; asceticism, 146, 150; and Buddhism, 143; cyclical time, 144, 147; fulfilling the five *mahavratas* (Great Vows), 149–50; Gandhi and, 143, 144n; influence on Indian history and religions, 143; karma/karmic defilement, 148–50; life, 148–49; Mahavira, 144–51; monastic communities, 146, 150–51; origins and the Tirthankaras, 144; path to liberation, 144, 149–51; principle of nonabsolutism, 149; reality, 149; rebirth, 62; renunciation of clothing, 146, 151; soul, 148–49; women/nuns, 151; world (underworld, middle realm, heavens), 147–48

Jambudvipa, 147–48
Jaspers, Karl, 1, 6
Jesus: baptism at the River Jordan, 22–23; birth and visit from the Magi, 36; and Satan, 34, 108; and the Son of Man, 35–36
jivanmuktas, 87
jñana, 73
Job, book of, 34, 168
Judaism: Axial Age, 1, 3; contemporary, 225; human conception and the soul's creation, 77; messianic anticipations, 35–36; Zoroastrian influences, 32–36
junzi. *See* gentleman (*junzi*)

Kalamas, 110
karma, 64–65, 226; Buddhism, 125, 128; cessation of, 149–50; classical Hinduism, 64–65, 67–68, 71; definition, 64–65; and ethicization of rebirth, 64–65, 67–68, 71; Jainism and karmic defilements, 148–50; removing, 150
Kierkegaard, Søren, 81
King, Martin Luther, Jr., 185
Kisagotami, 135–36
knowledge: Brahman as unknowable, 80; Confucian moral self-cultivation and love of learning, 186–87; *jñana* (*gnōsis*), 73; Noble Eightfold Path and cultivation of wisdom, 127; *shramanas'* goal of a unified field theory (Theory of Everything), 72–73; *shramanas'* quest for liberating knowledge, 71–73, 85–87; Vedantic school (Upanishads), 75–83, 85–88, 89; Vedic ritual and religion, 72
Krishna, 94–95
Kubera, 45

Laozi, 155, 201–2, 221

Legalism, 198–99
li, 188–91; dignity and manners, 188–89; in public ritual, 190–91; Xunzi's view of, 198
liberation: the Buddha's awakening under the bodhi tree, 108; Hindu quest for, 67–73, 94–95; Jainism, 144, 149–51; and karma, 149–50; liberating knowledge, 71–73; Mahavira's attainment of perfect enlightenment, 146; Mahavira's discipline for attaining, 149–51; *samsara* and the problem of rebirth, 62, 68–73; and *shramanas*, 69–73; through devotion, 94–95. See also *moksha; samsara*
lingam, 41, 91
love: Confucian love of learning, 186–87; Confucius and the quality of *ren*, 181–82; Confucius on filial piety and, 182; Mengzi on parental love, 196; Mohists on virtue of universal love, 181–82

Magi, 36
Mahavira, 144–51; and the Agam Sutras, 146; asceticism and mortification, 146; attainment of perfect enlightenment, 146; birth and parents, 145; and the Buddha, 145; discipline for attaining liberation, 149–51; followers and disciples, 146; and Jain worldview, 146–49; life story, 145–46; renunciation and becoming a *shramana*, 145–46; renunciation of clothing, 146, 151. See also Jainism
Mahayana Buddhism, 141, 199, 221
Malunkyaputta, 125
manas, 46
Mandate of Heaven (*tianming*), 167–68, 178
mantras, 53

Mao Zedong, 199
Mara, 108
Matthew, Gospel of, 36
maya, 82, 87
Maya, Queen (the Buddha's mother), 100, 135
Mazda. See Ahura Mazda
meditation: and the Axial Age's inward turn, 228; Buddhist, 108, 131, 135; Confucian, 186; Gotama's first teachers, 104; Indus Valley Civilization, 85; Vedantic school, 85–86
Mencius, 194, 195
Mengzi (Mencius), 194–97; on evil/human evil, 196; on filial piety and parental love, 196; and government's role in promoting the good, 194–95; on heaven, 197; and innate human goodness (*ren xing*), 194–97; life of, 194; Parable of Ox Mountain, 196
mental discipline: the Buddha's understanding of the undisciplined mind, 129–31; and Buddhist meditation, 131; Noble Eightfold Path, 129–31
Mitra, 12
Mohists, 181–82
moksha, 69; experience of, 87; *shramanas* and, 69–73, 85–87
monasticism: *bhikkhus/bhikkhunis*, 111, 135–36; Buddhist Sangha, 133–36; Jain orders, 146, 150–51; women monastics, 135–36
monotheism, 23
morality/moral obligation and responsibility: Axial Age and, 25–26; Confucianism and moral cultivation, 173, 176–77, 185–92, 197–98; "ethicization," 28; Noble Eightfold Path (wholesome action and the Five Precepts), 128–29; Zhou

theology, 166–68; Zoroastrianism, 25–26, 27–28, 29–30
Mozi, 181
music and the arts, 172–73, 187

Nachiketas's dialogue with Yama, 55–57, 60, 69
Nanak, Guru, 22–23
Neo-Confucianism, 199
nibbana: and *arahants*, 125, 133; Fourth Noble Truth and the Noble Eightfold Path, 126–32; negative language of, 124–25; and *parinibbana*, 125, 136–37; Third Noble Truth, 123–26
Niebuhr, Reinhold, 2–3
Nietzsche, Friedrich, 123
nirguna Brahman, 79–80, 90, 93
Noble Eightfold Path, 126–32; cultivating wisdom, 127; developing moral conduct, 128–29; disciplining the mind, 129–31; right action and the Five Precepts, 128–29; right livelihood, 129; right speech, 129; skillful concentration, 131; skillful effort, 131; skillful intention, 127; skillful mindfulness, 131; skillful understanding, 127, 131–32; Triple Practice, 127–31
nonabsolutism, principle of, 149
not-self (*anatta/anatman*), 119–22
Nowruz ("New Day") festival, 31–32

Pali Canon, 98, 99, 101, 105, 109, 138, 141; and the Suttas, 98, 99, 138
paradise, 30, 34
parinibbana, 125, 136–37
Parsis, 31
Period of Warring States (or Period of One Hundred Philosophers), 3, 170, 191, 194, 196, 197, 201, 217
politics and government: Confucian virtue and governance, 191–92, 194–95; Daoist political philosophy, 210, 213–16; Daoist practice of *wu wei*, 213; Mandate of Heaven, 167–68, 178; Mengzi on, 194–95; noninterference and minimalist governance, 215–16; Period of Warring States, 3, 170, 191, 194, 196, 197, 201, 217; Shang dynasty, 163; Zhou dynasty, 167–68
Prajapati, Queen, 135
prayer: Indo-Iranian, 31; *shrauta* rites and Brahmin priests, 53; Zoroastrian, 31
preaxial period: East Asia (preaxial China), 155–63; South Asia (Indo-Aryans), 10, 43–57; South Asia (Indus Valley Civilization), 39–42, 43, 52; West Asia (Indo-Iranians), 9–19
Proto-Indo-European (PIE), 9–10
Puranas, 89
purity, ritual: Hindu bathing rituals, 42; Indus Valley Civilization bathing facilities, 41–42; Zoroastrian, 31
Purusha, story of the, 50–52, 78

Qin dynasty, 165, 182, 198–99
quantum physics, 118

Rahula (son of Gotama), 135
Rajchandra, Srimat, 144n
Ramanuja, 88
Ramayana, 89
reality: *anekanta* (Jainism), 149; and Axial Age recognition of ultimate mystery, 231; impossibility of discussing ultimate reality (Hinduism), 82–83; and *maya*, 82
rebirth: Ancient Greece, 61–62; Axial India, 61–65, 67–68; Buddhism, 62; "good" or "bad," 67–68; Jainism, 62; karma and the ethicization of, 64–65, 67–68, 71; metaphors/

analogies, 62–63; precursor notion of "redeath," 61; and *samsara*, 62, 68–73, 87–88; Sikhism, 62; Upanishadic passages (*The Supreme Teaching*), 62–64. See also afterlife; death

redeath, 61

reincarnation. See rebirth

religions/religious traditions: Axial Age understandings, 223–28; change and development over time, 223–24; different functions in culture/within a society, 224–25; interreligious encounters and influences, 224; personal transformation of the individual, 226–28; and problem of the self, 226–28; prophets' transformative experiences at age thirty, 22–23, 99, 101–2, 103, 145–46

ren, 180–82, 194–97

ren xing, 194–97

renunciation: Gotama's, 104–5, 107; Mahavira's, 145–46. See also *shramanas*

Rig Veda, 10, 43, 44, 45–47, 50–52, 88; cosmogony and story of the Purusha, 50–52; hymns concerning death and afterlife, 45–47; on Soma, 15–16, 18; on worship of Indra, 18

rita/asha, 12–13

ritual: Buddhist Sangha councils and question of, 139; Confucian moral development and interior dimension of, 189–91; fire rituals, 15, 31, 52–53; gods of, 12, 15–16; Indo-Aryan, 44; Indo-Iranian, 14–16; *li*, 189–91; prayer, 31; ritual purity, 31, 41–42; Soma, 12, 15–16, 18, 53; Vedic *shrauta* rites, 52–53; and the *zaotar* (Iranian priest), 21–22; Zoroastrian, 30–32. See also sacrifice

sacrifice: and cosmic maintenance, 5–6, 14–16, 50–52; Indo-Aryan, 44; Indo-Iranian animal/blood sacrifices (*yasna*), 15; and seven-stage Avestan cosmogony, 13–14; story of the Purusha, 50–52; Vedic *shrauta* rites, 52–53

sage: Confucian ideal, 178; Daoist, 210–12, 216

saguna Brahman, 90

Sakyas, 99

samsara, 62, 68–73; liberation through devotion, 94–95; and *maya*, 82; and rebirth, 62, 68–73; the reevaluation of the world, 68–69. See also *shramanas*

Sangha, 133–36; daily meditation, 135; discipline and structure (rules of communal life), 135; dissemination of the Dhamma, 133–34, 135; First Buddhist Council, 138; gatherings to settle doctrinal and practical disagreements, 138–39; local monastic communities, 134–36; question of divine worship, 139; question of ritual practice, 139; women, 135–36

Saoshyant, 29, 35–36

Satan, 34, 108

satya, 143, 150

Schulz, Charles M., 212

Second Noble Truth, 115–19

self, concept of: *atman*, 46, 76–77, 227; Axial Age and individual selfhood, 3–4, 6, 225–28; the Buddha's, 119–22, 227; Confucianism on self and community, 227, 230; Daoism and self-effacement, 211–12, 227; the Five Aggregates of Being, 121–22; not-self (*anatta/anatman*), 119–22; religion and the problem of the self, 226–28; Upanishads, 75–77,

227; Vedantic school, 75–77, 227; Vedic, 46, 76. *See also* human nature

sexuality: Five Precepts and sexual misconduct, 128–29; Indus Valley Civilization, 40–41

Shang dynasty: concept of virtue, 161–63; divination practices, 157–58; end of, 165, 167; heaven and earth, 158–61; religion of, 156–63, 168. *See also* East Asia, preaxial (ancient China)

Shangdi (Di), 159, 166

Shankara, 88

Shiva, 41

shramanas, 69–73; and the Daoist sages, 211–12; Gotama and the story of the Four Sights, 101–4; Gotama as, 104–5, 107; and *jñana*, 73; Mahavira, 145–46; meditation, 85–86; quest for liberating knowledge, 71–73, 85–87; relationship to ordinary householders, 70–71. *See also* asceticism

shrauta rites, 52–53

shruti, 44

Shvetambaras (the white-robed), 151

Siddhartha, King (father of Mahavira), 145

Sikhism, 23, 62

Soma: and the god Indra, 18; and Indo-Iranians, 12, 15–16, 18; Vedic *shrauta* rites, 53

Son of Man, 35–36

Song dynasty, 194, 199

soul/souls: Abrahamic traditions' view of conception and, 77; Confucianism's little attention to, 176–77; Jainism, 148–49; and Upanishadic *atman* (higher self), 76–77, 227; Vedic *atman*, 46, 76

South Asia: advent of Indian Axial Age, 54–57, 60–61; Buddhism, 97–141; classical Hindu era, 54–95; Indo-Aryans, 10, 43–57; Indus Valley Civilization, 39–42, 43, 52, 61n; Jainism, 143–51; preaxial India, 10, 39–57

Spring and Autumn Age (Zhou dynasty), 170, 171

The Spring and Autumn Annals, 170

Sri Lanka, 137, 140, 141

stupas, 137–38, 139, 140

Suddhodana, King, 100–101

suffering: the Buddha and The Four Sights, 101–4; and change/impermanence, 112; Daoist political analysis, 214–15; *dukkha*, 111–14, 115–19, 123–26; First Noble Truth, 111–14, 115; the Four Noble Truths, 109–32; Second Noble Truth and cause of, 115–19; Third Noble Truth and cessation of, 123–26; Zoroastrianism and, 30

Surya, 45

taijitu symbol, 206–7

Taiwan, 161

tanha (thirst/craving), 116, 123–24

Tatia, Nathmal, 151

Theravada Buddhism, 141

Third Noble Truth, 123–26

Thoreau, Henry David, 215

Three Sovereigns and Five Emperors, era of, 156

tian, 166–67, 178

Tibet, 68, 141

Tillich, Paul, 181

time: *avasarpini* (cycle of decline), 147; cyclical, 33, 47, 144, 147; Jainism and cyclical, 144, 147; religious traditions' change and development over time, 223–24; *utsarpini* (cycle of ascent), 147; Zoroastrianism, 33

Tirthankaras, 144. *See also* Mahavira

Tolstoy, Leo, *The Death of Ivan Ilyich*, 102–3

Tomb-Sweeping Day (Taiwan), 161
transcendental consciousness, 4–5, 231
Triple Practice, 127–31
Triple Refuge, 139
Trishala, Queen (mother of Mahavira), 145

Uddaka Ramaputta, 104
Upanishads: *atman*, 76–77, 227; and axial reevaluation of Vedic ritual system, 55–57; Brahman, 79, 80; *Chandogya Upanishad*, 81, 85; *Isha Upanishad*, 79; *Kena Upanishad*, 80; *Maitri Upanishad*, 82; on meditation, 86; Nachiketas's dialogue with Yama, 55–57, 60, 69; rebirth metaphors/analogies, 62–64; *The Supreme Teaching*, 62–63, 86, 87. *See also* Vedantic school
Ushas, 45

Vajrayana Buddhism, 141
Varuna, 12, 19, 45
Vedantic school, 75–83, 85–88, 89; *atman*, 76–77, 227; Brahman, 78–80, 89, 90, 93; Brahman-*atman*, 80–82, 87–88; concept of the self/human essence, 75–77, 227; discussion of ultimate reality, 82–83; the knowing that leads to *moksha*, 85–87; meditation, 85–86; philosophical problems, 87–88; rebirth, 62–64; three subschools of Hindu philosophy, 88. *See also* Upanishads
Vedas, 44; cosmogony and story of the Purusha, 50–52; hymns concerning death and afterlife, 45–47; Indo-Aryans, 44, 45–47; Rig Veda, 10, 15–16, 18, 43, 44, 45–47, 50–52, 88; and *shruti* (revelation), 44
Vedic Period: axial reevaluation, 55–57; *brahman*, 53–54, 78; caste/stratification of humanity, 52; *devas*, 12, 44–45, 139; Nachiketas's dialogue with Yama, 55–57, 60, 69; philosophical turn, 59–60; ritual and religion, 44, 47, 49–54, 72; role of knowledge, 72; *shrauta* rites, 52–53; story of the Purusha, 50–52, 78. *See also* Indo-Aryans; Upanishads; Vedas
Vesak (Buddhist holiday), 137
virtue, concept of: ancient Chinese religion, 161–63, 191–92; Axial Age compassionate and mindful virtue, 228–29; Confucian ideal of *ren*, 180; Confucian moral self-cultivation, 185–92; and filial responsibility, 162–63; Mandate of Heaven given to a virtuous ruler, 167–68
Vishnu, 91, 139

Warren, Robert Penn, 156
water: and the *Dao*, 207–8; Indo-Iranian deity, 11, 14; and seven-stage Avestan cosmogony, 13–14; and Zoroaster's prophetic call, 22–23
Wen, King, 165
West Asia: preaxial Indo-Iranians, 9–19; Zoroastrianism, 21–36
Western philosophical tradition, 1
Whitehead, Alfred North, 1n
wisdom: the Confucian gentleman, 182–83; Noble Eightfold Path and cultivation of, 127. *See also* knowledge
women: *arahants*, 135–36; *bhikkhunis* and the Buddhist Sangha, 135–36; Indus Valley Civilization terra-cotta figurines, 40–41; and Jainism, 151
worship: ancestor reverence, 160–61, 162, 168; *Bhagavad Gita* on, 94–95; Buddhist Sangha gatherings on question of, 139; Confucius on, 176–77, 231; contemporary Hindu goddess worship, 41; Hindu iconography and idolatry, 92–93;

Hindu personal devotion, 88–95;
Indo-Iranian nature deities, 11, 14;
Indo-Iranian worship of Indra,
18–19, 44–45; Indus Valley goddess
worship, 40–41; liberation through
devotion, 94–95; Zhou worship of
Tian, 166–67. *See also* gods/
goddesses
Wu, King, 165–66
Wu Jing (the Five Classics), 187
wu wei, 213

Xunzi, 197–98

Yama (King of Death), 45, 46;
Nachiketas's dialogue with, 55–57,
60, 69
Yashodhara (wife of Mahavira), 145
Yashodhara (wife of Siddhatha Gotama),
101, 135
yazatas, 24
Yeats, William Butler, 205
Yi Jing (book of divination), 165, 187
yinyang, 206–7

zaotar, 21–22
Zarathustra, 19. *See also* Zoroaster
Zen Buddhism, 125–26, 224
Zhang Daoling, 221
Zhou dynasty, 162, 165–70; *Book of
Odes* and theistic problem of evil,
168–69; early rulers, 165–66; East
Asian transition to the Axial Age,
165–70; folk religion, 168–69; and
life of Confucius, 171–72; Mandate
of Heaven (*tianming*), 167–68;
morality, 166–68; Period of Warring
States, 3, 170, 191, 194, 196, 197,
201, 217; political and cultural
changes, 165–66; Spring and
Autumn Age, 170, 171; theology,
166–69; Western Zhou/Eastern
Zhou periods, 170; worship of Tian,
166–67
Zhuangzi, 216–20
Zhuangzi (book), 200, 215–16, 217–20;
acceptance of change/
impermanence, 217–19; butterfly
dream, 220; "Inner Chapters," 217
Zoroaster, 19, 21–36; and Ahura Mazda,
22, 23, 25, 31, 227; and the Gathas
(Verses), 21–22, 24–25, 30; legacy,
27–36; life, 19, 21–26; moral
sensitivies, 22; as priest (ritual
specialist), 21–22; as prophet, 21–23;
rejection by his community, 30;
visionary experience and prophetic
call, 22–23
Zoroastrianism, 21–36; afterlife and
paradise, 30, 34; Ahriman (evil
deity), 24–25, 34; bodily
resurrection of the dead, 29;
celebrations (festivals), 31–32; Day
of Judgment, 33; dissemination of,
30; eschatological cosmological
drama, 28–29; heaven and hell,
33–34; human beings' role, 29–30;
human moral responsibility, 25–26,
27–28, 29–30; influences on
Abrahamic traditions, 32–36;
innovations, 27–29; movement
toward monotheism, 23; practices/
rites, 30–32; prayer, 31; ritual purity,
31; sacred fires, 31; *Saoshyant* (future
redeemer-judge), 29, 35–36;
suffering, 30; theistic dualism and
moral qualities of the gods, 24–25;
theology, 23–25; time and history,
33

www.ingramcontent.com/pod-product-compliance
Lightning Source LLC
Chambersburg PA
CBHW051937290426
44110CB00015B/2013